ISBN 978-0-266-95135-3
PIBN 10914598

REPORT WRITING

THIRD EDITION

by

CARL G. GAUM

Member American Society of Mechanical Engineers
Professor in University Extension
Rutgers University

HAROLD F. GRAVES

Professor of English Composition
The Pennsylvania State College

and

LYNE S. S. HOFFMAN

Assistant Professor of English Composition
The Pennsylvania State College

NEW YORK

PRENTICE-HALL, INC.

1950

PREFACE

The preface to the first edition is still applicable: "Nowadays reports play a large part in public and corporate affairs. As a natural consequence, an increasing number of men and women must know how to write them. When no standardized form is furnished, it is often difficult to develop a logical arrangement for a report and to present clearly and emphatically the facts and ideas which it must contain. This book, which supplies certain principles of composition and rhetoric to the special field of the report, is intended to be helpful to those writers who are either inexperienced or less effective than they would like to be.

"The report writer must meet several requirements. To borrow a term from public speaking, he must be 'audience-minded'; that is, he must write with an appreciation of his reader's point of view. He must be clear and accurate. He must have the ability to determine what to include and how to arrange it. In this book the authors have tried to hold in mind these common demands and to point out reasonable and effective methods of meeting them.

"The materials of the text are so arranged that the student may advance progressively from the simple problems to the more complex. The business letter is chosen as the proper approach, both because it demands somewhat less skill in organization than many longer forms, and because its relationship to all report writing is so close. The student's practice begins with the writing of letters and short compositions, in which he can find interest because of their obvious relationship to the practical reports of business and industry. With this foundation laid, he is prepared to attack the more complicated problems."

That the principles laid down in the first edition have been found pragmatic is evidenced by the increasingly wide adoption of *Report Writing* in both industry and the classroom. Consequently no deviation in principle is to be found in this edition.

The new edition does incorporate the following improvements:

1. The integration of the material on the planning, organizing, and writing of all reports into a section of three consecutive chapters which carry the student completely through the process

of creating a report—from the gathering of the raw data to the revision of the manuscript.

2. At the request of many users—a more extensive "handbook" treatment of the general problems of composition.

3. A modernization of the treatment of the business letter and of problems of mechanics peculiar to technical writing (e.g., abbreviations, numbers, compounding, graphic presentation).

4. An even closer relationship with industrial practice and attitude through citation from style manuals, letters, memoranda, and actual reports.

5. The integration of all specimen reports, with provocative questions and comment, in one section following the text.

6. New illustrative material.

7. Expanded treatment of the summary and the abstract; of interpretation; of memoranda; of footnotes and bibliography; of interviewing, sampling, and the questionnaire; and of graphic presentation.

8. An up-to-date and classified bibliography.

For invaluable suggestion and material the authors are indebted to the following:

From The Pennsylvania State College: Professor Edward J. Nichols and the other members of the Department of English Composition; Professors Charles L. Kinsloe and E. B. Stavely of Electrical Engineering; Professor Lawrence Perez, Civil Engineering; Professor Michael Cannon, Chemical Engineering; Professor John R. Brachen, Landscape Architecture.

From the University of Virginia: Professor Joseph Vaughan, Head of the School of English, College of Engineering.

From Rensselaer Polytechnic Institute: Professors Fred Abbuhl and the late Homer Nugent.

From government and industry: Dr. John A. Hipple, Jr., Head, Atomic Physics Section, and Dr. Hugh Odishaw, Assistant to the Director, The National Bureau of Standards; Dr. R. E. Birch, Director of Research, Harbison-Walker Refractories Company; Mr. Michael Baker, Consulting Civil Engineer, The Baker Engineers; Dr. G. D. Byrkit, Patent and Library Supervisor, The Mathieson Alkali Works (Inc.); Mr. Paul Truesdell, Universal Oil Products Company; Mr. B. H. Saltzer, Engineering Administrator, Wright Aeronautical Corporation; Dr. W. E. Kuhn, Manager, Technical and Research Division, The Texas Company; Mr. H. D. Barber, Vice President, Erie Railroad Company; Mr. J. C. Reed, Manager, Research and Product Development, American Radiator and Standard Sanitary Corporation; Mr. W. E. McCullough, Chief Metallurgist, Bohn Aluminum & Brass Corporation; Mr. Douglas B. Hobbs, Aluminum Company of America; Mr. R. W. Mumford, Vice President, and the late William R. Cushman, Power Engineer, of the American Potash & Chemical Corporation; Dr. J. A. Hutcheson, Assistant Director, Westinghouse Research Laboratory; Dr. R. S. George, Hercules Powder Company; Mr. F. J. Sanders, Technical Manager, The Standard Oil Company (Ohio); Mr. E. J. Billings, Executive Assistant, The Babcock & Wilcox Co.; Dr. D. T. Rogers, Assistant Director of Technology, Jones & Laughlin Steel Corporation; Mr. John C. Long, Manager of Publications, and Mr. Louis H. Winkler, Chief Metallurgist, Bethlehem Steel Company; Mr. Henry S. Walker, Director of Research, The Detroit Edison Company; Mr. Richard J. McFalls, Plant Manager, Cluett, Peabody & Co., Inc.; Mr. G. J. Brown, Editor of *Our Sun,* Sun Oil Company; Mr. Bernard R. Jones, Technical Data Section, Ethyl Corporation; Mr. W. H. Herman, Chief Research Engineer, Pennsylvania Department of Highways; Mr. Osborn H. Graves, Department of Regional Studies, Tennessee Valley Authority; and especially Mr. T. O. Richards, Head of the Laboratory Control Department, and Mr. Ralph A. Richardson, Head of the Technical Data Department, Research Laboratories Division, General Motors Corporation; and the editors of the American Standards Association.

C. G. G.
H. F. G.
L. S. S. H.

TABLE OF CONTENTS

FIGURES

CHAPTER 1

THE DEMAND FOR REPORTS

SOME MEN tell their story in reports; they have no other means of making their work and knowledge useful. That is why employers so often write the colleges, "Send us men who can write decent reports too."

What do they mean by "decent reports"? Many critics in recent years have pointed to the faults they want to see eliminated. They have charged government bureaus with writing "gobbledegook"—that heavy jargon that demands more reader energy than the content justifies. In industry, employers charge that too many reports are not clear, direct, and pertinent; executives, they say, waste too much time trying to get the answers out of bad reports.

"No report is better than what's in it." Surely no amount of style and form, coherence and emphasis, can make a good report out of unreliable information and bad judgments. A report is more than "English," just as any other good piece of writing is more than letters, commas, and semicolons.

But on the other hand, no amount of solid investigation and brilliant thinking is likely to become very useful until it is communicated to others. If a man's work calls for reports, then his work is no better than his reports.

That is why students preparing for places of responsibility want to know more about the modern art of report writing.

What is a report? A report is the communication of information to clients, superiors, or employers. One essential ingredient is *fact,* new information. The report writer has something new to tell. Another characteristic is the relationship of writer to reader; the writer is responsible to the reader. The President reports to the stockholders; the General Manager reports to the President; the Superintendent reports to the General Manager; the Engineering Department reports to the Superintendent; and Sam Witham, Assistant Engineer, reports to the head of his department. In practice, however, this order is reversed, because the

President's reports to the stockholders rely upon, are based upon, all the others.

The ultimate basis of any good report is *facts*. That means direct observation, experiment, inspection; experience, research. Sometimes, it is true, the reports of executives or of recognized authorities seem to be no more than general ideas and opinions; but what we must remember is that the facts leading to these opinions were gathered and reported earlier, and the opinions are dependent upon those facts.

The characteristics of a reported fact are these: (1) It is limited to direct observation, and (2) it is expressed in unambiguous terms. For example:

> Fact: "The flue gas contained 10 to 14% CO_2."
> Opinion: "Such gas is so dilute that it could not be used for obtaining the partial pressure of CO_2 needed in the carbonating unit."

Note that the statement of "fact" presumes a direct investigation, firsthand observation by somebody; note also that the terms "flue gas," "10 to 14%" and "CO_2" should mean exactly the same things to everybody. On the other hand, the opinion statement draws a conclusion from these facts; the conclusion depends upon standards previously set for what is "needed in the carbonating unit" as well as upon the new facts.

By definition, then, a report must be more than vague "ideas" and "opinions." The ideas must have a solid basis in fact.

The modern report is one of the most interesting developments of the last century. The growth of the technical professions, the extraordinary increase of great business organizations, and the widening activities of municipal, state, and federal governments have all led to the increased need for written communications within each group. The larger organizations demanded greater specialization. Executives became increasingly dependent upon subordinates and experts. So there developed this complex system in which many intermediate positions form a connecting chain from the lowest subordinate to the organization head. And so developed the written report, needed to carry the specialist's information to the policy-makers and to provide a permanent record.

Who writes reports? That the writer of a report is responsible to his reader does not always imply that he is inferior. Directors of a corporation are responsible to the stockholders, but not inferior to them. The President of the United States is responsible to the citizens. The architect and the consulting engineer are responsible to their clients. Responsibility does not imply either social or economic inferiority. It does imply definite duties to be fulfilled.

The extent of the art of report writing in modern life has already received some mention. In numerous fields it is a regular, if not a routine, duty. Some of the more prominent of these fields are considered in the following paragraphs.

Engineers. No other form of writing has so much importance for the engineer as that of reports. Probably in his earliest professional work he will be forced to furnish some sort of written records to his superiors. As he advances he finds that his reports increase in length and complexity. He is called upon for greater skill in composition, for more ingenuity. The engineer's reports vary from the simple account of a simple job, often made in a brief letter or on a prepared "form," to a detailed account based on an extensive examination, and leading to important recommendations. By his reports an engineer's ability must often be judged. Many examples of the general success or failure of engineers may be traced to proportionate success or failure in the composition of their reports. As T. O. Richards and Ralph A. Richardson of the General Motors Corporation have said, "Success in engineering and research depends as much upon the ability to present an idea convincingly as it does upon the ability to perform calculations and experiments." [1]

The many situations in the engineering professions calling for reports can hardly be enumerated. Consider the hundreds of problems that call for a recording and communication of facts: highway, building, bridge, dam, or sewer construction; electric power developments; questions of water supply; selection of sites for every sort of development; examination of mining properties; development of oil fields; tests of machinery and materials; means for improving plant efficiency; in fact, all the problems that engineers must face.

Research scientists. Today thousands of reports result from the investigations and research of scientists, presenting to interested persons information about new scientific and technical discoveries.

---

[1] In *Technical Writing*, an address given by Thomas O. Richards, Head of the Laboratory Control Department, and Ralph A. Richardson, Head of the Technical Data Department, at Ann Arbor, June 11, 1941.

New classifications, new types of machinery, new interpretations, new developments in scientific theory—all these call for recording in the form of reports.

Government departments constitute one of the most important producers of such reports; yet there are many other organizations that publish valuable new scientific and technical information—colleges and universities, scientific and technical societies, museums, and groups formed for the advancement of learning in special fields. Such reports, as we have previously noted, are ordinarily highly technical in tone and diction, and often highly theoretical.

Architects. The modern architect must maintain contacts, not alone with his own organization, but with his clients and the contractors.

Within the organization he receives reports from his employees or from consulting experts. Usually these reports are short, and they are frequently in the form of letters or memoranda. The "work book" in the drafting room is an interesting record, containing as it does all information necessary for those making plans and specifications. It may legitimately be classified as a report, although it consists not of one, but of many separate subjects.

It is customary for the architect to deliver the plans to his client in person in order that he may be able to explain, interpret, and, if necessary, defend them. But, when a meeting of architect and client is impossible, the architect may employ a written explanation or report. When recommendations for important developments cover a period of years, and when a considerable number of people will be interested in plans for the future, the architect's or landscape architect's report is sometimes printed. The printed form is adaptable, however, only for developments of public interest, such as city planning, or a program for improving college buildings and grounds.

In his relations with client and contractor the architect customarily makes his communications orally; but, even after information has been so delivered, or agreements so reached, it is essential in many cases to furnish a written record, or "confirmation," of what has taken place. The value of such records is obvious.

Agriculturists and foresters. The agriculturist's reports are usually public in character, and are often to be classified as "scientific research." In most instances they are published under national, state, or experiment-station authorization, and are distributed gratuitously or at small cost to all persons who desire the information they contain.

The forester is more frequently called upon for reports in connection with the routine work of his profession. The "forest engineer" deals with a complex and difficult type of report that covers extended investigation of great timber properties. If his work is to be valuable, he must possess considerable skill both in organization and in communication of material.

General administrators. The executive functions of modern business include the interpretation and presentation of facts from the point of view of organization policy. Periodic reports are regularly written by many executives. These reports, usually made annually, cover new developments, comparisons with previous periods, the outlook for the future, and specific recommendations. Such reports are usually dependent upon numerous professional and routine reports from specialists and subordinates. They are condensed and generalized. They concern themselves only with the broad features of the work. Boards of directors, stockholders, and taxpayers are the groups of persons to whom the more important administrative reports are directed.

Who reads reports? The reader of a private report is generally acting in some executive capacity. That is, he uses the report to help him reach decisions and determine policies. It is as an executive that the chief engineer receives reports from his assistants; he, in turn, must report to other executives. The production manager, the sales manager, and the general manager all receive reports from men responsible to them; and they in turn report to those in higher executive positions. Often, of course, the executive reader has far less technical knowledge than the writer of the report; so technical data must be translated for him to understand.

The consultant's clients read his reports in order to understand what he has done and what he advises. Commonly, of course, these clients are laymen without the consultant's technical background.

The public reports of government agencies are intended for two broad classes: the taxpayers and the special interest groups. Taxpayers read reports of a general, nontechnical nature as they read their newspapers. The special groups, however, have a practical interest in reports that touch their own wants; statisticians, importers, farmers—hundreds of professional and occupational groups find reports fitted to their needs and often read at least semi-technical exposition with interest.

The private reports of experiment stations, museums, professional societies, and scientific foundations are often technical in nature, intended for technical readers.

Readers of reports, then, are of all kinds; but only rarely do they have the same technical or specialized background as the writer. Always, if the report is worth writing at all, the reader lacks the knowledge the writer has to convey.

Qualifications needed by the report writer. Good report writing may not require genius, but it does require preparation. Anyone with average acquirements can learn to write the reports demanded of him, provided he knows the essentials and is willing to study and practice.

The first requirement for success is *experience* in the general field with which the report deals. The untrained observer overlooks important details and fails to distinguish the important from the irrelevant. Broad training and knowledge come first.

Such experience and background are largely responsible for the power of *accurate observation*—the most essential quality in the list. The report writer must see the thing as it is.

Ability in *analysis and judgment* follows closely after observation. The writer must pick his problem apart, discover its component elements, and reason to sound conclusions.

Freedom from preconceptions, essential in all scientific procedures, makes original and accurate work possible. To "know" what you are going to find before you investigate closes your eyes to all conflicting facts and leads to absurd mistakes. Background and experience are useful only when the observer remains capable of viewing each new situation with fresh eyes and open mind.

Common sense demands concentrating on essentials, emphasizing the significant, and adapting to the situation at hand.

Accuracy of expression cannot be minimized. To express false conceptions accurately does not make them more true, but at least it enables the reader to discover their falsity more easily. To hit the nail on the head is as desirable as to have a nail to hit.

Finally, the report writer needs an *understanding of the reader.* He senses the reader's wants and interests, recognizes his education and background, understands his needs. He learns to write differently for different persons. He adopts the rule: "The reader is always right."

The guiding principles. Unlike the literary artist, the report writer composes neither for his own entertainment nor for that of his reader. A report must be a thoroughly useful document. The reader usually wants the information. The writer's satisfaction is in giving it to him in the most economical and agreeable way possible. A few guiding principles will help. Keep these in mind. Apply them to every rule, every suggestion, that you find in this book:

1. *Save the reader's time.* The reader's time comes first, your time second. Clear typing; simple statements; elimination of all excess verbiage, repetitions, and jargon; the use of tables of contents, clear titles and subtitles, well-labeled tables and figures; and good summaries in prominent places (especially at the beginning) with full topic sentences to start each paragraph—these are some of the devices that help readers to get what they want fast.

2. *Remember the reader's needs.* Tell not all you know, but all your reader wants to know. Answer his questions, as stated or implied, and nothing more.

3. *Make the report objective.* The emphasis is not on the writer, but on the findings and conclusions. Personal feelings, personal accounts, are generally out of place.

4. *Use restraint.* Use the language of scientific thinking. Avoid all exaggerations. Use few superlatives such as "very," "exceedingly," "absolutely," and "ideal." Guard your undemonstrated conclusions with particular care. Never say "facts prove" unless they do prove—beyond all possible doubt. Understatement is more fitting in reports than overstatement.

5. *Interpret the raw facts.* Tables and charts are not enough for a full report. Significant items must be taken out for emphasis; meanings must be added. It is the writer's job to explain.

6. *Provide for future reference.* Most reports of importance are filed for possible later use. Hence they must be as understandable ten years from now as they are today. That accounts for the need of full titles, full explanations, and full data.

7. *Give attention to appearances.* Neat, attractive copy appeals to the eye. It reflects your good taste. It is easier to read.

Study these rules; refer to them constantly as you write your reports.

Exercises

Suggestions for study. To secure immediate interest, and to make the actual writing of trial reports less superficial, you should begin your work by choosing a number of subjects for reports to be completed at a later time. Then begin your investigation of those subjects, keeping eyes open for facts and ideas, making plans for observations at first hand, interviewing persons who may help you, or communicating with individuals or with organizations. If you have in mind definite subjects for development, moreover, you will give more attention to the study of principles of composition than you otherwise would.

Before you begin the actual composition of long reports, however, you should have some immediate experience with the less complicated types. In order to provide such practice, and to introduce the whole subject of report writing, we make our approach through the business letter. Letters are not only closely related to reports—very frequently they *are* reports. In writing them, you learn the value of conciseness, of saying at once the thing you want to say, and particularly of meeting your reader's demands.

Subjects for development. You are expected during your study to write several long reports, from 1000 to 4000 words in length. You should select your subjects at once. If possible, choose subjects with which you have had actual experience, or with which you can now become acquainted.

Address every report to a definite reader. Decide, when you choose your subjects, to what reader or readers you will address your discussion, and what position you, as the writer, are supposed to hold.

The following subjects are intended to be suggestive:

1. For a periodic report (monthly, quarterly, semiannual, or annual), providing a record of accomplishments for the period and a comparison with similar periods of the past:

A college society or fraternity	A college department
An athletic team or association	A town, village, or borough
A chamber of commerce	A finance committee
A small corporation, from president to stockholders	
A labor union, from an official to the members	

A department or official of a manufacturing concern:

Production department   Safety supervisor
Cost department   Health officer
Personnel department   Plant foreman
Maintenance department   Sales manager

2. For a progress report, covering the progress made in a project not yet completed:

A pilot-plant or laboratory experiment
A dam, a water system, a road, or a building under construction
A term paper
A housing or slum-clearance program
An extended study of efficiency in shop, laboratory, office
An investigation of some phase of labor-management problems
The erection and equipment of an addition to a plant
The conversion of a plant to a new product

3. For an examination report, covering facts discovered through an investigation or inspection:

Inspection, calling for description and explanation:

A water-supply system   A timber cruise of a small tract
A heating system   A traffic problem
Fire-protection equipment   A mine
A power plant   A recreational area
A sewage disposal plant   A harbor or naval base
A broadcasting station   An airport
A geological study of a small area   A commercial garage
Material used in a local factory, laboratory, or office

Examination, calling for a discussion of the comparative value of:

Two automobiles   Safety devices for mines
Road materials   New machinery for a factory
Bridge materials   New equipment for a mine
Heating systems   Types of airplane motors
Coals (fuel values)   Diesel or gasoline engines
Group insurance plans   Types of cameras
Air-conditioning systems   Types of building insulation

Examination, calling for an independent report:

Methods of paying workmen
Methods of profit sharing
Methods of local taxation
Theories of zoning or of slum clearance
Theories of municipal government
Manufacturing industries of a city
Workmen's compensation laws in the United States
Pension or retirement plans
Methods of regulating traffic on city or state highways
The gardens, forests, or mineral resources of your state

Examination, determining the reasons for:

Distribution of students in different courses
Varying living costs in several towns
Difference in price of two similar products
Different types of architecture found in a town
Differences in fertility of farms in the same region
Strikes in the state
Decrease in profits in some industry
The greater durability of some material

4. For a recommendation report, which reaches a decision, advocates a policy or action, and presents facts in support of the writer's position:

Plans:

Better layout of a factory	Drainage for a mine
A real-estate development	Slum clearance
Establishing a city park system	Central heating
Substitution of buses for trolleys	

Elimination of grade crossings in the county
Program for decreasing accidents in a factory or mine

Selection of sites:

A theater	A drive-in market
A gasoline station	A chicken farm
A branch office	A golf course
A fish hatchery	An artillery range
A new factory	A dam
A summer hotel	A county hospital

Advisability of action:

Installing fluorescent lighting
Installing new machinery
Installing parking meters
Building a municipal airport, autocamp, or hospital
Changing a method of management or manufacture
Buying a store, a farm, a factory, a mine

5. For a "search of the literature," which integrates, summarizes, and perhaps interprets the published information on some technical or scientific material or process; the information to be obtained by an exhaustive search of *current* technical periodicals and bulletins (see the bibliography, Appendix B):

Newly discovered synthetics, isotopes, antibiotics
Special uses of the air-borne magnetometer, or the mass spectograph
Special uses of atomic energy
New treatments for certain diseases, such as fluorination for dental caries and streptomycin for tuberculosis
New methods of oil prospecting, coal mining, job evaluation, profit sharing
New uses for known materials

CHAPTER 2

THE REPORT IN LETTER FORM

Relation between letters and reports. The short report, with which our study ought naturally to begin, is customarily in the form of business correspondence. Furthermore, all report writing conforms more or less to the standards, customs, and conventions of the letter. It demands little observation to note many points of similarity between the two forms, and to see how dependent the one actually is upon the methods of the other.

The modern report, as we have observed, is a comparatively new type of writing that has developed a form and style in keeping with the demands of a mechanical and industrial age. Like the business letter, the report is written for definite and practical ends. Neither kind of composition is intended primarily for the pleasure of writer or reader. The substance is always more important than the form; or, to put it perhaps more exactly, the form must be suited to the subject. The aim of both letter and report is to give necessary information clearly and adequately, but concisely.

The one striking dissimilarity is in the evidence of personality in the style. A modern letter is informal and personal. It attempts to establish a close and friendly contact with the reader. The writer makes frequent use of the pronouns "I" and "you." A report, on the other hand, is in the main impersonal—objective. Any personal relationship between writer and reader is consciously subordinated. Only the *facts* are deemed important.

Business correspondence is now entering upon a new period of development—a period in which we recognize more and more insistence upon courtesy, directness, good English, and attractive appearance. A similar insistence, if somewhat later in developing, is steadily growing in the field of reports. No longer are careless, poorly organized, rambling reports and letters likely to be tolerated. The demand for better reports, like the demand for better letters, is being recognized and fulfilled.

Functions of the Letter

Dependence upon the reader. In both routine correspondence and report writing, the writer is very dependent upon the wishes of his reader. Favors may be asked sometimes, or demands made, but in most instances a routine business letter is eagerly awaited and eagerly read. So is a report. The reader expects something from both. He demands that the composition cover thoroughly the necessary ground and then stop. Irrelevancies, side issues, thoughts unconnected with the central business of the message —these disturb him and distract his attention. Routine business letters, like reports, must be brief but thorough.

The kind of routine letter that most closely resembles the report is the "answer to inquiry." Such a letter is, in fact, a report in every sense except that the writer does not have the same responsibility to his reader. Let us now consider the typical letter of inquiry, and the typical answer to it.

The letter of inquiry. The writer of a letter of inquiry wants certain information or advice that another person is able to supply. Sometimes his inquiry may lead to direct and immediate profit to the person or the company addressed. At other times, however, the person addressed has nothing immediately to gain; the writer asks a favor of him, stating in his communication his exact wishes and courteously requesting answers to his questions.

Study the following examples for both form and content. An analysis of such letters as these will disclose the following characteristics:

1. The first paragraph is a "contact" paragraph, presenting directly the business of the letter, and usually indicating the reason for making the request.

2. The inquiry itself is worded and arranged in such a way as to make the answering of it as easy as possible.

   (a) Often, if the inquiry consists of more than one specific question, each question is given a paragraph by itself.

   (b) If the writer desires to give particular emphasis to each specific question, he may adopt special devices: numbering each question, indenting the section containing questions, or employing a spacing scheme different from that found in the rest of the letter. Use of a numbering system gives a questionnaire-like appearance distasteful to some

CUSHMAN CHEMICAL COMPANY
Trona
California

January 14, 1949

Mr. Richard Woolett, Head
Testing and Instrument Division
Eastman Salt Products Corporation
Gunderson, Pennsylvania

Dear Mr. Woolett:

Our manufacturing division contemplates replacing its present recording flow meters with
Johnston equipment. We understand that you, after
considerable investigation, have already made this
change.

Would you be willing to let us know what consideration led you to choose the Johnston meters,
and how satisfactory they have proved since their
installation? We are especially interested in the
answers to the following questions:

1. How much maintenance do these meters require?

2. How much is their accuracy affected by changes in
the temperature of the liquid?

3. What kind of replacement and parts service do
you get?

We will appreciate any information you can
send us, and we look forward to the opportunity of
returning the favor.

Very truly yours,
CUSHMAN CHEMICAL COMPANY

R. Paul Campbell

R. Paul Campbell
Purchasing Agent

RPC:gch

Carmel Products Co.,
200 Rock Mill Road,
Carmel (5), New York,
February 21, 1949.

Professor John Truby, Head,
Department of English,
State University,
Albany (12), New York.

Dear Professor Truby:

As one of your former students, I am appealing to
you for some specific information on modern practice
in the business letter.

Since one of my present jobs is to set up a "style
sheet" for our company correspondence, I would appreciate your help in selecting the most appropriate
letter form. The textbooks I have consulted leave
me in doubt about the following:

1. Which letter style is most desirable today — the
block, modified block, indented, or military?

2. What punctuation is necessary, what optional?

3. In the salutation is it courteous to address a
stranger by name or should one use "Dear Sir," or
"My dear Sir"?

4. Is it proper to itemize questions as I am doing?

5. Where should the "Attention" line be placed?

6. Is a "Subject" line good practice, and if so
where should it be placed?

I shall be grateful for any information you are
willing to give me on these points — and on any
others you believe troublesome.

Respectfully yours,

Stephen Cornell

Stephen Cornell
Executive Assistant

sc/mk

readers unless they are fundamentally interested in the material.

3. The letter of inquiry is tactful, exhibiting an appreciation of the expected favor, explaining the reason for desiring the information, and when possible offering service in return.

Answers to inquiries. The answer to inquiry bears a striking resemblance to a short report. To be sure, the relationship between writer and reader is seldom the same: the writer is usually granting a favor rather than performing a routine duty. But it is the object of both forms of composition to present definite information. If the writer intends to grant the request at all, his answer is determined rather definitely by the one who put the questions. The scope of the answer, if not fixed, is at least implied. Courtesy will demand that the answer cover the ground and no more.

The following example and the letter reproduced on page 17, then, are in the form of simple reports. Each of them either supplies all the information requested or directs attention to other sources of knowledge.

NEWTON SALT PRODUCTS CORPORATION
Gunderson
Pennsylvania

January 22, 1949

Mr. R. Paul Campbell
Purchasing Agent
Cushman Chemical Company
Trona, California

Dear Mr. Campbell:

Replying to your letter of January 14 regarding our Johnston flow meters, I am very glad to send you what information we have.

We chose the Johnston meter for several reasons:

1. Though the original cost is greater, the instrument is more fully guaranteed than other flow meters.
2. The original cost includes installation and recalibration by Johnston engineers.

3. The recorder can be placed at a considerable distance from the meter body and orifice plate without time lag. As you know, this proves especially important in controlled chemistry processes where one or two men must be in constant touch with many elements.

4. Actual flow tests satisfied us that the Johnston meter was never less than 99% accurate over a considerable range of flows, densities, and temperatures. I am enclosing a copy of the report made from these tests.

The meters, without exception, have proved completely satisfactory since installation. We have seldom had any difficulty at all with the recorders or meter bodies. Occasionally the mercury in the latter has become dirty and required cleaning. In some of the lines carrying heavy solutions of salt we have had to remove and clean the orifice plates at intervals of a month. About the only other maintenance costs we have incurred result from periodic tests and calibrations of the recorders.

We have had little occasion to order replacements or parts. The few times that we have needed such service it has been very prompt. There has been some difficulty in obtaining monel orifice plates, but of course this is in no way peculiar to the Johnston instrument.

I hope that this information is what you need. If I can be of any further assistance, please do not hesitate to call on me.

Yours truly,

Richard Woolett

Richard Woolett, Head
Testing Division

rw/gfc
Enclosure

The letter which follows, in addition to serving as an example of the "answer to inquiry," also contains definite instructions on letter *form* and is itself a good example of the modified block.

State University
Department of English
Albany 12, New York
February 24, 1949

Carmel Products Co.
200 Rock Mill Road
Carmel 5, New York

Attention Mr. Cornell

Gentlemen: Subject: Business Correspondence

I am glad to offer what suggestions I can in response to your letter of February 21. Practice in business correspondence is, of course, anything but uniform, but for purposes of selecting a particular style sheet I believe I can answer your questions with reasonable brevity.

1. The two letter styles most in use today are the block (which you used) and the modified block (which I am using). The only difference lies in the indention of the paragraphs in the letter body. The modified block is somewhat more common but not necessarily more desirable. I'd suggest you choose either of these and forget the others. The indented form is fast disappearing (from a typist's point of view it is inefficient), and the military style is generally considered too brusque.

2· "Open" punctuation is used almost exclusively. It is definitely preferable because of its simplicity. In open punctuation the only marks at the end of the lines in the formal parts of the letter are the colon after the salutation and, less often, the comma after the "Yours truly" or its substitute. Internal punctuation follows the usual rules of course; a comma between name and title, city and state, day and year. Incidentally, the city zone designation follows the city without parentheses.

3. The trend in salutations is to personalize, to address even a stranger by his name. Why not?

4. It certainly is efficient to itemize questions and answers as you and I have done. Many authori-

ties state that a separate letter should be written
for each subject discussed. This seems unneces-
sarily wasteful of time and materials. Itemization
seems a good solution.

Carmel Products Co.   2   February 24, 1949

    5. The "Attention" line should be placed as I
have illustrated above. My personal preference is
to address the individual directly. However, its
use is desirable when the company's name would identify a filed carbon copy (particularly the second
sheet) more readily than would the individual's.

    6. The "Subject" line is used by some reputable
firms, but most prefer to refer to the subject in
the opening sentence of the letter body. For quick
reference, a subject line, placed as I have placed
it above and underscored, is efficient.

    I would like to add one suggestion about a
seemingly inconsequential matter — the folding of
the letter for enclosure in the ordinary small business envelope. It is easy to avoid the trivial but
unnecessary irritation caused by improper folding.
Thus:

    1st: Fold the face-up letter horizontally so that
        the bottom edge falls a quarter to a half
        inch below the top.
    2nd: Fold the right-hand edge one third of the
        width.
    3rd: Fold the left-hand edge to the right, just
        short of the crease created by the previous
        step.
    4th: Insert the letter into the envelope with
        the fold to the back and the open edge up.

    I am pleased to be of this small assistance,
and shall be equally pleased to answer any further
questions that may come up.

                  Sincerely yours,

                  John Truby

                  John Truby, Head
                  Department of English

jt;eb

Such letters are similar in essentials—in style and organization —to regular short reports. Consider the plan:

1. The first, or "contact," paragraph presents the subject and aim of the letter.

2. The second paragraph, if the letter is very long, may be a summary of the information that follows.

3. Each question, whether stated in the letter of inquiry or inferred from it, is answered in a separate paragraph, in the order of its presentation in the letter of inquiry.

4. The final paragraph usually expresses a willingness to serve and expresses hope that the reader will be satisfied with the data supplied.

The reader's attitude. The reader of any answer to an inquiry is naturally interested in its contents—he asked for them. To satisfy him, therefore, the writer need only come to the essential point without delay, and cover the details only so thoroughly as to meet his reader's needs.

So with the reader of a report: usually he, too, has a definite motive for desiring what is to be found there. The need to stimulate new interest is slight, and the devices of the short-story writer worth little. The subject itself arouses interest. This is especially obvious when the reader has himself made a request for information.

The letter of instructions. The letter of instructions—from employer to employee, from superior to subordinate, or from client to expert—deserves a good deal of the report writer's attention. Such a letter is sometimes sufficiently detailed to outline the investigation demanded and the subjects to be covered by the report. At other times it is general, permitting the report writer to use his own best judgment in investigation and in writing. But the letter of instructions is always a real guide to the one who receives it. Whether short or long, it may have an important bearing upon the construction of the report.

The letter of inquiry often asks a favor, which the addressee may or may not wish to grant. But the letter of instructions actually makes a demand. The writer of such a letter is ordinarily paying for services, or he holds a position that entitles him to give orders. Yet, as the following examples show, the tone is scarcely less courteous and the arrangement little different.

— 1 —

KENT & HALSEY

Inter-Office Communication

January 7, 1950

Mr. N. B. Sanborn
Engineering Department
Mojave Plant

Dear Sanborn:

The Mojave hospital reports show a constant increase in the number of cases of soda-ash burn treated. Several of these cases have caused the company considerable expense in lost time as well as money. Will you investigate and report with recommendations as soon as possible?

Sincerely yours
(*Signature*) .
Bart Watson
Vice-President

This letter of instructions leaves all methods of investigation and presentation to the writer. He must employ judgment in determining how far he shall go, and how he may best present his findings. The letter calls for a definite investigation and implies the purpose of the report.

The following letter is somewhat more specific, both in explaining the purpose of the report and in defining its scope. The report writer who is so definitely instructed usually will find it advisable to follow the same order as that outlined in the letter. It is significant to observe that Dr. Bush does so in his response, the letter of transmittal accompanying the now-famous Bush Report.

— 2 —

The White House
Washington, D. C.
November 17, 1944

Dear Dr. Bush:

The Office of Scientific Research and Development, of which you are the Director, represents a unique experiment of teamwork and cooperation in coordinating scientific research and in applying existing scientific knowledge to the technical problems paramount in war. Its work has been conducted in the utmost secrecy and carried on without public recognition of any kind: but its tangible results can be found in the communiques coming in from all over the world. Some day the full story of its achievements can be told.

There is, however, no reason why the lessons to be found in this experiment cannot be profitably employed in times of peace. The information, the techniques, and the research experience developed by the Office of Scientific Research and Development and by the thousands of scientists in the universities and in private industry, should be used in the days of peace ahead for the improvement of the national health, the creation of new enterprises bringing new jobs, and the betterment of the national standard of living.

It is with that objective in mind that I would like to have your recommendations on the following four major points:

First: What can be done, consistent with military security, and with the prior approval of the military authorities, to make known to the world as soon as possible the contributions which have been made during our war effort to scientific knowledge?

The diffusion of such knowledge should help us stimulate new enterprises, provide jobs for our returning servicemen and other workers, and make possible great strides for the improvement of the national well-being.

Second: With particular reference to the war of science against disease, what can be done now to organize a program for continuing in the future the work which has been done in medicine and related sciences?

The fact that the annual deaths in this country from one or two diseases alone are far in excess of the total number of lives lost by us in battle during this war should make us conscious of the duty we owe future generations.

Third: What can the Government do now and in the future to aid research activities by public and private organizations? The proper roles of public and private research, and their interrelation, should be carefully considered.

Fourth: Can an effective program be proposed for discovering and developing scientific talent in American youth so that the continuing future of scientific research in this country may be assured on a level comparable to what has been done during the war?

New frontiers of the mind are before us, and if they are pioneered with the same vision, boldness, and drive with which we have waged this war we can create a fuller and more fruitful employment and a fuller and more fruitful life.

I hope that, after such consultation as you may deem advisable with your associates and others, you can let me have your considered judgment on these matters as soon as convenient—reporting on each when you are ready, rather than waiting for completion of your studies in all.

Very sincerely yours,
(s) Franklin D. Roosevelt

Dr. Vannevar Bush,
Office of Scientific Research and Development
Washington, D. C.

It is apparent that the organization of letters of instruction is not particularly different from that of letters of inquiry. Although in his letter, President Roosevelt has thought it necessary or desirable to introduce his letter with background material, ordinarily the first paragraph, as in all letters, is "contact." It states the business of the letter—in this type it calls immediate attention to the task before the reader. Sometimes that single paragraph is deemed sufficient. Perhaps more often, however, the report writer must be provided with certain information that will make his instructions clearer to him, and the desirability of outlining the needed information is often evident.

The completeness of a letter of instructions depends upon several things. Frequently the writer is himself unfamiliar with the full requirements for an investigation; he has insufficient technical background to know with any definiteness what will be needed. He does know, however, the broad problems that must be solved. In such situations the executive's letter of instructions will leave all details to the discretion of the specialist. In other cases the writer of such a letter is himself a specialist addressing a subordinate or assistant. Here the nature of his instructions will depend chiefly upon how much confidence he is able to place in the initiative and wisdom of his subordinate. There are also times when the nontechnical executive is possessed of general information about the particular problem, which the specialist must have if his work is to proceed readily. Whenever he does, he will naturally convey such information to his readers in his letter of instructions.

The extent of the instructions will, in general, depend upon the knowledge of the man giving them and upon the specific knowledge, ability, and good sense of the man who is asked to do the work.

The letter report. When the information demanded in a report requires no more than two or three pages, it is sometimes written as an ordinary letter. Since the business letter form is thus frequently employed by the report writer, he must understand it thoroughly.

The similarity between an answer to an inquiry and a short letter report will be evident from a study of the following examples.

— 1 —

KENT & HALSEY

Inter-Office Communication

January 14, 1950

Mr. Bart Watson
Vice-President
Office

Dear Mr. Watson:

I have completed the investigation you requested in a communication of January 7 regarding the number of hospital cases of caustic burns suffered by employees of the Soda Products Plant.

The burns are chiefly assignable to preventable causes. Most of the trouble could be avoided by enforcement of rules already prescribed by the Safety Committee. I am convinced that 90% of the cases can be eliminated by putting the following recommendations into effect:

1. Employees—Some men are much more susceptible than others to the soda-ash irritation. There is no effective method of preventing them from getting the "rash," and their cases are the most serious. They should be transferred to another plant where they will not be subjected to caustic dust.

2. Clothing—The Safety Committee's rule with regard to clothing to be worn in this plant is too general. Men should not be allowed to work unless fully protected by dust-proof clothing, or more accurately, dust-resistant clothing. This would mean gloves, caps, long sleeves, and heavy leather shoes.

3. Showers—The men should be made to take showers after each shift. A shower-room should be provided and the men should be allowed to use it on company time if the rule is to be effective.

4. Cuts, etc.—No one should be allowed in the plant with even a small uncovered cut or abrasion. Very serious infections are liable to result from such serious carelessness. The foremen should be told emphatically to check on this.

5. Hours—The men in the Soda Products Plant work the usual 8-hr shifts, winter and summer. The evaporating units and rotary dryers make the place very uncomfortable for men properly clothed even in winter. In summer it is practically unbearable. This is especially true in the dryer room, the hottest and dustiest place in the plant. This situation can be somewhat alleviated by having the men in the dryer room change off with the men in the burkeite yard or those on the Dorr thickener, but the only really feasible solution, in my opinion, is a 6-hr shift (dryer room only) and the installation of some induced-draft ventilators.

6. Auxiliary conveyors—Many of the more serious cases of soda-ash burn —almost all of those in which the lungs and throat are affected—result from a breakdown in the conveying system. These breakdowns are unavoidable despite the micromax-thermocouple control of the dryers, for sometimes the filter cake feeding the dryer is too damp, forms into lumps, and clogs the conveyors. The dryers cannot be stopped without losing several hours' production; consequently, there is nowhere for the soda ash to go except on the dryer-room floor. Installation of an auxiliary conveyor (one would suffice for both units) would eliminate this hazard.

7. Washer—Installation of a dust-washer (spray type) over each of the magnetic separators would not only eliminate much of the plant dust but would permit return of the dust, in solution, to production.

I trust this is the information you desire.

Yours truly,

The foregoing letter, though written in response to very general instructions, follows a logical plan. The first paragraph presents the exact business of the report. The second paragraph provides a general summary of the conclusions reached after the investigation. Then follow definite recommendations, each in a separate paragraph. Note the use of subtitles. In a letter of some length, covering several points, such a method of calling the reader's attention to each section is advantageous.

The letter that follows is of a different type. Described as a "confirmation" report, its object is not to supply new information or advice, but to provide a written record of an understanding, or of information, previously reached or conveyed orally. Such letters are frequently needed as records, written and signed, and therefore binding, to prevent oversight that might be expected if every person concerned were obliged to depend entirely upon memory. The confirmation report may sometimes serve as a contract, or as an amendment to a contract. Again, it may be a pure information report, unusual only in that the facts contained in it are already known to the reader.

— 2 —

JOHN H. WALKER
Landscape Architect
Newton, Illinois

August 3, 1950

Mr. Albert C. Russe
612 Fourth Avenue
Chicago, Illinois

Dear Mr. Russe:

This letter is written in confirmation of the oral understanding reached in our conference of August 1, at which you and Mrs. Russe, Mr. P. H. Smith, Field Manager of the Carter Construction Company, and I were present.

Plans and specifications were read and approved in part as follows:

It was agreed that the proposal of the Carter Construction Company be accepted for all the roads shown on the plans and as specified, except the connecting service road shown on the plans as Road "B." Mr. Smith agreed to deduct $1250 from his proposal for the omission, leaving a total sum of $5690.

Mr. Watson was authorized to order the necessary flagstone for the paths shown on the plans, to be delivered at the nearest freight station at $430, and to be laid by the Carter Construction Company for the sum of $350 in accordance with their contract.

Grading was authorized according to plans and specifications at rates named in Mr. Smith's proposal:

"A"	$ 930
"B"	695
"C"	1980
"D"	2265
Total	$5870

Other work outlined in the specifications was omitted at this time. The contract is to be prepared at once by the Landscape Architect, signed by the Carter Construction Company, and then sent to you for your approval and signature.

Very truly yours,

The confirmation report is usually short, since it covers only the important features of a single conference. It may appear either as a business letter or as a memorandum (see page 34).

These examples of the short letter report will serve to illustrate something of the nature of report writing. Sèveral characteristics may be briefly pointed out:

AMERICAN RADIATOR & **Standard Sanitary**

CORPORATION

OFFICE OF MANAGER
RESEARCH AND PRODUCT
DEVELOPMENT

P O Box 1226
PITTSBURGH 30, PA.

September 26, 1948

Professor Lyne S. S. Hoffman
Department of English Composition
The Pennsylvania State College
State College, Pennsylvania

Dear Professor Hoffman:

Your inquiry about the ability of the present-day
engineering graduate to write reports is of considerable personal
interest to me -- I spend a good part of my time reading those
reports.

Actually the technical students we get today are very
much all right in their technical training. However, the same
mistake is being made today as when I went to school; there is
not enough appreciation of a thorough command of simple, concise
English. In our department we have mechanical, ceramic, metallurgical, electrical, and chemical engineers. But those who use our
reports are seldom, if ever, technical men, and our greatest
difficulty is in getting our people to write up their reports in
simple, everyday English that everyone understands. The value of
the report is lost when a busy executive is forced to wade through
a maze of technical terms. He just doesn't read the report.

If you can get the technical student to understand that
his ideas are of no value unless he can "put them across" and
that he cannot put them across except by the use of simple everyday
English that doesn't require the reader to keep a dictionary or a
glossary of technical terms at his elbow, then he will be a welcome
addition to any engineering or research department.

Yours very truly,

JCReid

Manager

mjd

Serving the Nations' Health and Comfort

ARSS-2331 MGR. RSRCH.

FIG. 1. The Letter Make-up

1. The report is *direct*. It wastes no time in coming to the point. It states its business, and usually its conclusions, at the outset.

2. The report is *concise*. It does not ramble or digress.

3. The report is *considerate* of the reader. It sets out to supply him with what he wants and needs, with no more and no less.

The letter of transmittal. The conventional letter form often plays a part even in long reports that are not written as letters. Such reports are often introduced by letters of transmittal. This use of the letter is discussed in Chapter 7, Preparing the Manuscript.

Note: Since the **letter of application** is not directly related to our subject but is important to many readers, it receives special treatment in Appendix A.

Mechanics of Letter Writing

Although there are several acceptable forms for the modern business letter, it follows many very definite conventions. A recognition of the best usage is an advantage that few can afford to ignore. The young man especially, whatever his work, should exemplify the best practices in modern letter writing.

For the reasons already mentioned in "Professor Truby's" letter (pages 17–18) only the block style and its modified form are considered relevant to the purposes of this book. Consequently, all the discussion and all illustrations are limited to these two forms.

The brief set of instructions that follows will serve as an adequate guide for most business correspondence. For detailed treatment of the letter consult one of the references listed in the bibliography, Appendix B. These specifications are those for the modified block, but this style differs from the block only in its indention of the letter paragraphs.

Paper

If the letter writer is not supplied with company paper, he should select white paper of good quality and standard size (8½ by 11 inches). Half sheets are sometimes justified for very short letters, but even then the carbon should be on a standard sheet for efficiency in filing. Intracompany correspondence may be written on paper of various colors for easy identification of department, division, or plant source.

Typing

Unless impossible, all business letters should be typed and a carbon copy made for reference. Care should be taken to see that the typewriter ribbon is satisfactory and the type clean.

Ink

Though a few reputable houses use blue ink, black is still the rule. If the letter must be handwritten, only black, blue, or blue-black are acceptable.

Make-up of the letter

Heading. Since the first page of most business letters is written on a sheet bearing the firm's letterhead, only a date line is commonly required. The complete and unabbreviated date is absolutely essential. It sometimes appears directly under the letterhead, more often under it and to the right so that it just reaches the right-hand margin. If there is no printed letterhead, the typed heading appears in the upper right-hand corner, just over the date, and with its longest line just reaching the margin:

> 444 Fifth Avenue
> New York 22, N. Y.
> March 21, 1950

Inside (introductory) address. The inside address includes the name of the person or group to whom the letter is directed, and sufficient address to make mistakes in identification (particularly of the filed carbon) impossible. It begins on the left-hand margin at least two lines below the heading:

Mr. Paul Andrews		Mr. Bryant Fitch, Head
Vice President		Research & Development
Prentice-Hall, Inc.	*or*	Nicholson Products Co.
70 Fifth Avenue		2210 Wacker Drive
New York 11, N. Y.		Chicago 14, Illinois

A certain amount of juggling of the elements of the inside address is possible when it improves the appearance of the block. But an individual or company name must agree in spelling and abbreviation (if any) with the form used by the owner, as in a letterhead for example.

Attention line. When the individual's name is known it is generally better to address him directly, but if the letter desires a prompt response from the *company*, not from any particular person (who may be out of town, for example), then the attention line serves a useful purpose. When the attention line is employed it follows the inside address, two lines below and two above the salutation, usually against the left-hand margin.

Salutation. The salutation is the polite form of address that introduces practically all letters (all block and modified block). It is placed on the left-hand margin two lines below the inside address or, if one is used, the attention line. The formal salutations are *Dear Sir, Dear Madam, Gentlemen, Mesdames.* Slightly more formal is the *My dear Sir* type. Sensibly, the trend is very clearly in favor of addressing the individual directly, as *Dear Mr. Keeler,* or *My dear Mr. Keeler.* **Note:** When an attention line is used the salutation should address the firm, not the individual.

Subject line. Though it is efficient for quick reference the subject line is relatively uncommon. When used, it should be prominently displayed (see letter, page 17). Its use does not eliminate the necessity for an immediate statement of the business of the letter in the letter body.

Letter body. The letter body, of course, contains the message of the letter. It is centered on the page and divided into comparatively short paragraphs, which are more effective in holding reader attention. The first paragraph begins two lines below the salutation and is indented, usually about ten spaces.

Complimentary close. It is customary to close a letter with a conventional phrase: *Yours truly, Respectfully yours, Sincerely yours, Cordially yours,* or the like. The exact phrase used should have some relationship to the message of the letter or with the writer's attitude toward his reader. *Sincerely yours,* for example, indicates a spirit of friendliness and informality. *Yours truly,* on the other hand, is the proper close for an impersonal business communication. *Respectfully yours,* again, should be used only when the writer actually intends to emphasize his *respect* for the reader, and today is usually confined to the communications from a subordinate to his superior.

The complimentary close appears two lines below the letter body and on a line by itself. Preferably it begins on the vertical line established by the heading or date line or directly at the center of the page.

Signature. Every letter should be signed by the writer. Occasionally the company name comes first, followed by the writer's name, as follows:

> Very truly yours,
> BOWMAN & NICHOLS, Inc.
> *Michael Cannon* (signed)
> Michael Cannon
> General Manager

The present trend, however, is to omit the company name in the signature if it appears on the letterhead:

> Very truly yours,
> *Michael Cannon* (signed)
> Michael Cannon
> General Manager

Supplement. When it is desirable to know who typed the letter for writer's signature, a supplement is used. It is typed flush to the left-hand margin. A number of forms are acceptable. If, for example, in the close above Mr. Cannon's secretary is named Eleanor Black, the supplement could appear:

> Very truly yours,
> *Michael Cannon*
> Michael Cannon

MC:eb
> General Manager

Or, perhaps more efficiently,

> Very truly yours,
> *Michael Cannon*

Michael Cannon: eb
> General Manager

If the letter encloses other material, a notation to that effect is added directly below the supplement:

MC:EB
2 enclosures

Second page. Identification of a second, or third, page of a letter is made possible by typing the addressee's name, the page number, and the date across the top of the page:

Dr. Vannevar Bush   Page 2   November 17, 1944

Envelope. The address should appear on the envelope in complete form. It should be blocked. If an attention line is used on the letter, it should be placed in the lower left-hand corner of the envelope.

Spacing

The appearance of the letter is greatly dependent upon intelligent spacing. Generous use of white space has much to do with making the letter attractive. The letter should give the appearance of being framed on the page, with its "center" slightly above the center of the page.

Margins. The width of all margins depends, of course, on the length of the letter, but it is better to use two pages than to crowd a long letter onto one. Left and right margins of an inch and a half are suggested for the average letter, with an inch the minimum. Except on some electric typewriters, an even right-hand margin cannot be achieved, but there should be as little variation as possible in the length of the lines.[1] Overall appearance is improved if more white space is left at the bottom than at the top.

Between the parts of the letter. A good rule of thumb is to double-space between the parts of the letter, double-space between paragraphs, and single-space everything else. This rule should be tempered by good judgment in several instances:

1. When a letterhead is used, the date line may be variously placed to produce the best appearance.

2. In short letters, the inside address is often dropped more than two lines below the date line.

3. In short letters, the complimentary close is occasionally dropped more than two lines below the last paragraph of the letter body.

4. In all letters, sufficient space should be allowed for the pen-written signature, even at the cost of triple-spacing between the complimentary close and the typed signature.

5. In very short letters, appearance can be greatly improved by (a) widening all margins, and (b) double-spacing the text but *not* the heading or inside address. If more than one double-spaced paragraph is used, the indention must be employed, but usually no extra spacing between paragraphs is required.

6. The subject line is generally placed on the same line with the salutation—with a minimum of five spaces between.

---

[1] Division of a word at the end of a line should be avoided if possible. If divided, the word must be divided between syllables. Never divide a very short word, and never separate a one-letter or two-letter syllable from the rest of the word.

MAKING IT FAR BETTER: SOME SUGGESTIONS

Repair job for a run-of-the-mill letter in time-worn, wordy technique.

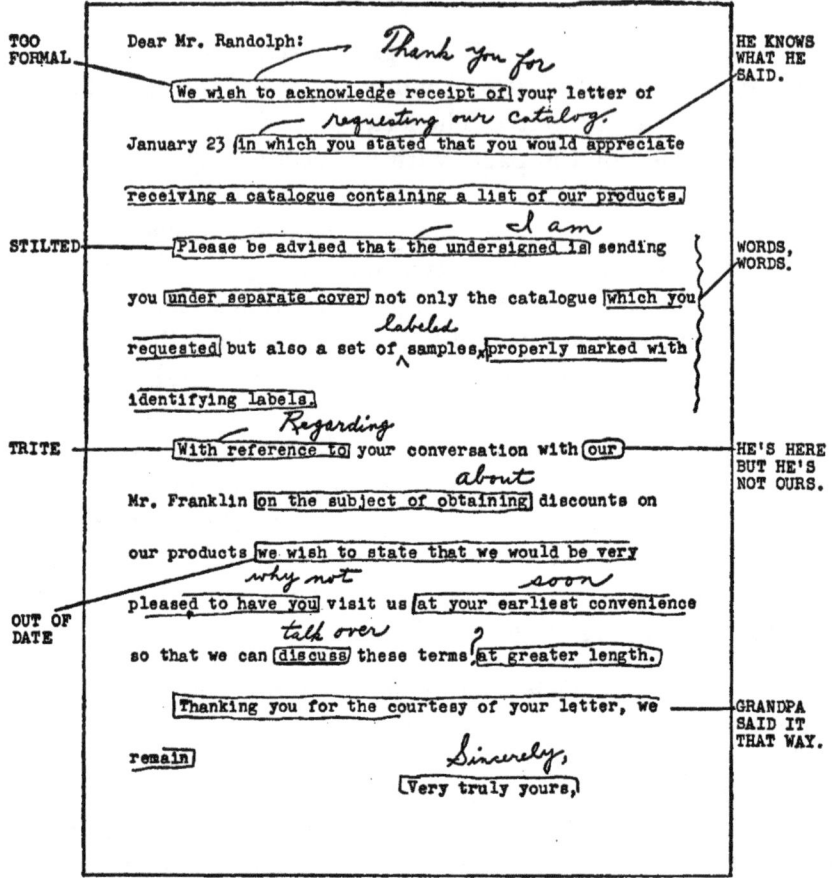

Fig. 2. Letter Style (*Courtesy of the Sun Oil Company*)

32

7. The supplement is placed on the same line with or a little below either the typed signature or the title of the signer.

Second page. The second page is *not* centered on the page. It begins two lines below the identification.

Punctuation

The predominantly used open punctuation is simple but fully satisfactory. The formal parts of the letter require no end punctuation except the colon after the salutation, the comma after the complimentary close, and a period after an abbreviation. Internal punctuation follows the standard rules for all punctuating. Commas must be used between city and state, day and year, name and title (when on same line); a colon is used after the word *subject* on the subject line; and usually either a colon or a virgule (/) between the elements of the supplement.

Capitalization

Capitalization offers no difficulty peculiar to the letter. It is worth noting that the *dear* in *My dear Sir* or *My dear Mr. Smith* is not capitalized, and that only the first word in the complimentary close is begun by a capital.

Abbreviations

In the best modern business correspondence, abbreviations of all kinds are usually avoided. If abbreviations are used (as in inter-office communication), they should be used consistently.

Words like *company, corporation,* and *incorporated* are abbreviated in titles *only* when they are abbreviated by the firm itself in its legal name. When in doubt, spell in full. In addresses it is preferable to spell out the names of numbered streets unless the numbers require more than two words.

Notes on style

A good business letter states its business courteously but directly, without trite or commonplace expressions. In the past, business correspondence was characterized by numerous abbreviations and other expressions in a sort of commercial code that could be found nowhere else. Modern letters use the language of speech, carefully avoiding the letter-writing jargon of the last century. The following rules should be observed in all letters:

1. Do not write the entire date in figures: *5–8–49*. Always use the conventional form: *May 8, 1949.*

2. Omit the letters *-st, -nd, -rd, -th* after the day of the month. Write *June 3,* not *June 3rd; May 5* not *May 5th.*

3. Avoid the participial conclusion. Leave the reader with a clear, firm impression of your letter. Instead of *Hoping this will please you,* or *Trusting that this will meet with your approval,* write *I hope this will please you,* or *I trust that this will meet with your approval.*

Memoranda

Memoranda have become increasingly important in business and industry. They serve most of the purposes of the letter (especially of the letter of instructions), *but* their use is nearly always restricted to interoffice, interdepartmental, or intershop communication. Consequently they differ from the letter in make-up, content, and style:

Make-up. Both the full- and the half-sheet memoranda are illustrated on succeeding pages. Carbon copies are fully as important for most memoranda as for business letters. When a half-sheet memorandum is used, a full-size carbon is made for filing. Note:

1. There is no indention.
2. There is no end punctuation.
3. There is no salutation or complimentary close.
4. The subject is in capitals.
5. The illustrations are self-explanatory.

Content. The memorandum deals with only one subject.

Style. The primary function of the style should be to save both reader and writer time. Courtesy is sacrificed for conciseness.

An example of the use of the memorandum for other than departmental purposes occurs in the "confirmation" report, where a written record is desirable to avoid possible misunderstanding:

MEMORANDUM

Client:	Albert C. Russe, Chicago, Illinois
Property:	Longshore Boulevard, Benton
Persons at Confer-	Mr. & Mrs. Russe
ence (July 7,	P. H. Smith, Field Manager, Carter Constr. Co.
1949):	John H. Walker, Landscape Architect

Plans and specifications were read . . . .

Office Memorandum • UNITED STATES GOVERNMENT

TO   : Hazel Lewis, Supervisor, Stenographic and   DATE. November 1, 1945
         Office Training Unit, Chattanooga
FROM   : Charles O. Libbey, Head, Office Methods Staff, Knoxville

SUBJECT: STYLE FOR INTEROFFICE MEMORANDA

This is an illustration of the standard office memorandum prescribed by the Bureau of the Budget for all Government agencies.

The items in the heading begin two spaces from the preceding colons, and the body of the memorandum uses the left margin established by the placement of the heading. The right margin may be slightly narrower than the left; the bottom margin should not fall below the minimum of one inch.

Since the Government memorandum requires the date to be typed on the same line with the name of the addressee, in some cases it is necessary to use two lines for the name and office address. Information following the word "From" is typed on one line, leaving a blank line before the subject.

Titles of courtesy, <u>Mr.</u>, <u>Mrs.</u>, and <u>Miss</u>, are omitted before the names in the heading. Classification titles are not necessary when the organizational unit provides a satisfactory address. No punctuation is used at the ends of the lines in the heading. The "To" and "From" lines should be parallel in content.

Paragraphs begin flush with the left margin. Single spacing is used within the paragraphs, double spacing between them.

The initials of the dictator and the typist appear for reference. This is true even when the person who dictated the memorandum is not the person who signs it. In that case it is unnecessary to precede the initials with those of the signer since his name is typed on the "From" line. Only one set of reference initials would indicate that one person both composed and typed the memorandum. If changes were made after the stenographer transcribed the memorandum and the final copy was typed by another person, the initials of the latter would take the place of those of the transcribing stenographer.

The nature of the attachment is not given in this memorandum; therefore it is described after the word <u>Attachment</u>. If more than one unidentified attachment were sent, the word <u>Attachments</u> would be followed by the listing of the name of each.

Carbon copies of the memorandum are to go to the two persons whose names are listed in alphabetical order. Note that the address must be

Fig. 3a. Memorandum Make-up (First Page) (From *Manual of Standard Secretarial Practice,* Tennessee Valley Authority, 1945)

Office Memorandum • UNITED STATES GOVERNMENT

-2-

TO : Hazel Lewis   DATE: November 1, 1945

FROM : Charles O. Libbey

SUBJECT: STYLE FOR INTEROFFICE MEMORANDA

given for each person listed. The name of the person to receive a
given copy is underscored with colored pencil. Since these addresses
are on the second page of the memorandum, a mailing slip will be
attached to each copy repeating the name and address underscored on
the second page.

That an attachment is being sent to one person who is to receive a
copy of the memorandum is indicated by the word Attachment in parentheses after the name and address. Two copies of the memorandum without the attachment are being sent to one person. as indicated by the
note in parentheses following the name.

This page illustrates the set-up for the second and subsequent pages
of a memorandum. Each page after the first is numbered with an Arabic
numeral centered two lines below Office Memorandum • United States
Government and preceded and followed by a hyphen. Titles, organization
units, and locations are omitted after the names in the heading. The
subject is repeated on each page, and the text begins on the fourth
line below.

EML:BC
Attachment: "Manual of Standard Secretarial Practice"
CC: Nelson T. Barr, Office Methods Staff, Chattanooga (Attachment)
    Myrl E. Lawrence, Stenographic and Office Training Unit,
      209 AB (2 copies)

FIG. 3b. Memorandum Make-up (Second Page)

STANDARD FORM NO. 64

Office Memorandum • UNITED STATES GOVERNMENT

TO   : Glenn A. Dooley, Chief Personnel Officer   DATE: November 1, 1945

FROM   : Charles E. Lex, Jr., Chief, Office Service Division

SUBJECT: STYLE FOR INTEROFFICE MEMORANDA

Attention of Arlene Snure.

The half-size memorandum paper is used for short messages. The record copy is made on full-size buff onionskin.

The text begins two lines below the subject. If an attention line is necessary, it is written as the first paragraph of text. This memorandum illustrates a signature form preferred by some dictators. The single set of reference initials indicates the person who composed and typed the memorandum.

Charles E. Lex, Jr.

EML

FIG. 4. Half-page Memorandum

Exercises

1. Write a letter of inquiry and the answer to it. Choose one of the following situations:

(1) A friend writes for information about the kind of work in which you are engaged.

(2) One employer writes to another, asking for information about an applicant for a position.

(3) A man wishes to open an account with a department store. The store writes to the man's bank, asking for information about his credit rating.

(4) A student writes to a technical or business man for help in the preparation of a report for one of his courses.

(5) A farmer writes to the experiment station in his state, asking for recommendations concerning the best cows to purchase.

(6) A dean is carrying on an investigation to determine the advantages and disadvantages of final examinations. He writes to other colleges for their experiences.

(7) A young man, who is thinking of entering the insurance business, writes to an uncle who is district manager of a large insurance company, asking him for advice and suggestions.

2. Write a letter of instructions and a letter report answering it.

(1) The business manager of a college newspaper asks an assistant to find out why several prominent local stores do not advertise in the paper.

(2) The office manager of a company asks an assistant to determine the cause of increased expenditures for office supplies.

(3) You are appointed by your employer to investigate the character and ability of a young man who is applying for a position.

(4) The president of a college asks a member of each fraternity to report to him concerning the week-end activities of the students.

(5) The football coach instructs the manager to make a report on the condition of equipment before the first practice.

(6) A fire insurance company writes to one of its agents for a report regarding the risk involved in insuring a local grocery store.

(7) A party political leader of a district requests information from one of his lieutenants about the probability of electing the party nominees.

(8) A client writes to his architect, asking why a certain requested change in the plans has not been carried out.

(9) A newspaper owner, learning that a story appearing in the paper contained untrue statements, asks the city editor for an explanation.

3. Rewrite the following letters, making the necessary corrections and satisfying yourself that the arrangement and expression are good:

(a)

Chartersville Vermont;
Novem. 6, 1948

George A. Semple
Worcester Vermont.

Dear Mr. Semple,

I am herewith asking information about John H. Phelps, who says he was employed by you from June 1939 to Sept. 1941. He seems like a good man, but I know nothing about his past record. Does he get along well with men? He said he had charge of about fifty employees with you. Does he have a good education? He talks well, but I don't know much about him. Why did he leave you? He says he was successful with you.

Respectively yours,
(s) *Casey Kent*
General Manager

(b)

Temple, Texas
August 6, 1950

Mr. James K. Roamer,
Pres., The Rutherford Constr. Co.
Rutherford, Texas.

Gentlemen:

The work is going along all right.
Fifteen new men got in last night, and we put them to work today.
Last week we finished the excavation. It took so long because we were short of help. Now we have enough men to go ahead rapidly.
All material is here. Kennedy saw to that last week. We can let you know more by the end of this week.

Yours truly,

(c)

211 1st St.
Ellington, Ill.
Je. 6, 1950

John Hipple, M'gr
Tudor Furniture Corp.
Chicago

My dear sir,

In reply to your most esteemed favor of the 7th instant, I beg to submit at this time my report on this investigation carried on during the course of the past few months. Two men and I carried on this investigation. It began rather late in July. The enclosed report gives a more or less full account of it.

As per your instructions I can advise you that every indication points to the fact that the plant is in a satisfactory condition, all things considered.

Too many men are being employed, as the report shows. The number could, no doubt, be cut down with profit to every one concerned. There is some antiquated machinery which is in need of replacement if full efficiency is desired. The report is divided into three parts, the third part of it dealing with the matter of transportation, which, I believe, you might consider important in this case. Transportation facilities are better now that the new branch line has been completed by the United Builders of Rahway, New Jersey.

That should mean an increase in our business without a doubt. The other two men who worked with me, named Jones and Henderson, proved to be very helpful and they are deserving of a great deal of credit. Hoping the report will please you, I am

Yours,

CHAPTER 3

FUNDAMENTAL FORMS OF COMPOSITION

PRACTICE in the writing of short letter reports is excellent training for the longer types. We may discover most, if not all, of the same elements in both. The general aim of the writer is the same, whether he writes one page or a hundred—to set forth essential facts, opinions, or conclusions as clearly and as concisely as possible. Few qualities are worth more than these in report writing.

Reports are expository in tone. Frequently their only aim is to transmit information; and, even when the writer wants to convert his readers to a new idea, a new policy, or a new plan of action, he still holds to the calm and unbiased tone of exposition. The emphasis always appears to be upon facts and explanations, not upon opinions. The style is businesslike and matter-of-fact. "Fine writing," description for the sake of emotional effect, suspense, and every kind of exaggeration are not for the report writer. His reader is busy and practical-minded; the tone of the report must fit the reader's mood.

The report, even when comparatively short, may combine a considerable number of elements, or simple forms, of composition with which every writer should make himself familiar. The student who has tried his hand at a few letter reports has probably encountered difficulties even with these. The longer and more complicated the report, the more apparent becomes the necessity of knowing how to develop the simple forms that comprise the whole. Our study has begun with a consideration of some short reports, viewed as units. We may now profitably turn to an examination of the elementary parts of report writing.

The General Plan

Every report must, of course, follow a carefully developed outline or plan. It must be remembered, however, that no plan can be determined arbitrarily by anyone other than the writer himself—and he must develop it to meet the requirements of his

40

particular situation. Consequently the following generalized out-lines of reports should not be regarded as inviolable models, but only as skeletons typical of a great number of modern reports.

There are two basic methods of arranging report material, the inductive and the deductive. The inductive method presents the material much in the order it was acquired by the writer:

> Introduction
> > Statement of the Problem,
> > defining the subject, the
> > scope, and the purpose
> Text, Discussion, or Body
> Conclusions
> Recommendations (if any)

In such a report the conclusions are induced from the data offered in the main body of the report. Today, this type is most used for reports of experiments.

The deductive method presents the conclusions first and the data which produced them second:

> Summary or Abstract
> Introduction
> > General background
> > Definition of subject, scope, and purpose
> Conclusions
> Recommendations (if any)
> Text
> Appendix (when necessary)

The plan itself explains its increasing popularity with industry. As Mr. Richards and Mr. Richardson of General Motors Research Laboratories point out,[1] "This type of report suits people in various positions, who are interested in the work from various points of view. The busy executive, interested only in the highlights of the investigation, may read only the foreword, conclusions, and recommendations. The engineer, on the other hand, may be interested in the details supplied by the discussion, and the young fellow who does the work will probably have to wade through the appendix. . . ."

As emphasized before, these are not intended to serve as standardized outlines, but only as bases for the study of such fundamental forms of composition as are needed in the construction of reports, such forms as the following:

---

[1] Reference already cited in footnote 1, page 3.

1. Summary
2. Definition
3. Descriptive exposition
4. Narrative exposition
5. Interpretation of facts and ideas
6. Argument

If we turn to either of our generalized outlines, or to the specimen reports in the second section of the text, it is not difficult to see how these forms enter into the development of a report. The summary is invariably needed, often at the end as well as the beginning. Definition is necessary for the statement of object and scope as well as for the explanation of ambiguous or technical terms. Descriptive exposition is required to present a clear picture of apparatus, of grounds or buildings, or of some work of construction. Narrative exposition enters into the explanation of procedure, plans for carrying out a project, or records of past achievements. Exposition of facts and ideas makes possible an interpretation of phenomena, of statistics, or of data that the author has collected. And argument is often the controlling purpose of the whole report; it is particularly linked with recommendations. All these forms are familiar and useful tools to the report writer.

Even this short explanation should suffice to show the importance of the study to be undertaken in this chapter. It is not enough to know that these forms exist in the report; nor is it enough to know the place they occupy. The real question is, How may these fundamental forms be used effectively? Good report writing clearly depends upon a proper construction and relation of the parts. If the parts are incoherent and hazy, the whole cannot be logical and clear. It is characteristic of the successful report writer that he never overlooks any detail, never neglects any device that will make his work clearer or more effective.

The following discussion and illustrations aim to help the student develop his ability in constructing each section of his reports.

The Summary

A summary is an abridgement of the report or of significant parts of it, written to save the reader's time and to simplify the whole subject for him. It may be a general condensation of all sections of the report; it may be an epitome, setting forth only the chief points of significance; or it may be an extended statement of conclusions developed logically from the facts and evidence in the text.

The nature of the summary will depend upon the kind of reader addressed, the purpose of the report, and the position of the summary in the report. When placed at the beginning, it is usually an epitome or abstract of the whole report. Placed at the end, it is usually detailed and complete—not a mere restatement of main headings, but a presentation of conclusions arising from the discussion.

The following quotation serves a double purpose: in the first place it explains the need for the summary, and in the second, it is itself an informative summary of what one major industrial concern expects in its reports:

We start the report with a short foreword which gives general background information on the project. It defines the subject, scope, and purpose of the work, and makes reference to any correlated reports on the subject. The conclusions come second. They summarize the results of tests and discoveries made, and are short, concise statements which those who may not be entirely familiar with the subject can understand. This part of the report will often be written to sell the investigation or discovery to others. These two parts of the report are the most difficult for most technical men to write satisfactorily because they summarize the entire work in simple language. They are written for the person not familiar with the details of the subject, particularly the executives who must make engineering decisions. . . . The foreword and the conclusions together should state the problem and interpret the results in such a way as to make it unnecessary to read further to base a decision on the work . . . done. It has been evident to us that it is impossible to make these two parts of the report too elementary. We never had a report submitted by an engineer in our organization in which the explanations and terms were too simple. . . . Even the best engineer is not an expert in all lines. A busy executive cannot possibly take time to go through all the details of every report, even though he may have engineering training. . . . It is the duty of the engineer, in his report, to do the summarizing for the executive.

The report gets more technical and detailed as we get away from the front cover. The third section contains the recommendations, if there are any. These are simple, forceful statements, frequently without explanation. They may recommend future work on the subject or the action that should be based on the conclusions of the work.

The final part of the report is the discussion. This is the body of the report and contains the methods used in the investigation, the detailed data which were obtained, and the calculations. This part of the report substantiates the conclusions and the recommendations. . . . The discussion uses drawings, curve sheets, photographs, and other illustrative material. If there are any elaborate mathematics in the report, we prefer to move them out of the discussion and put them in an appendix at the end of the report.[2]

---

[2] General Motors reference already cited in footnote 1, page 3.

Introductory summary. As the preceding summary indicates, the best modern practice favors a summary at the beginning of the report, a plan quite in keeping with the desire to simplify the reading as much as possible. In published reports of a technical or scientific character, this summary is customarily an *abstract*. In reports addressed to executives it may be a very brief *epitome*. Yet in some public reports the introductory summary is several pages in length, rather popular in style, and complete enough in itself to make it unnecessary for laymen to read further.

In the reports of specialists the summary is often an "epitome." No attempt is made to mention in it every phase of the report, all the methods, materials, and devices that are employed. It includes only the most important and significant conclusions. And it is very brief. When a letter of transmittal accompanies a report, the epitome will usually be found there. Some of the specimens in Chapter 7 illustrate its position and nature. Regardless of where it appears or how long it is, such a summary touches upon only those points that are essential from the executive standpoint.

For example:

— 1 —

It seems evident that construction of the proposed by-products coking plant at Hippleton would not be profitable until the coke market improves.

— 2 —

The tests indicate, as the body of the report shows, that replacement of the present cast-iron pipe in the Glauber Salt Plant with wrought-iron pipe would effect a substantial long-time saving despite the heavy initial cost.

— 3 —

The investigation shows that the actual flow of saturated sal soda solution through thin-plate orifices is 21% greater than our theoretical calculations indicated, and that no appreciable back-pressure is evident.

The longer introductory summary which follows is considerably more detailed and specific, but actually it represents less than a page and a half of a 40-page report:

INTRODUCTION AND SUMMARY

The carbonizing properties of Hill-bed coal from Hickey No. 1 mine, Cherokee County, Ala., were determined by Bureau of Mines-American Gas Association tests at 500°, 600°, 700°, 800°, 900°, and 1000° C and by expansion tests. The investigations also included chemical analyses, agglutinating and plasticity tests, assays at high and low temperatures, and oxidation tests. Blends with high-volatile A Pittsburgh-bed coal were carbonized by the BM–AGA method at 900° C.

The Hill bed, as it is known locally, belongs to the Lee formation and therefore is of Pennsylvanian age. The bed was 25.5 inches thick in the Hickey No. 1 mine and 14.5 to 24.5 inches thick at six points in the vicinity where core samples were drilled. The unwashed sample contained 6.1 percent ash and 0.9 percent sulfur. The washed sample, which was used in most of the tests, contained 3.1 percent moisture, 21.8 percent volatile matter, 72.8 percent fixed carbon, 2.3 percent ash, and 0.5 percent sulfur, as carbonized, and its ash fused at 2400° F. The coal contained 77.2 percent fixed carbon on the dry, mineral-matter-free basis and therefore ranks as medium-volatile bituminous. The agglutinating value determined on a silicon carbide-coal mixture of 15:1 was 7.4, and the maximum plasticity determined by the Gieseler method was 73 dial divisions per minute at 468° C.

Yields of carbonization products from the washed sample in the 18-inch BM–AGA retort at 900° C were: Coke, 79.3 percent, and, upon the basis of per ton of coal carbonized, gas, 10,300 cubic feet; tar, 6.7 gallons; light oil in gas, 1.71 gallons; and ammonium sulfate, 20.8 pounds. Except for the 500° C coke which was pebbly, the cokes made at all temperatures were well-fused, medium- to fine-grained, and moderately fissured. The 900° C coke from the washed sample contained 1.7 percent volatile matter, 95.0 percent fixed carbon, 3.3 percent ash, and 0.5 percent sulfur. It had the following physical properties: Apparent specific gravity, 0.82; 1½-inch shatter index, 81.7; 1-inch tumbler index, 70.9; and ¼-inch tumbler index, 77.3. The 900° C coke from the unwashed sample contained 8.2 percent ash and 0.8 percent sulfur; it was more abradable than the coke from the washed coal, as shown by its tumbler indexes (1-inch, 66.4; and ¼-inch, 74.6). The coking power of Pittsburgh-bed coal was increased significantly by blending with 20 percent Hill (washed) coal; raising the proportion of Hill coal to 30 percent did not materially strengthen the coke from the blend. The heating values of the 900° C gas were 526 Btu per cubic foot and 2710 Btu per pound of coal; this gas contained 140 grains of hydrogen sulfide per 100 cubic feet.

As anticipated because it ranks high in the medium-volatile classification of bituminous coals, Hill coal expanded during carbonization. The expansion determined in the sole-heated oven and calculated to a charge density of 55.5 pounds per cubic foot was 20.3 and 14.8 percent for the washed and unwashed samples, respectively. The blend containing Pittsburgh coal contracted in the sole-heated oven and developed a maximum pressure of 1.7 pounds per square inch in the vertical expansion-test oven; therefore, it is considered safe for carbonization in byproduct ovens.

Results of oxidation tests in air at 100° C for periods of 3.9, 8.1, and 13.6 days showed that Hill coal oxidizes more rapidly than Pittsburgh-bed coal from the Warden mine and requires less oxygen to effect a decrease in coke strength.[3]

The introductory summary of some public reports constitutes a report in itself. Hence the term "double report," which is rather commonly used today. The first part of a double report, often re-

---

[3] From the Bureau of Mines Technical Paper 703, *Carbonizing Properties of Hill-Bed Coal from Hickey No. 1 Mine on Lookout Mountain, Cherokee County, Alabama*, by J. D. Davis and others, 1947.

printed in newspapers, is nontechnical and interesting to laymen. This initial portion has sometimes adopted a style not very different from that of the newspaper "special feature." It covers all matters that have value and interest to the general public. The second part is given over to technical details.

The abstract. The abstract, the term often given to technical summaries, presents in bare outline the whole substance of a technical report, paper, or experiment. Its importance to the report writer can scarcely be overstated. Since most abstracts represent a 95 to 98 percent reduction of the report or article abstracted, the saving in reading time is beyond estimate. Few technical men who wish to keep abreast of progress in their fields possess the time to wade through the tremendous volume of technical literature confronting them in the form of reports, papers, bulletins, and articles in periodical publications. The abstract provides a highly efficient short-cut; for the good abstract will either supply the reader with as much information as he requires, or it will make it clear that he will not be wasting his time by reading the entire piece. In fact, the advantages of the abstract have become so widely recognized that many companies and professional technical journals require the insertion of an abstract at the beginning of every report or article.

The abstract is important to the report writer in another way. Such publications as *Chemical Abstracts, Ceramic Abstracts,* and *Metallurgical Abstracts,* together with the even more specialized but private compilations found in company libraries,[4] are invaluable to the investigator who wishes to learn what has already been done in his field of inquiry. And what others have done for him he must do for them.

The problem of condensing a long report into an abstract only two to five percent its length is not a simple one, even when the report is the writer's own. The reader must be told about the subject, the purpose, the scope, the apparatus, the method of procedure, and the conclusions of the report—and anything else deemed sufficiently important to demand such emphasis. The presentation of material in the abstract almost invariably follows the order employed in the report. Also, the abstract follows the

---

[4] See "Abstracting Research Reports" in the *Journal of Chemical Education,* Vol. 25, p. 130, March 1948, by L. C. Stork and K. C. Cousins of the Texas Company.

same tone (often the same phrasing), and, most difficult of all, it must maintain the same emphasis. For even the experienced writer, abstracting is a skill acquired only through painstaking practice, but the novice will be aided by the following instructions:

1. Calculate how many words five percent of the original will allow you.

2. Construct an outline of the report, probably by referring to the table of contents and the table of illustrations, charts, curves, and the like.

3. Indicate on this outline the parts most emphasized in the report by reason of their positional, spatial, or logical importance; for example, the purpose, the conclusions, and the recommendations.

4. Allot a proportionate number of words found in Step 1 to each major part of the outline, allowing more to the parts selected in Step 3.

5. Summarize each part in the allotted number of words, or in fewer. Remember that too many words used for any one part will distort its emphasis.

   a. Use numerals for all numbers.

   b. Use abbreviations when you are sure the reader will understand them.

   c. Do *not* omit *a, an,* and *the.*

   d. Do not include tables or graphic presentation of any type. Instead simply mention that a curve (etc.) showing such and such is to be found in the report.

   e. If you have too many words, this is the time to revise. Check your phrasing first: Reduce clauses, especially qualifying clauses, to phrases; and phrases to single words. Then, if necessary, reduce several specific statements to one general one.

6. Integrate your sections and again revise your writing, supplying enough transition between the parts to make the writing consecutive.

Examine the following abstracts:

— 1 —

The special requirements that must be fulfilled by a shunt intended to be used in surge-current measurements are explained. A tubular shunt with coaxial potential leads that meets these requirements is described, and factors affecting its design are discussed. A theoretical derivation of the "skin effect" in this type of shunt at high frequencies is given in one of the appendices.

The advantages of using a mutual inductor for obtaining oscillograms of the rate of change of current during a surge are outlined, and several types of mutual inductors developed especially for this purpose are described. Theoretical derivations, given in the appendices, indicate that the concentric-tube mutual inductors described in this paper can be used to measure the high-frequency components of a current surge up to 70 megacycles with less than 10 percent error.

Several shunts and mutual inductors of the designs described in this paper were constructed for use in the high voltage laboratory at the National Bureau of Standards. Their complete description and oscillograms showing results obtained with them are included.[5]

As contrasted with the table-of-contents type of abstract illustrated above, the following example actually summarizes the content of the report, including the results.

— 2 —

CRACKING WITH CATALYSTS

Abstract

During the past five years the fluid catalytic cracking process has received intensive study. An accelerated program of installation has been instituted because of the necessity of providing sufficient aviation base stock. The catalyst used, of the so-called fluid type, is a powder intimately mixed with vapors in the reaction chambers. In general, the UOP catalyst is of the synthetic silica-alumina type, which has definite superiority as to yield and octane rating of the base stock over that of the natural clay type. The important process variables are temperature, pressure, space velocity, and length of process period; and these must be carefully controlled in order to insure the quality of the product. A table and a diagram are included to show the effect of operating conditions and conversion on product distribution.

Stocks with appreciably lower boiling points, such as kerosene, are more refractory and require more severe conditions; they produce stocks that are less olefinic than a typical gas oil. Conversely, heavier stocks are more easily cracked, and yield more unsaturated products.

Higher yields can be obtained in catalytic cracking on recycle operation just as in thermal cracking. The methods of finishing the product include catalytic retreating, "polytreating," and sulfuric-acid treating.

Two types of commercial units are discussed: the single-stage unit and the two-stage unit. These units are characterized by considerable operating flexibility. At this time the many large commercial installations are the proving and developing grounds for the economic feasibility of the process. These activities have attracted the necessary venture capital. The results of this development and testing will later be translated into small economical units so necessary for the small refiner in his competition in the high octane gasoline production field.[6]

---

[5] Abstract of the National Bureau of Standards Research Paper RP1823, *Shunts and Inductors for Surge-Current Measurement,* by John H. Park, September 1947.

[6] From the Universal Oil Products Booklet No. 254, *Cracking with Catalysts,* by C. L. Thomas and others, April 1944. Courtesy of Mr. Paul Truesdell.

The summary is important not alone in the development of the whole report, but in that of the separate sections. If a report is written after this plan, the reader finds it easy to grasp its general idea, or that of any section, and has less difficulty in understanding the importance of the facts contained in it. Even more important, in some cases, is this additional advantage: The reader can skim through a report so arranged, reading the introductory summary and topic-sentence summaries, without being forced to wade through a mass of details.

The final summary. An introductory statement or summary may not eliminate the necessity for a conclusion. To be sure, a formal conclusion is now unpopular with a good many writers and with many readers as well. The rhetorical flourish, or "persuasive" conclusion, is even more out of place. The conclusion, if it belongs in the report at all, should be more complete than the first summary, more reasoned, and certainly more than a dull restatement of points already well fixed in the reader's mind. Whereas the introductory summary may be read by those who do not themselves intend to read the whole report, the final summary seldom is. The introductory summary is a simple statement of generalizations, without proof. The final summary is dependent for its proof upon the facts set forth in the text; it points back to those facts, and reasons from them to its conclusions. For example:

— 1 —

CONCLUSIONS

Even though the gradients were of the order of 400,000 volts per cm, the large currents observed could not be explained on the basis of quantum-mechanical field emission. Eyring and Millikan[1] in 1926 found it necessary to use an electrometer to measure the currents produced by 106 volts per cm gradients at thoroughly outgassed surfaces. Anderson[2] in 1935 measured currents of the order of 0.1 microamp from $\frac{1}{4}$ cm^2 area at gradients and total voltages comparable with those used here. This current density would give 0.2 ma over our area of 500 cm^2. He "conditioned" his surfaces by sparking and a hydrogen discharge. In this experiment the surfaces were treated by sparking and heat.

A possible explanation of these large currents would be the following mechanism: An electron liberated from some sharp point or region of low work function on the cathode would strike the anode and liberate and ionize an absorbed gas atom. This heavy ion, upon striking the cathode, would liberate one or more secondary electrons.[3] The process would continue until an equilibrium value was reached.

A detailed study of sparks or impulsive breakdowns was not made, since the excessive steady current emission made it difficult to go to the highest voltage. It seems clear that it would not be possible to make a satisfactory

high-voltage condenser unless different methods of conditioning the surfaces
were developed.[7]

[1] Eyring and Millikan, *Physics Review,* Vol. 27, p. 51 (1926).
[2] Anderson, *A.I.E.E. Journal,* Vol. 54, p. 1375 (1935).
[3] Linford, *Physics Review,* Vol. 47, p. 279 (1935).

— 2 —

VI. Summary

1. Commercially heat-treated 24S–T aluminum alloy sheet (0.064 in.
thick) was artificially aged for various periods at 350°, 375°, 385°, and 400°
F. The tensile properties resulting from artificial aging and the resistance of
the aged materials to stress-corrosion cracking in NaCl + H_2O_2 solution and
(for some of the materials) in a marine atmosphere, were determined.

2. The maximum yield and ultimate tensile strengths obtained in this
alloy were independent of the aging temperature between 350° and 400° F.
The optimum results were obtained by aging the material approximately
20 hr at 350° F, 5 hr at 375° F, 3 hr at 385° F, and 1½ hr at 400° F.

3. The effect of the aging treatment at 385° F was more pronounced on
the tensile properties in a transverse direction than on those in a direction
parallel to the direction of rolling. The yield strength of the transverse specimens of the commercially heat-treated material was increased approximately
40 percent above an initial value of about 45,000 lb/in.², and the ultimate
tensile strength approximately 3 percent above an initial value of about
70,000 lb/in.² The percentage elongation was reduced to about one-third of
the initial value of 18. Effects of the same magnitude were observed for the
parallel specimens, except that the yield strength was increased only about
25 percent above an initial value of about 50,000 lb/in.²

4. Corrosion damage was measured by losses in elongation and ultimate
tensile strength. Elevated-temperature aging of materials for short periods
compared to those necessary to obtain the maximum mechanical properties,
increased the susceptibility of the material to corrosion. However, for aging
periods sufficiently long[3] to produce maximum physical properties, the resistance to corrosion of the artificially aged material was generally at least
equal to that of the commercially heat-treated material exposed without elevated-temperature aging. The ultimate tensile strengths of specimens exposed
under stress in the sodium chloride-hydrogen peroxide solution were reduced
as much as 30 to 35 percent for material aged for short periods of time. The
reduction was only 10 to 15 percent for specimens aged for periods sufficiently long to produce maximum tensile properties. The same amount of exposure of unaged material reduced its ultimate tensile strength by 11 to 32
percent.

Losses in tensile strength and ductility of anodized material aged 3 hr or
longer at 385° F and exposed for 6 weeks under stress in the marine atmosphere were small; the maximum loss in ultimate tensile strength was 1500
lb/in.², a loss which is probably not significant in this case; the maximum
loss in ductility was represented by specimens in which the percent elongation was reduced from 7 to 5.

[3] In some instances, also for aging periods up to three or four times the minimum
necessary to produce maximum physical properties.

[7] From Westinghouse Research Laboratories Report, *Electrical Breakdown Between Cylinders in Vacuum,* by H. S. Siefert, August 1942.

Specimens aged for 6 hr or longer at 375° F and subsequently exposed without surface protection by anodic treatment for 6 weeks in the marine atmosphere were generally no more severely damaged than the commercially heat-treated material exposed without artificial aging. For one lot of unaged material the effect of stress was marked in increasing the corrosion damage; the ultimate tensile strength of the stressed specimens was reduced 9 percent, as the result of 6 weeks of exposure in the marine atmosphere, compared to 1 percent for the unstressed material; the percent elongations on the two sets of specimens were reduced 53 and 17 percent, respectively. However, there was little difference in the corrosion damage to specimens that had been aged 6 hr or more at 375° F whether they were exposed stressed or unstressed in the corroding media.

The maximum losses in tensile strengths and ductilities of unstressed panels, exposed without surface protection to the weather (marine atmosphere for 1 year) or to tidewater (intermittent immersion for 14 days), were found in specimens aged 1 to 2½ hr (at 385° F).

5. Intercrystalline corrosion in some degree was found in all of the aged materials on examination after exposure in any of the corroding media. The intercrystalline corrosion was most severe in specimens aged for short periods of time; as the aging periods were increased to or beyond those necessary to produce the maximum values of yield strength, for the various aging temperatures, the intercrystalline corrosion became less general and less severe than that found in specimens aged for the shorter periods.[8]

Definition

Definition obviously has an important function to perform in the average report. The writer usually possesses a specialized vocabulary, very useful to himself in his routine work, but often much beyond the comprehension of his reader. Furthermore, the writer may wish to use terms in a restricted sense, and so to eliminate all possibility of ambiguity by early, if arbitrary, definition.

Object and Scope. The first need for definition arises at the beginning of the report. The writer must clearly define his subject. Of course, the title page should be as complete and adequate in its statements as good sense permits, but even the most carefully stated title must often leave much unsaid—much that the letter of transmittal or an early section of the text should develop.

The object, or aim, of a report is often stated in a single sentence. Seldom does it require any long explanation. While the *object* is general, the *scope*, on the other hand, must be explained in rather specific terms. A report on "Profit Sharing" may have for its object merely "to determine the advisability of adopting some

---

[8] From National Bureau of Standards Research Paper RP1788, *Effect of Artificial Aging on Tensile Properties and Resistance to Corrosion of 24S–T Aluminum Alloy*, by Hugh L. Logan, Harold Hessing, and Harold E. Francis, May 1947.

system of profit sharing in the Meddan Machine Works." The statement of the scope must, however, not only define exactly what the writer means by "profit sharing" in his particular discussion; it must further explain the boundaries set, the extent of the investigation covered by the report, and the definite limitations set either by those authorizing the report, or, through necessity, by the writer himself. A section headed "Scope" should, therefore, consist of a very clear definition of the ground covered in the report.

The following examples illustrate the use of definition in these early sections of the report:

— 1 —

Object. The object of this report is to determine the advisability of erecting a substation at Mannington.

Scope. This report discusses the investigation carried on during the past month, presents such facts as seem important for reaching a sound conclusion, and offers the recommendations that the engineers agree upon as advisable. The need for such a substation, the choice of a site, the engineering problems involved in construction, and the financial considerations are the matters that receive chief emphasis.

The following passages illustrate a simplified form of presenting both object and scope:

— 2 —

Investigations concerned with the sewer and drainage problems of Braxton are complete. Recommendations for such works naturally must depend upon (1) topographical and geological conditions, (2) existing sewers and drains, and (3) available methods of sewage disposal. The following report, therefore, covers these three considerations.

— 3 —

It is the purpose of this paper to discuss some of the fundamental principles of cracking catalysts and the catalytic cracking process, to give typical results over rather wide ranges of operating conditions and charging-stock quality, and to describe certain important developments of the present design by the Universal Oil Products Company.[9]

The purpose of any definition is to set limits or boundaries for the matter defined, to avoid "double meanings," and to make misinterpretations impossible. The simplest form is known as the "logical" definition, the dictionary form, which consists of three

---

[9] Paper already cited in footnote 6 on page 48.

parts in a single sentence: the term, the genus, and the differentiae. Note these examples:

Term	Genus	Differentiae
A machine	any combination of mechanism	for utilizing or applying power
Engineering	art	by which the mechanical properties of matter are utilized in structures and machines
"This report"	(report) on location	to determine the best site for the proposed factory

Definitions differ in length according to the development of the third part, the differentiae. The first two parts usually allow of little elaboration or development, but a great deal of discussion may be needed for a satisfactory differentiation.

The order of these logical definitions is the natural, or obvious, order. A sentence made up of the three elements mentioned usually provides the best topic sentence for a detailed definition. It summarizes and condenses the whole definition, so that the details which follow are more understandable.

Technical Terms. Perhaps a more difficult problem than the definition of object and scope is that of defining technical terms that are used in the discussion of a subject. The writer must first know his reader's educational equipment. To define technical terms for a specialist in the field would be ridiculous. To define them for a layman who is totally unacquainted with the field is often a necessity. Unfortunately, the dividing line between the technically trained and the technically ignorant is by no means a sharp one. Many executives who are quite lacking in formal technical education understand and use numerous specialized terms. In answer to the report writer's question, "When and how shall I define?" the only reasonable suggestion is this: *Study your reader. Know all that you can know about him.*

The following examples illustrate good practice.

This definition concerns a term in common use which the writer wishes to employ in a restricted sense:

— 1 —

Unfortunately, different meanings are assigned to the word "rate," as applied to domestic service. The best measure of the cost of service to the consumer is *the whole amount paid for electric service during a given period, divided by the number of kilowatt hours of electricity used during that period.* As the term "rate" is sometimes used, it refers only to the energy charge, or is otherwise not inclusive, and, in certain situations and for certain classes of service, may be very misleading.

Here is the definition of a term with which the reader is assumed to be unfamiliar:

— 2 —

The septic tank is a sedimentation tank designed and operated so as to foster the decomposition of the settled solids in the absence of oxygen. It was originally believed that this process was capable of nearly complete conversion of the deposited solids into liquids and gases; experience has shown, however, that this view is not justified, and that the proportion of solids thus converted is much less than at first supposed. Furthermore, such tanks, unless covered, frequently give off offensive odors, produce black and foul effluents, and present numerous operating difficulties.

In the following definitions two terms are differentiated:

— 3 —

The term *sewage* is used here to refer to human waste matters, together with the polluted water of the household—such as water from bathing, scrubbing, dish washing, clothes washing, and food cleansing. The *sewerage system* refers to the system of piping designed to carry off any or all of these wastes.

— 4 —

A facsimile broadcast station is a station which transmits still pictures by means of radio for public use. A special recorder machine must be used in conjunction with the radio receiver in order to print the photograph or other still object so received. Thus, while television is able to transmit moving images, facsimile is limited to reproduction of still pictures, print, writing, symbols, and so forth.[10]

Before the writer defines a technical term, he should first inquire of himself whether he may not avoid the term entirely. Nothing is more confusing and uninteresting than an exposition that is constantly interrupted by the definition of terms. The inexperienced writer may profit greatly by reading the semitechnical articles that are to be found in numerous modern periodicals. Seldom are such articles cluttered with definitions. Writers have learned to *translate* technical facts into common language, rather than to hold to their specialized vocabularies. Translation into simple language is, when it is possible to use it, a better method than

---

[10] From *Radio: A Public Primer,* by the Federal Communications Commission.

definition. It is, of course, a more difficult process, but the appreciation of the layman will be sufficient reward.

Even without having for comparison the long technical report on which the following popular translation is based, the reader will see that the former must have been highly technical. The writer here has given a report both accurate and understandable to the layman:

Better methods have long been sought for manufacturing rubber goods from the latex, or sap, of rubber trees. Rubber is not soluble in water, but latex and some other forms of pure and compounded rubber can be suspended in water by dispersing them into very minute globules. These "suspensions," or "dispersions," for some purposes resemble a solution, although in other respects they are quite different. In water dispersions the globules of rubber carry negative charges of electricity; consequently, when a current is passed through them, the minute bits of rubber go to the positive pole, or anode. Some searchers for new methods gave attention to this knowledge.

In 1922, S. E. Sheppard and L. W. Eberlin, working in a laboratory of the Eastman Kodak Company, at Rochester, New York, and Paul Klein, A. Szegvari, and a large staff in Budapest, Hungary, found independently that pure and compounded rubber could be electrolytically deposited from water dispersions upon metal or ceramic molds, in a way somewhat like electroplating with metals. The former group was trying to cover metals with adhering coats of rubber deposited from water dispersions, and the latter to make rubber goods directly from latex.

Each investigator was practically interested in the improvement of the quality of rubber goods. They knew that, when the solid, dried crude rubber was worked upon a mixing mill in the rubber factory, the rubber substance was altered, depolymerized, as the chemist says, and thereby became softer and weaker. They knew that the less rubber was heated or worked, the better was its quality. They also knew that research of chemists in recent years had shown how vulcanization may be carried on at lower temperatures than formerly and the necessary sulphur combined with rubber with a minimum of loss of quality. Certain substances, known as "accelerators," possess the property of permitting vulcanization to be accomplished at relatively low temperatures. However, if these accelerators were incorporated in the usual mixing mill, the temperatures would be sufficiently high to cause vulcanization during mixing, and to spoil the goods.

These men conceived the plan of so depositing rubber on forms, from latex, that the rubber particle itself was not altered, and made the astonishing discovery that electro-deposited rubber had the highest quality ever observed. Many were the problems to be solved before this was made practical. It was necessary to incorporate other substances to be deposited simultaneously on the anode, such as sulphur, zinc oxide, and carbon black. These last two substances are necessary in rubber goods to give toughness. A long investigation was carried out to find means to disperse them in water, mixed with the latex particles, without coagulating the latex. A noteworthy achievement, which has made the anode process possible, has been the discovery of the means by which these rubber layers may be freed from bubbles; for, when an electric current is passed through a solution, bubbles of gas are formed on anode and cathode. So the men hit upon the scheme of surrounding the anode with a porous clay diaphragm. The anode is, therefore, immersed in electrolyte inside a porous clay cell or dish and the rubber particles, together with those of zinc oxide, sulphur, etc., are deposited upon this porous so-called "anode diaphragm." Thus the rubber, as it collects, forms a continuous, homogeneous, tough covering of uniform thickness. Any thickness up to an inch or more is practicable. Rubber thus formed is stronger than rubber prepared by the old methods, and is free from gas or air holes. Therefore, it is permissible to use less thickness for some purposes.[11]

Descriptive Exposition

One of the most difficult forms of composition used by the report writer is description, or "descriptive exposition." The writer's purpose in using descriptive passages in his report is to give his reader a clear conception of the appearance of a machine, a device, a dam, a mine, a mill, a structure, or a property; or he may use them to explain the general plan or the underlying principles of the object. The development of either purpose calls for rather specific language and a plan somewhat similar to that employed by the writer of pure description.

Especially in technical documents, descriptive writing is often exceedingly difficult. The object calling for description is usually somewhat complicated; it consists of numerous important elements or parts. Since the writer naturally knows much more about the object than his reader and since his interest is usually in details, he often neglects to present a unified picture of the whole. He is unable to place himself in the position of the person whose knowledge is limited. Too often the technical writer begins a description with a detail of minor significance, continues to pile up details, and fails utterly to make his reader see the relationship of the parts to the whole.

Before beginning a descriptive exposition, the writer must consider his reader's mind. What are the questions which there demand immediate answer? If it is some new device that the writer wishes to explain, he may summarize his reader's questions as follows:

What is it called?
What is its use?

---

[11] "Molding Rubber with Electricity," Engineering Foundation Research Narrative, No. 125. Reprinted by permission.

What, briefly, does it look like?

What is the principle of the thing?

These, clearly, are the questions that you would ask if a friend remarked, "I just saw a very interesting machine in operation."

Such questions must be answered at once in the development of a descriptive exposition. Before the reader has simple answers to these questions, descriptive details can have little meaning or interest for him.

In this, it will be seen, we return to our much-emphasized rule: *Give a general impression first.* In the description of a machine, the first paragraph may contain its name, its purpose or use, its general appearance, and its working principle. In the description of a piece of property, the opening discussion may give it a title by which it may later be called, and may set forth general conclusions concerning the dimensions, the important features, and the surroundings. Such information must logically come first. To begin with hairsprings or cogwheels, with bushes or shingles, means hopeless confusion to the reader and the possibility that he will never know what the writer is trying to tell him.

After the reader's preliminary questions are answered, the writer may proceed to develop the details of description. The method to be used must depend upon the purpose to which it is to be put. The writer's first step is to form in his own mind a picture of the thing he intends to describe. If he is chiefly concerned with external appearance, he should attempt to form a mental *photograph*. Sometimes, of course an actual photograph, or a set of photographs, is included as a further aid to the reader; but, whether such mechanical means for clearness are present or not, the writer himself must have a clear vision. If principles or relationships are of first importance, the writer should form a mental *diagram* as the basis for his development. Since the photograph is so useful in giving a picture of external appearance, it will be the writer's best guide when appearances are the aim of his description. The photograph, however, is of little worth in showing the working principle, or the position and the relationship of parts. On the other hand, diagrams usually give no impression at all of external appearance, but they are much more useful than photographs in indicating how the parts are related. It is unnecessary at this point to consider the advisability of inserting actual photographs or diagrams in the report. The important thing to remember here is that the writer himself must visualize photographs or diagrams if his writing is to be logical and clear.

To make a discussion of details that is logical is seldom easy; but, if the writer has visualized his subject clearly, he has made an excellent start. Wherever possible, he should attempt to adopt some chronological order, borrowing the chief characteristic of narrative forms. For example, a machine may be described by considering the parts in the order in which they are set in motion. A description of a mill may follow the flow sheet. A description of property may proceed in the order of an actual or imaginary trip around it. A student's inspection-trip report, covering a visit to a manufacturing plant, easily adapts itself to the narrative order, although it is essentially descriptive. Such a report may logically be divided into three main parts:

1. General information as to size of plant, kind of output, and so on (introductory sentence or paragraph)

2. Main features of the plant (treated either (a) in the order of observation, or (b) in the order in which the manufacturing process proceeds)

3· Writer's conclusions concerning the character of the plant and its methods of operation as a whole (final paragraph, or series of paragraphs)

The chronological order is evidently the easiest to follow. Where a descriptive exposition can adopt such an order, the writer is wise to develop his discussion in this way.

Perhaps the most useful suggestion that can be given to the writer of descriptive exposition is that he employ plenty of comparisons. Every reader knows some devices and properties which are, at least in some respects, similar to those being described. The writer must make use of this knowledge; he must point out these similarities. Such procedure is a dictate of common sense in all writing. The general principle of leading "from the known to the unknown" is universally recognized as sound.

Comparisons, to be sure, are useful only when one of the things compared is familiar to the reader, and only when the object used for comparison has a constant form. If you have never seen a calorimeter and know nothing about it, it is of no use for a writer to compare some new device to it. Likewise, it is worth little to compare some structure to a "building" or a "boat," because buildings and boats have various forms, and the reader has no means of knowing which form the writer had in mind when he developed his comparison. If these dangers are recognized, however, the report writer may proceed with discrimination to discover objects for comparison that are known to his readers and that will enable him to explain the unknown in the light of the known.

The following example of descriptive exposition is worth studying:

APPARATUS AND TEST PROCEDURE

The apparatus is shown diagrammatically and in part in Figure 5. It consists essentially of a revolving specimen rack with a capacity of 96 specimens so mounted that the specimens travel through three compartments. The largest of these is a high-humidity thermostat, the temperature of which is regulated by the temperature of a layer of water beneath the specimens. Humidity, air circulation, and water circulation are maintained by pumping the thermostatted water through a nozzle positioned in the free space in the center of the specimen rack and directed downward in such a way that the water does not strike the samples. The compartment is also provided with baffled sprays to supplement the dew formation that occurs on the samples and to provide means of securing intermittent run-off.

A small glass-walled compartment is used for drying. Air is forced upward through it by the blower shown in the diagram. The air temperature is controlled by resistance heaters in the air duct.

Refrigeration is accomplished in the adjoining compartment, in which the samples pass close to the walls of a metal jacket through which precooled liquid is circulated.

The specimens are sheet tensile blanks, 0.75 in. by 12 in. by 22 ga. They are suspended rigidly on stainless-steel wires between the upper and lower rings of the specimen carrier in a position normal to the radius of the rings. The openings between adjacent compartments are thus very narrow. The atmosphere from one compartment is prevented from entering the next compartment by maintaining a slightly reduced pressure in the small vestibules that are provided between them.

The space beneath the three compartments is used to house the operating equipment; namely, the compressor, thermostat, and circulating pump for the refrigerating liquid, air blower for the drying compartment, pump for the circulating water in the high-humidity compartment, controls for the sprays, and suction pump for the vestibules.

With this apparatus it is possible to attain complete uniformity of treatment of the individual samples, a wide range of wetting conditions, controlled temperature of the three phases of the cycle, and complete independence of the wetting, drying, and cooling conditions.[12]

[12] H. Pray, Battelle Memorial Institute; and J. L. Gregg, Bethlehem Steel Co.: *An Accelerated Atmospheric Corrosion Test.* Courtesy Mr. John C. Long, Manager, Publications, Bethlehem Steel Co.

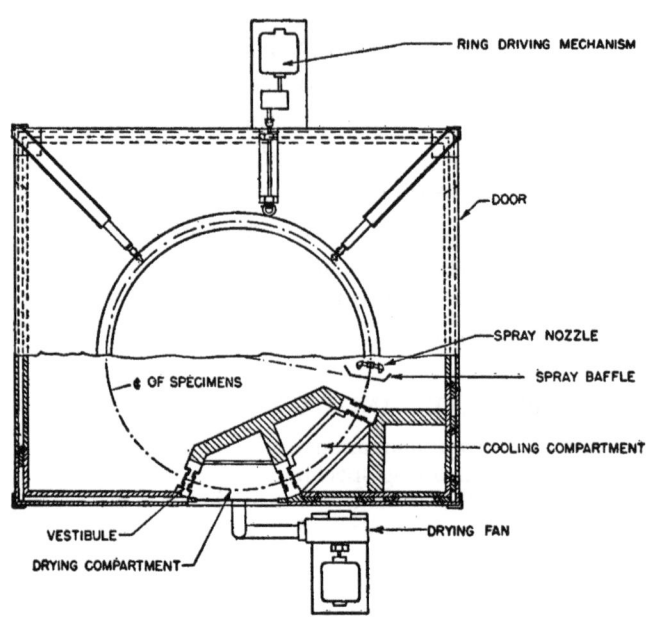

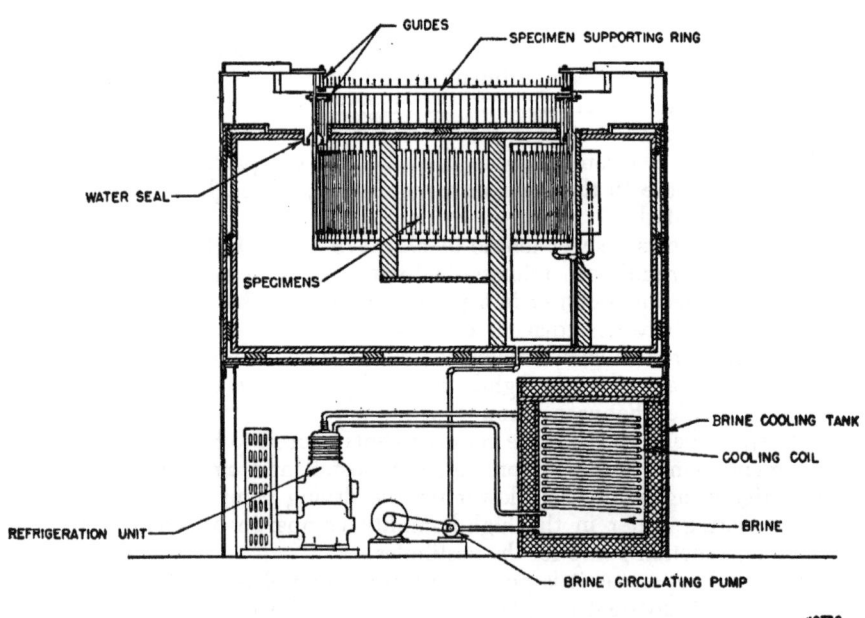

Fig. 5. Diagram of Test Apparatus

10750

60

Narrative Exposition

Descriptive exposition, as has been suggested, may often advantageously follow a chronological, or narrative, order. Possibly no method employed in exposition is easier to write and easier to understand. The narrative form is thoroughly concrete, not abstract. It is interesting, chiefly because it is not passive—it *moves*. It holds attention by constant change, and the change in a narrative is a normal and logical one that the mind readily follows.

If chronological order is recommended for descriptive writing, when the aim is to explain appearances and relationships, it is obviously even more desirable when the writer wants to emphasize action. The account of an undertaking, a process, or an operation is not nearly so troublesome as some other problems of report writing, for the reason that the narrative exposition form is the one best suited to the development of such subjects. The writer stresses action, and consequently employs narrative exposition, when he wants to explain an experiment, a new process of manufacture, the story of a completed project, the record of work accomplished in a day, a week, or a month; or when he wishes to make suggestions for work to be carried out in the future. Sometimes the entire report may be a single chronological account of this type. Again, such order may be used only in single sections, for the narrative element is frequently important even when the report as a whole follows no such order. So long as the writer can direct the attention of his reader to his account and lead in a straight path from stage to stage, his problem presents no difficulty.

It is essential, however, that the reader know at the outset where he is going, and why. In a report, the account of a process or operation is of no value for its own sake. There must always be some practical purpose for including such an account. Every narrative exposition found in reports must therefore begin with a "summary of the story," enabling the reader to grasp further details with more understanding and interest. One object of such a summary may be to let the reader see the *purpose* of the process or procedure. Another may be to show its *extent*. Still another is to indicate its *direction*. Unlike the novel or short story, narrative exposition makes no attempt to hold a reader in suspense. Because the first requisite is to make him understand, there is no reason for keeping him curious.

This "summary of the story" varies according to the needs of the case. The following examples illustrate the correct practice of holding the reader in expectancy, without keeping him in suspense as to the outcome.

The following introduction stresses the *purpose* of explaining the process:

— 1 —

Concrete ducts, in spite of the time required for the successive layers to set, are now being used extensively underground. The reason for their low cost under most circumstances, and for their practicability, will be more apparent after a discussion of the method of laying them.

The following introduction emphasizes the *extent* of the undertaking that is explained:

— 2 —

This interesting work of construction, which occupied 425 men over a period of four months, involving an expenditure of $1,700,000, is now complete. Although it began in May with peculiarly unfavorable weather conditions, efficiency in management brought it to a conclusion late in August, several days ahead of schedule.

This short introduction emphasizes *extent* and *result:*

— 3 —

Work today has been concerned entirely with continuing the tests begun last week. So far the results have hardly been promising.

The following introduction outlines the steps or stages in the process, suggesting both *extent* and *direction:*

— 4 —

The principal operations in the manufacture of mercury-in-glass thermometers are cleaning, filling, and graduating the glass tube.

This last example illustrates an emphasis upon all three—*purpose, extent,* and *direction:*

— 5 —

A series of tests was made to compare the results obtained when the fuel savers were used with those obtained with the boiler alone, and with the sliding damper in the fuel door closed but not sealed. Runs were made at various rates of steaming, as fixed by the size of the orifice on the steam outlet, and with a constant steam pressure of approximately four-pound gage. At each rate two tests were made, which differed only in the amount of coal fired at one time. The amounts were usually either 30 or 50 pounds, though in some tests other amounts were used. The regular tests averaged about 16 hours in length, the shortest being 10 and the longest 18 hours. The fuel used on a test varied from 220 pounds to 400 pounds, depending upon the rate of steaming. Readings of the important data were taken every fifteen minutes. One sample of coal from each lot delivered was taken for analysis.

Most of these summaries of the story are simple enough, but the need for them is apparent. Before he is asked to follow the steps of the chronological account, the reader ought to be told what the story is about and where it is headed.

After such an introduction, the account frequently proceeds in a straight line from one step to the next without complications, and the writer seldom runs into serious difficulties. Complication, of course, may arise. In some processes, for example, a number of different steps are progressing simultaneously. Again, there may be alternative methods of doing the same work.

If two or more steps proceed simultaneously, each must naturally be carried to its conclusion before another is brought into the discussion. To skip from one to the other is needlessly confusing. If alternative methods must be explained, begin with the one most commonly used. Usually, all methods will have something in common, and the other methods may therefore be explained by contrasting and comparing them with the first. Once the problem has been carefully analyzed, these complications are not really difficult to overcome.

Note how the following narrative exposition is phrased in language intelligible to the layman:

RADIO BROADCASTING EXPLAINED

At some time or other you have observed, from a distance, a man chopping wood. You noticed that the sound of his axe reached your ears after your eyes had witnessed the actual impact. By the same token, a person at a radio-receiving set thousands of miles away can hear a broadcast sound before a person seated far back of the microphone yet within earshot of the actual proceedings.

This is because radio emissions travel with the speed of light—186,000 miles a second—as compared with only 1,120 feet a second for sound. Thus, it requires just about one-sixtieth of a second for a voice from Europe to be electrically wafted to your home receiving set!

Here is how a standard broadcast station works:

A person talks into the microphone as if it were a telephone. His voice sets up varying vibrations in the microphone. The lower the pitch the slower the vibration. These vibrations have various intensities and frequencies. "Intensity" means the degree of sound, and "frequency" refers to the number of sound waves which can be transmitted in a given length of time.

In the microphone these vibrations are converted into electrical current having the same frequency and intensity characteristics as the sound delivered into the microphone. After being checked and double checked at the studio, these electric impulses are sent over leased telephone wires to the individual transmitting station (usually some miles distant), or to other radio stations carrying the same broadcast. This is the method used in so-called network broadcasting.

These electrical vibrations which represent the voice or music in the studio are sometimes called the audio wave. They are greatly amplified in intensity—sometimes millions of times—before they are imposed upon the "carrier wave" at the transmitter. The carrier wave is the one assigned to the radio station by the Federal Communications Commission—that to which the dials on the radio receiver must be tuned in order to hear the station.

The intensity and the frequency of this wave are constant, and by itself it cannot transmit any music or speech. In order to do this it must be varied in some way in accordance with the fluctuations of the audio waves. This is called modulation. In the standard broadcast band the audio waves are imposed on the carrier wave in a manner to cause its frequency to remain constant and its amplitude (or power) to correspond with the audio waves. This is called amplitude modulation. In contrast, frequency modulation varies the frequency of the radio wave while the amplitude remains constant.

These modulated radio waves are then put on the air by the transmitting antenna. They radiate from the antenna tower as waves moving with the speed of light and proceed in all directions. Some of them follow the contour of the ground and are called ground waves. Others dart upward and are called sky waves. The former give the best daytime reception. At night, however, the sky waves are forced back to earth by a ceiling of electrical particles which science calls the "ionosphere." This nightly rebound gives the listener a choice of more distant stations.

Radio waves pass through buildings and other objects, of course, to absorption and interference. As in the case of artificial ripples on water, radio vibrations weaken with distance. Seasonal disturbances and sunspot periods can also disrupt and throw them off their course.

Standard broadcast stations in this country transmit 550,000 to 1,600,000 waves a second. They are known as long-wave stations because the waves they transmit are actually long. At 550,000 waves a second, the distance between the crests is 1,800 feet. This is known as wave length. A station transmitting 550,000 waves a second is said to have a frequency of 550,000 cycles. This corresponds to 550 kilocycles (1 kilocycle equals 1000 cycles) which, for the sake of convenience, is the usual marking on your receiving set dial. ("Kilo" means 1000 and "cycle" refers to a complete swing of an electric vibration. Thus, kilocycle is a short way of denoting a thousand of these vibrations or oscillations a second. By the same token, a megacycle is equivalent to 1000 kilocycles.)

The so-called short-wave broadcast stations transmit from 6,000,000 to 25,000,000 waves per second. These are sent out one after the other so rapidly that the distance between their crests is only about 37 to 150 feet. It is a paradox that short waves go farther than long waves. That is why international broadcasts are on short waves.

Standard or AM amplitude modulation is transmitted in three simultaneous waves. The fundamental frequency or carrier wave is accompanied by two other waves, one immediately above and the other immediately below the main carrier. These are called side bands. The distance separating the main frequency and its companion frequencies is known as the modulation frequency.

The modulated radio wave from the radio station transmitter is picked up by the home receiving antenna. That is to say, it sets up in the receiving antenna modulated radio frequency current having the same frequency and the same varying intensity as the radio frequency currents in the transmitting antenna. In the receiver the carrier wave and the audio waves, of which the modulated wave is comprised, are separated by a device called a detector or demodulator. The carrier wave is shunted off into the ground. Having done its job it is no longer needed. The audio waves, however, are sent to the loud-speaker, or telephone headset, where they are transformed back into the sound waves that you hear.[13]

Interpretation of Facts and Ideas

The last form of exposition to need mention in connection with report writing is the most abstract of all. The student who has had any experience with laboratory reports knows the importance attached to "theory." Figures, results, data of all sorts, usually play an exceedingly important part in any report. Tabular or graphical methods of presentation are often employed. Such facts as appear in tables and charts, however, frequently need interpretation, comment, and explanation. Sometimes, too, the facts are of such a nature that tabulation is impracticable. In all these situations the writer adopts the form of discussion that we call "interpretation of facts and ideas."

Such a form of exposition, being so largely abstract, allows of no definite chronological order. Neither does it allow the writer to visualize his subject matter so clearly as in descriptive writing. The report writer's best guide is a study of his reader. Let him begin with these questions:

What does my reader need to know?
How much does he know about this subject now?
How may I best link my new information with his knowledge?

If he is able to answer the first two questions, the third will seldom trouble him for long.

The writer must always begin such abstract exposition with those aspects best known to his reader, proceeding thence to aspects that are new and unfamiliar. He adopts the familiar method of going from the known to the unknown. The general tendency in every reader's mind is to reach out for something that he recognizes in terms of his own experience.

In abstract discussion there is more danger than elsewhere of

---

[13] From *Radio: A Public Primer,* by the Federal Communications Commission, 1941.

omitting an important part of a section, of covering the same ground several times, or of throwing certain sections out of their normal place in the whole text. The best safeguard is a carefully constructed outline, based upon the writer's answer to the question, What does my reader need to know? Usually a thoughtful analysis of the reader's needs will bring to light some general questions which, it is reasonable to suppose, he will want answered. These form the skeleton of the discussion and enable the writer to put his facts and ideas into their proper positions.

The following exposition obviously attempts to answer certain questions that are assumed to be in the reader's mind:

The accompanying table shows the following significant facts: first, that sales for February, 1948 are $2126 less than for the same month last year; second, that the total cost for selling during the month was $103 more than for the same month of last year; third, that only one district, the Tri-State, showed substantial gain.

Since the situation at first glance is so discouraging, these figures require an explanation. February 1947 was the second best month of the year. The order from Maxwell and Company alone, which came during that month, amounted to $1250. This concern has since that time distributed purchases more evenly over the year, so that our order from them in February 1948 amounted to only $230. Other important orders in February 1947 were those of Dickinson's, Randolph & Swift, and Breck. These firms are at present experiencing a serious slump, a condition for which our sales organization is in no way responsible.

The increase in selling cost is accounted for by a minor change in the office personnel, a change that will eventually be profitable.

There is nothing in these figures, therefore, to cause the least pessimism. Our business is steady, if not sensational, and most of the salesmen bring promising reports.

The procedure for analyzing and interpreting data, especially when they are presented in a table or curve, can sometimes follow a definite pattern such as the following:

1. Selection of the most significant facts and restatement in words

2. Definition of any terms too vague or too technical for exact reader comprehension. It is particularly essential that units be precisely identified

3. Reasoned statement of the causes of these phenomena, and possibly an estimate of their effect on other elements of the problem under discussion

For example, an examination of a table (Step 1) might show that in 59.6% of a state's automobile accidents mature and experienced men were at the wheel. Before this fact could be meaningfully evaluated it would probably be necessary to define (Step 2) "mature," "experienced," "automobile," and "accident." If it was found in Step 2 that the "mature and experienced" man was a male 24 to 50 years of age with at least two years' driving experience, then Step 3 might point out that the particular phenomenon is not so significant as it at first seems. For there were five times as many male registered drivers as women, and of every five men four belonged to the 24–50 year age group. Furthermore it could be pointed out that men drive a very great proportion of road hours, especially if "automobile" includes commercial vehicles as well as passenger cars. Finally, if the table was compiled in an effort to learn what kind of driver represents the greatest highway hazard, then comparisons should have been made on equal bases —that is, how many men in each age-group were involved in accidents, *per capita, per registered driver,* or *per 100 road hours driven,* the choice of unit depending on the use to which the information was to be put.[14]

Argument

Thus far the discussion of the forms of composition has been limited to exposition, that form which aims only to enlighten or inform. Nearly all reports, it is true, adopt the tone and spirit of exposition, use its devices, and depend upon the application of its principles. Nevertheless, the actual aim of a good many reports is argumentative. To a certain problem there are several possible solutions, each of which has its advocates. The writer's aim may be to find the right solution, to recommend it, and to secure the adoption of his recommendation. Such a report, in aim at least, is argument. Public reports addressed to citizens must very often point to a need for definite improvements and advances. Citizens must be persuaded to support changes that the writer deems essential. Occasionally, too, argument plays an incidental and contributory part even in reports that are mainly expository in purpose. Whenever the writer recommends or advises a particular line of action or policy in regard to which differences of opinion have heretofore existed, we may term his work an argument.

The term "conclusions," used in connection with our discussion

---

[14] For information on statistical analysis and interpretation refer to the bibliography, Appendix B.

of summaries, is often confused with the term "recommendation." Conclusions, it should be noted, are important generalizations. Recommendations, on the other hand, are suggestions for improvement growing out of these generalizations. "Conclusions" state that something *was, is,* or *will be true.* "Recommendations" point toward action; they state that something *should be done.* The difference will be clear from a study of the following sections:

CONCLUSIONS

The conclusions drawn from the study follow:
1. The expenditures for accounting, for so-called "efficiency direction," and for time study, are larger than for any similar period in the past.
2. These increased expenses do not seem warranted by the advantages that have been, or are likely to be, obtained.
3. Unless it is possible to cut the cost of overhead substantially, profits will be seriously affected.

RECOMMENDATIONS

As a result of this study, the following recommendations are presented:
(1) Mr. Tenny should be placed in charge of the accounting department.
(2) The directors should abandon the "efficiency system," which has proved costly and ineffective.
(3) In the future no more than three engineers should be assigned to time study.
(4) Mr. Griffith should be instructed to reorganize the shipping department according to the plans that he has suggested, and he should be given full authority in that department.

An argument is not merely assertive and contentious. If the student has such an impression, he should erase it immediately from his mind—certainly, for the purpose of report writing. The kind of argument that has a place in reports is calm, reasoned, and businesslike. Except in its purpose, it has very little in common with political oratory and appeals to the jury.

The normal order of argumentative discourse is worth considering. Most thorough arguments follow a plan somewhat as follows:

1. A discussion of the problem: What is it? Wherein is it important?

2. Presentation of the dominating factors that should determine a decision, the "issues" in the problem

3. A comparison of the several solutions or "sides" of the question; presentation of facts and "evidence"

4. Conclusions and recommendations

This, in its essential features, is the plan of very many reports.

The reader is seldom definitely antagonistic to the writer's recommendations. Usually he is neutral. Very often, however, he *must be shown,* and the writer finds it necessary to justify his recommendations carefully and logically. Unlike many "persuasive" arguments addressed to antagonistic groups, the recommendation report usually places the general decision of the writer at the beginning—in the letter of transmittal, or in a section headed "Summary of Report," or sometimes even "Recommendations." This position of the decision is, however, in keeping with traditional argumentative practice, where the "proposition" is the first statement in the argument. Such a practice has definite advantages when the reader is open-minded and wants to know the writer's conclusions immediately.

In the development of an argumentative report, the letter of transmittal assumes an exceedingly important place. Such a letter may tend to increase the reader's interest in the question, to emphasize its importance, and to show the need of a solution. It may have the further argumentative value of advancing the writer's claim to attention by setting forth the extent of his investigations, the advice and help that he has received, and the soundness of his methods. The letter of transmittal may be personal and direct. It may serve as an excellent introduction.

Note that the plan of the "normal" argument is almost exactly that of regular scientific procedure. These points are taken up in turn:

1. What is the question?
2. What are the governing factors that will determine a decision?
3. What are the facts?
4. What conclusions can be drawn from these facts?

It is natural that reports which advance a thesis should be written in this order.

The issues, or the factors governing or determining a decision, must occupy a position of prominence in the argumentative report. Frequently, of course, they may be included under "Scope." After they have been determined and presented to the reader in the report, the later discussion may be subdivided accordingly. For example, in a report concerned with the selection of a particular type of bridge, the issues were determined as follows:

1. Which type is best suited to the needs of the situation?
2. Which type is advisable from the standpoint of cost?
3. Which type is most acceptable to the public?

These three questions then determined the three chief divisions of the text proper:

I. Adaptability
II. Cost
III. Acceptability

The further steps in the development of an argumentative report need little discussion at this time. The most important part of the report, from the standpoint of sound argument, is that concerned with facts and evidence. Since everything hinges upon that, the writer must be particularly careful to develop it logically. He must be wary of hasty conclusions, unsatisfied with mere surface impressions. Logic and the laws of scientific procedure are the report writer's guides.

The kind of argument presented to the public or to a legislative body often differs from that presented to business executives or technical specialists. Sometimes such an appeal is strong in persuasive qualities, actually resembling the conventional political arguments.

Exercises

In each of the following assignments a definite reader group should be selected and named.

1. Abstract a chapter from one of your technical textbooks.

2. Abstract an article on a technical subject from some such periodical as *Fortune* or *Aviation*.

3. The president of a corporation, in his annual report, desires to include the following facts:

> Profits the preceding year had been $47,000.
> Profits this year were $22,000.
> One hundred more men were employed.
> Sales increased about three percent.
> Expenditures for new building amounted to $20,000.
> The sales manager resigned in July.
> A course in salesmen's training was adopted.
> The poorest sales were in the New Jersey district.
> It is recommended that only one salesman remain in that district.

Write his introductory summary.

4. Define the object and scope of a report on one of the following subjects:

> Selection of a method for increasing a city's water supply
> The use of light metals in the ———— industry
> Labor-management problems in the ———— industry
> Methods of oil prospecting
> A laboratory experiment
> Uses for a new material

5. Define one of the following terms in a short paragraph, adapting the dictionary definition for a specific report:

Factory	Catalyst	Slide rule
Pilot plant	Isotope	Curriculum
Laboratory	Supersonics	Oxidation
Easement	Right of way	Alloy

6. Write a short descriptive exposition on one of the following subjects:

A dam	A pressure cooker
A bridge	A fractionating column
A power shovel	A flow meter
A sextant	A thermocouple & recorder
A pressure gage	A machine shop
A fire extinguisher	A quarry or mine

7. Write a narrative exposition based upon the following accomplishments:

> Orders received from seven concerns
> Foreman given instructions for work
> Machine repaired
> First order filled and shipped in three days
> Other orders followed rapidly
> Shipping department worked overtime
> Final order shipped in eight days

8. Write a narrative exposition of one of the following:

> Drilling an oil well
> Multiple-effect evaporation
> A pilot-plant operation
> A production line
> An automatic control

9. Write an interpretation of one of the following:

> (a) The population of the city in 1935 was 47,320.
> The population of the city in 1940 was 69,287.
> The population of the city in 1945 was 78,962.
> The valuation of property increased 54 percent between 1935 and 1945.

FUNDAMENTAL FORMS OF COMPOSITION

The indebtedness of the city increased 27 percent in the same time.

The percentage of foreign-born men and women was 30 percent higher in 1945 than in 1935.

No important new projects were carried out by the city during these ten years; the increase in expenditures was due to a continuance of the same policies over a larger area and for a larger population.

(b) The student body in 1946 numbered 1710; in 1949 it numbered 1835; and in 1950 it numbered 2165.

The number of fraternities in 1946 was 15; in 1949 it was 19; and in 1950 it was 20.

The average number in a single fraternity has risen, from 28 in 1946, to 33 in 1950.

Students leaving college voluntarily during their first two years increased from 45 in 1946 to 107 in 1950.

The percentage of fraternity members leaving college voluntarily is less than half that of nonfraternity men.

(c) From 1900 to 1942 the average life expectancy of the American people increased from 49 to 69 years.

From 1925 to 1945 deaths from scarlet fever have been reduced 92 percent, from whooping cough 74%, and from measles 91%.

In the same 2 decades the death rate of children between the ages of 5 and 14 was cut 57%.

Cardiovascular disease, including chronic disease of the kidneys, arteriosclerosis, and cerebral hemorrhage, now accounts for 45% of the deaths in the U. S. Second are infectious diseases, and third is cancer.

Seven million persons in the U.S. are mentally ill and more than one-third of the hospital beds in this country are filled with such persons.

(Data from *Science, The Endless Frontier,* by Vannevar Bush. Washington: The U.S. Government Printing Office, 1945.)

(d) The following curves:

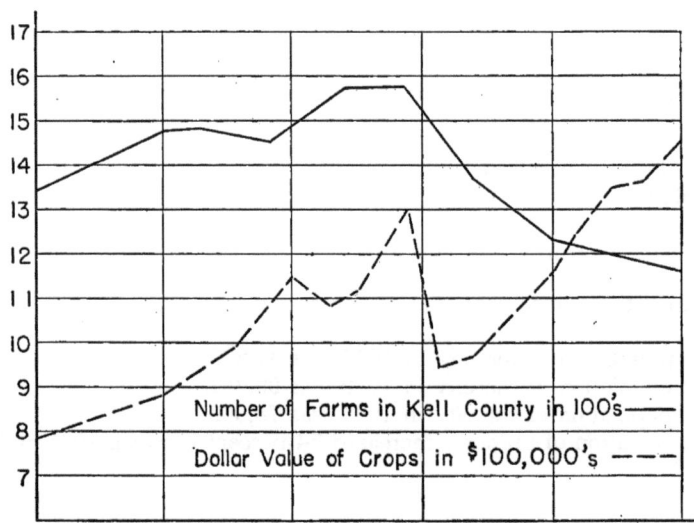

10. Develop an interpretation of, and an argumentative conclusion about, one of the following subjects:

Increase of wages since 1932, and the causes
Scholastic superiority of one group of students over another
Results of installing new machinery
Athletic results under a new coach
Strikes within a district during a year

CHAPTER 4

REQUIREMENTS IN STYLE

ALTHOUGH the foremost quality of a report is its truth, nevertheless the correctness alone of the data and conclusions will not make it effective. If the writer's statements are so worded as to mislead, confuse, or produce false impressions, his ability as an investigator amounts to little. Exactness of statement is just as necessary as accuracy in field work or research. A study of the first three chapters should have impressed upon the student the desirability of giving attention to details of style as well as to the selection of ideas. A consideration of certain specific problems in the style of reports follows.

The writing of most students is marred by more or less serious faults in construction. Unfortunately, too, the reports of some of the most reputable technical and business men and women exhibit ungrammatical and even incoherent sentence structure, hazy and ill-formed paragraphs, awkward and ambiguous expressions, and other similar violations of good use. Most of these men and women recognize that they have been handicapped by a weakness in expression, and they emphatically urge younger persons to improve themselves in the skillful use of the English language. It is, therefore, no waste of time to emphasize the principles of composition and good use.

We must admit that no uniform practice in the use of English obtains even among the most effective report writers. Prominent scientific and technical periodicals do not always agree in style. The student, therefore, must study the tendencies in the expression of his age, use his good sense and good taste, and adopt for his own composition those principles that experience shows to be most effective for his purposes. Business, technical, and scientific men recognize more and more the need of consistent standards in English; progress in the direction of general agreement is being made. The American Society for Engineering Education and the

American Standards Association have contributed especially to a general consistency in technical writing.

Probably the reader of this book has at least a fair grounding in the fundamentals of composition. More than anything else he needs to have his attention called to the special problems of the report writer, some recognized methods of improving composition, and a few rules regarding the mechanics of style.

General aims. "Style" in a report is not for the purpose of impressing or entertaining the reader. Style, the manner of writing, must fit the subject matter, the reader, and the writer. Report writing is a very practical business. The style of reports, therefore, must satisfy very practical requirements:

It must facilitate rapid reading. Most readers of reports have limited time. The writer, then, thinks less of his own time than of his readers'. If he can save time for both, well and good, but the readers come first.

The style *must convey the exact meaning.* There must be no ambiguity or uncertainty in the writer's message.

The style *must show restraint.* Exaggerations are out of place. Enthusiasms must be curbed.

The style, usually, *must be objective.* The report writer's emphasis is seldom on himself; almost always it is on *what is true, what happened, what has been observed.*

The style *must be clear for later reference.* Most reports are filed for the future convenience of specialists and executives.

The tone of report writing. If the writer is employed as a specialist or expert to carry on an investigation, it is usually expected that his attitude toward the work will be impersonal, and that his writing, too, will be impersonal. This is the situation especially when the writer is not well acquainted with his readers, or when his report is to serve as a preliminary to later reports written by others. If, however, the writer has a personal interest in the results of his report, or is addressing one or two readers whom he knows well, it is natural that his style will be considerably more informal. Like every kind of writing, a report adopts the style best suited to its reader. What does the reader want and expect in this report? A thorough consideration of that question precedes the actual writing.

The informal and personal tone, which is rare in report writing,

is illustrated by the following short passage. Such a tone is desirable if the writer is addressing friends and giving information
of a somewhat confidential nature:

> I checked the November shipment records with the local freight office
> and found that we have been charged with two cars more than our own
> records indicate. So far the explanation is still wanting, but I suspect that
> the mistake will be traced to our yard office. We are running the matter
> down now, and I hope to tell you something more definite in a day or two.

Such a style belongs more to the letter report than to a formal
type, in which objective details have first place and individuality
is subordinated.

Compare the following impersonal discussion with the one that
precedes:

> When the November shipment records were checked with the local
> freight office, it was found that the company had been charged with two
> cars more than the shipping department records show. The reason for this
> discrepancy has not been found, but indications point to an error in the
> yard office. As soon as a definite explanation can be made, it will follow.

Comments about the writer's professional standing and previous experience often have a legitimate place, customarily in the
letter of transmittal. The letter, in keeping with the modern
tendency of business correspondence, may be simple, informal,
and personal. It is usually best to have the letter carry the writer's
remarks about himself, and to maintain in the text itself a thoroughly objective attitude.

With some outstanding exceptions, therefore, reports are essentially objective and impersonal in tone. Such a convention leads to
a better emphasis—an emphasis upon the important facts. Scientific writing has always been characterized by an absence of
personal traits and subjective attitudes, because every effort is
made to subordinate the individual to the examination of objective phenomena. Report writing is similar. Personal pronouns are
rare. Instead of writing, "I carried on these tests," and "I examined
the sites," the author says, "These tests were carried on," "The
sites were studied," or "An examination of the sites showed . . ."

The writer's personality, of course, does count. Even when he
conscientiously avoids any direct reference to himself, his mode of
expression, his attitude toward his subject, his experience, and his
skill are all indications of his personality. The problem is primarily
one of emphasis. If he is writing informally to a friend, he keeps

the informal spirit. If he is developing an important document in which the facts deserve all the emphasis that he can give them, he writes formally and impersonally.

Make-up. Although this is not the place to discuss the general appearance of a finished report and the special graphical devices,[1] it must be apparent that these elements have a close relationship to style. Drawings, diagrams, maps, tables, graphs, and photographs are important means of simplifying an exposition and making a subject concrete to the reader. Even when these are accompanied by written explanations, they save time and trouble for the reader. A table, for example, is usually so clear that comparisons may readily be made from an examination of it. The same facts presented in written composition are confusing, heavy, and difficult to understand or interpret. One of the requisites of good style, therefore, is the use of tabular and graphical methods, instead of verbal exposition, whenever the former will furnish a more adequate impression. The writer must remember, however, that tabular and graphical elements almost always demand textual interpretation. A report that consists *entirely* of pictures, tables, and charts is very seldom adequate.

Again, the clearness of a report may be improved by a sensible use of subheads, or sectional titles. These subheads—Object, Scope, Summary, Financial Considerations, and similar titles—serve purposes of emphasis and are often important timesavers.

Our consideration of these matters, however, must be postponed while we confine our attention to the writer's use of language.

Adaptation to the reader. By this time the student is well aware of the necessity of making his report fit the interests, peculiarities, knowledge, and desires of his reader. However correct or excellent the form of composition that he adopts, the style is inadequate and poor if it is unsuited to his intended reader.

The engineer frequently addresses his colleagues, who are specialists like himself. At other times he is obliged to transmit his technical information so that a financier, a director, a stockholder, or a body of citizens will understand and appreciate its significance. The scientist may be obliged to write either for other scientists in his own field or for those outside. The architect must address both client and contractor. Executives address other ex-

---

[1] See Chapters 7 and 8.

ecutives, directors, stockholders, or taxpayers. Obviously, almost every report writer faces the difficult problem of adapting his information to different readers.

It is usually worth while to begin by attempting some sort of analysis of the individual reader, not to classify, but to differentiate him. For example, answers to the following questions are helpful:

What are his education, specific training, and experience?
How much information does he have on this subject?
What information does he want?
Has he indicated any prejudices?
Has he shown any preference for reports in a particular form and style?

In other words, specific information about an individual is worth much more than a general classification of a reader as "technical" or "semitechnical" or "lay." One reader likes details; another does not. One prefers bare facts, totally devoid of ornament; another must be interested, even entertained. Every writer must attempt to discover these personal traits.

Unfortunately, the instruction given in this book must be general. All that is possible here is to point out certain peculiarities of compositions for different classes, and to leave to the student the duty of further adaptation to his individual reader.

The first class of readers, then, may be termed "technical." Nearly every profession and business employs a considerable number of terms peculiar to itself—terms that have grown with the development of the profession or business, and that are known but slightly by outsiders. Such terms are specific; they save time for reader and writer alike, and they have meanings that no other terms can exactly convey. Specialists in all fields, therefore, must make themselves acquainted with the diction most useful in their field. A report addressed by the specialist to his colleagues employs technical style. Examine the following example:

— 1 —

The dam is of solid concrete masonry construction, designed as a gravity section. Its total length, 4648 ft, includes the powerhouse headworks, 950 ft long, and 2385 ft of ogee-type gate-controlled spillway section. To collect seepage water under the dam and prevent excessive uplift, a longitudinal drain was installed on the foundation 10 ft, 6 in. downstream from the face of the dam. Cross drains, 45 ft on centers, connect this drain to tail water at the toe of the dam. At all vertical construction joints riser drains connect the bottom drains to the inspection tunnel. To reduce seepage through the vertical construction joints, copper sealing strips were installed near the upstream face of the dam. Grout holes located 2 ft inside the upstream face of the dam were drilled in the foundation to a depth of 20 ft at 10-ft intervals and grouted under 25-lb pressure to form a cut-off wall against seepage through the foundation.

The dam and powerhouse are founded on rock at an average elevation of about 12 ft above sea level for the dam, and 7 ft for the powerhouse. The overhanging crest is an unusual feature of the spillway section. This permitted a curved surface, approximating the lower nappe of an overflowing stream of the depth of 22.5 ft, to be formed without increasing the width of the section beyond that required for stability.

The crest of the main spillway is fixed at elevation 86 and is surmounted by 50 Stony-type movable crest gates, each 22.5 ft high by 41 ft wide, operating in guides provided in concrete piers on the dam. Three regulating gates, each 10 ft high by 41 ft wide, have been provided adjacent to the powerhouses on a fixed crest at elevation 98.5 for use in finer regulation of the pool level. In the design of the spillway, an allowance of 4000 lb per linear foot was assumed, for ice pressure at the water surface. The gate piers, spaced 45 ft on centers, continue up above the pool level and support a runway at elevation 115, extending along the spillway section and powerhouse headworks, from which three electrically operated gantry traveling cranes operate the crest and regulating gates as well as the sectional head gates and trash racks, on the powerhouse. The gate piers also support the highway bridge which has replaced the old Conowingo Bridge inundated in the reservoir. The spillway section for the three regulating gates and 17 crest gates has been provided with a 20-ft-wide apron, curving up from the toe of the dam to an angle of 12½ deg with the horizontal, in order to prevent erosion at the toe of the dam.[2]

In spite of the occasional employment of technical diction, however, instructions and reports in practical work more commonly avoid strictly technical language. To what extent the specialist shall use his technical vocabulary depends, of course, upon the analysis that he has made of his reader. Often he writes in a style that is known as "semitechnical"—an adaptation for those who are largely unacquainted with specialized diction, but who nevertheless demand and need important technical facts. Something of the nature of this semitechnical style will be learned from an examination of the following paragraphs:

— 2 —

The Conowingo dam, of solid concrete masonry construction, is of the gravity-section type. Its total length is 4648 feet, which includes the headworks at the powerhouse and the spillway section.

Seepage of water under the dam is drained away to prevent excessive uplift. Seepage from vertical construction joints is reduced by copper sealing

---

[2] "Design of the Conowingo Dam and Headworks," *Journal A.I.E.E.*

strips. Grout holes drilled in the foundation every 10 feet carry liquid concrete (grout) under pressure to form a cut-off wall to prevent seepage through the foundation.

The dam is founded on rock at 12 feet above sea level and the powerhouse at 7 feet. An overhanging crest at the spillway section permits the properly curved surface for the overflow without increasing the gravity section of the dam. This considerably reduces the cost of the 2685 feet of the dam that go to make up the spillway. The spillway design assumes a pressure of 4000 lb per linear foot, for ice pressure at the water surface. Fifty movable crest gates surmount the main spillway at the 86-foot elevation. Regulating gates at the powerhouse maintain the pool level at the 98.5-foot level.

The gate piers, 45 feet apart, support a runway for the electric gantry cranes which operate the crest and regulating gates, section head gates, and trash racks. The piers also support the highway bridge which replaces the old Conowingo bridge, now inundated.

The spillway section has been provided with an apron whose upward curvature prevents erosion at the foot of the dam.

Although less common and less useful in reports, the "popular" style must occasionally be used. Municipal and government reports are often written primarily for the benefit of laymen. Sometimes it is desirable that popular interest be aroused in the subject. Then the writer makes his style as appealing as he can. The following short exposition has the "popular" tone that would serve to attract the layman:

— 3 —

The Conowingo dam, whose construction inundated a wide area, forcing the relocating of a railway line and the abandonment of a village and a number of farms, is a concrete structure of the familiar "gravity" type; that is, it is built so that its weight alone is sufficient to resist the overturning effort of the piled-up waters that it confines. Seepage of water under the dam, which would have an upward thrust, is drained away.

Its total length is 4648 feet, which includes the site of the powerhouse (the "headworks") and the 2385-foot spillway. The upper surface of the spillway, curved to fit the natural shape of the lower surface of the overflowing waters, is like a shelf, or overhanging crest. This crest gives the curve desired without requiring the entire height of the spillway section to have this full thickness, which is greater than the "gravity" section needs to sustain the pressure of the pent-up waters. Considerable saving of concrete is obtained by this arrangement. The engineers have allowed for a pressure of 4000 pounds for every foot of the length of the spillway, to resist the pressure of ice on the surface of the impounded waters.

Fifty movable and three regulating gates work as guides in concrete gate piers, those near the powerhouse controlling the level of the pool. The gate piers support a runway for the electrical cranes which raise and lower the movable gates. They also support the highway which replaces the old Conowingo bridge now submerged.

To prevent erosion at the foot of the dam, the "apron," or downstream surface of the dam, is given an upward curve at its "toe," that flings the swiftly rushing water upward and robs it of its wearing effect on the bed of the stream.

Suggestions for effectiveness. It is difficult to give the report writer arbitrary instructions concerning his style. He faces many different problems and situations. And yet it is possible to point to certain qualities that usually belong to successful reports.

1. **Directness.** Get down to your subject immediately. Come to the point at once. Carry the principle of "summarizing early" throughout the report. Spend no time in nonessential preliminaries. So far as is possible, adopt the "deductive" method of development; that is, begin each section with generalizations and then develop them by means of details. The reader, when he turns to your report, has general questions in his mind. "Is the plan worth anything?" he asks. "Is it practicable? What will it cost?" In beginning your discussion, avoid suspense. Do not keep him curious. Answer his questions briefly first, then give details at length. But tell him immediately what you are writing about, what you have found, and what the findings may mean to him.

The following paragraph, serving as a preliminary to more detailed discussion, is itself developed by the "deductive method":

Three plans put into effect during the past six months have been reasonably promising. First, we instituted conferences in each division, at which nearly every agent was present and through which we were able to outline general policies. Next followed visits to each section by the Production Manager, the Superintendent, and the President. While the executives, therefore, were learning something of the problems in the field, the agents had opportunity to acquaint themselves with the factory point of view. Finally, last month we called some of the leading agents from each division to the factory for special instruction. All these steps were definitely advantageous to the morale of the organization.

2. **Thoroughness.** Make your report so comprehensive that no reader need ask further questions as to what it is intended to explain. It is your own problem to determine exactly how much of your information should be included. You must make every point in the investigation clear. Support your recommendations, and make your explanations so detailed that misconceptions will be impossible. Much of your information you may throw away, but you must consider every question that is likely to arise either at once or at a later time. Remember those readers who will pick up your report next week or next month, but do not forget those who may come to it ten years later.

3. **Conciseness.** Satisfy yourself that every point, every statement that you make, is important enough to demand inclusion. Make the report just as short as is consistent with thoroughness and clearness. Waste no words. Although no report need be so brief as to be totally barren of interest, it should take up as little space and time as possible.

After the report is written, go over it carefully, crossing out every needless word, sentence, and paragraph. Mere adornment is a positive fault; digression is inexcusable.

Wordiness may result from an attempt at "fine writing." It may result just as often from a failure to bring related ideas together in sentences of reasonable length. Choppy sentences frequently lead to waste. Compare the following paragraphs:

A concrete spillway makes up a large section of the dam. This section begins at a point located along the river wall of the lock and it extends to the powerhouse intake. The whole spillway is 864 ft long and it is divided into 18 separate bays. The gates which are used for opening and closing the spillways are of the fixed roller type. Each gate is constructed of two parts. The reason for this is to provide a method sufficiently flexible for the regulation of the amount of water which is to be discharged through each section of the spillway. The gates are each 40 ft in width and 40.44 ft in height. Each of them can be raised or lowered by either one of the two heavy cranes which can travel back and forth across the operating deck of the spillway. The cranes have a capacity of 80 tons each. The crest of the spillway is approximately 30 ft above the surface of the natural rock below. And the piers are 66 ft higher than the crest. There is a concrete apron on the downstream side of the spillway. The engineers believed this was necessary to prevent erosion of the river bed.

The concrete spillway section, extending 864 ft from the river wall of the lock to the powerhouse intake, is divided into 18 bays. The spillway gates, of the fixed-roller type, 40 ft wide by 40.44 ft high, are built in two sections for flexibility in regulating the discharges. They are operated by either of two 80-ton-capacity traveling gantry cranes (from the operating deck of the spillway). The spillway crest is approximately 30 ft and the piers 96 ft above the natural rock. On the downstream side of the spillway a concrete apron prevents erosion of the river bed.

Both paragraphs present the same facts, but the one on the right is obviously easier to read and easier to understand. It costs less in reader-time.

The conciseness of the writer's expression has a great deal to do with the efficiency of his communication. Conciseness does not mean the elimination of minor ideas (as in condensation), so long as they are relevant. To the report writer it means the use of the fewest possible symbols (words) to represent a given number of ideas. It means the elimination of waste. It means the deletion (a) of unnecessary words; (b) of phrases for which a single word or fewer words can be substituted; (c) of clauses for which a word or a phrase can be substituted; (d) or of sentences which can properly be coordinated with, or subordinated to other sentences:

Wordy	*Concise*
(a) At the present time	at present now
(b) as a whole	entire
(c) which are known as gantry cranes	known as gantry cranes "gantry" cranes
(d) which is at the end of the corridor	at the end of the corridor
(a) these machines	they
(a) sum total	total
(b) most of the time	usually
(d) The building is too small. It is necessary for some of the classes to be held in the gym.	Since the building is too small, some of the classes must be held in the gym.
(1) The gates are 40 feet wide by 44 feet high. (2) They are operated by one of two cranes. (3) Both of these cranes are traveling cranes. (4) Each one has a capacity of 80 tons. (5) They are located on the operating deck of the spillway.	The gates, 40 feet wide and 44 feet high, are operated by either of two 80-ton traveling cranes located on the operating deck of the spillway.

Note: Sentences Nos. 1 and 5 at left have been reduced to phrases; sentences Nos. 3 and 4 to words.

4. **Clearness.** Make the plan of your report logical and easy to follow. Constantly guard against leaving some important matter unexplained or employing indefinite and incoherent language. Directness, thoroughness, and brevity play their part in making a report clear; good sentence and paragraph construction is essential. The too frequent use of definitions, as explained in Chapter 3, clogs the composition. Translation into "popular" or business language is the better method.

5. **Concreteness.** Though sometimes a difficult task, it is often

necessary to make your reader visualize the subject. Reports commonly employ "description," but too many so-called "technical descriptions" are essentially abstract. When possible, illustrate abstract statements with specific and concrete examples. Here is an illustration, restrained but concrete:

> Engineering works for the control and use of water vary in size from the Panama Canal and Boulder Dam down to farm terracing and trout-stream improvements. The same water may be used for irrigation, for hydroelectric power, for boating and fishing, for a city water supply, and for navigation. A dam may serve one or all of these purposes. Often the various beneficial uses are in conflict. A dam to be used for flood control must be emptied between floods, spoiling the lake for recreation purposes and seriously interfering with its use as a source of power.

Though writing is often criticized for being too general, too vague, it can be equally or even more vague to some readers when it is too specific. To say that the generators of a certain warship can produce a tremendous amount of electrical power (general) may be more meaningful than to say they have a total rated capacity of 80,000 kva (specific). For many readers it would be clearer than either to say that the generators produce enough electricity to supply the needs of a city the size of Portland, Oregon. Especially for laymen (stockholders and taxpayers, for example) the report writer must often make his facts vivid.

The paragraph. The paragraph is so important as a unit of the report that a great deal of the general effectiveness is dependent upon its construction. One must remember that a paragraph is more than an arrangement for providing breathing space, important as that function certainly is. The paragraph covers definite ground, builds up a single important idea or image by a series of related sentences, and has a necessary purpose in the development of the whole report. Good paragraphing demands more than haphazard subdividing.

In some forms of writing, the manner of constructing paragraphs is less important than in reports. The familiar essay, for example, follows no regular plan of paragraph development but takes any form that appears to be amusing, or original, or impressive. No such freedom is allowed the report writer. Customarily, his method is thoroughly logical, following a few obvious rules:

1. The opening sentence of the paragraph must be clearly indicative of everything the paragraph is to say. The reader of a

report often skips. His eye normally hits the first part of each section, the first sentences of many paragraphs. If important matter is hidden away in the middle of paragraphs, the hasty reader will miss it. The first sentence of a paragraph, therefore, should either indicate the exact subject of the paragraph, summarize its contents, or be clearly preparatory to the statements that are to follow. For example:

> Experiments were carried on by this company to determine the properties imparted to both cupola iron and electric-furnace iron by the addition of alloys.
> Let us observe one or two differences between the "leader" and the "executive."
> The operation of the electric oven is not radically different from that of other types.

These topic sentences, thoroughly typical of the best reports, introduce the subject of the paragraph.

2. The paragraph should be unified. It should confine itself to the subject indicated by the topic sentence. No digressions are permissible. For example, a paragraph built around the first of the sentences quoted above would include only the purpose and the general nature of the experiments that were conducted. A paragraph built around the second would confine itself entirely to differentiating the two terms "leader" and "executive." A paragraph based upon the third sentence would discuss the operation of the electric oven, emphasizing its similarity to "that of other types."

3. If consecutive statements in the paragraph repeat the same general idea, or illustrate a single point, they should be constructed in the same way. This rule is an aid to clearness and emphasis. Note the parallel construction in the following sections:

> The leader attracts a personal loyalty; the executive develops an organization loyalty. For one, the worker develops feelings of affection or even love; for the other, respect and obedience.

> There are three ways of bringing the two materials together: (1) by adding solid Cu to liquid Al, (2) by adding solid Al to liquid Cu, and (3) by adding liquid Cu to liquid Al.

4. The paragraphs of a report should follow each other naturally and logically. They should be connected in thought, and their connnection should be made apparent by the employment of transitional devices. Shifting the normal word order or

using words that indicate a relationship between a new paragraph and the one that precedes may help the transition:

To meet this need, new equipment seemed essential.
Nevertheless, the work continued successfully.
In a similar manner, new tests were conducted on the Barton valves.
Thus it seemed apparent that a new experiment must follow.
In spite of this serious loss, however, our sales increased substantially.
Of equal value in establishing good morale is the York plan.
Following these preliminary studies, the investigators turned to a more intensive examination of the obvious hazards.
To explain such expenditures, a new practice has been instituted.
All of these observations lead to but one conclusion.

Each of these sentences, by means of the words in italics, establishes a link between the part which precedes and that which follows.

5. Paragraphs should be of average length, neither so long as to tire and confuse the reader, nor so short as to appear choppy and incomplete. Short paragraphs or those consisting of a single sentence, though commonly employed in sales letters, are seldom sufficiently dignified and complete to meet the demands of a long report. Such short paragraphs do not usually emphasize the principal ideas and place them in a position of prominence, as they should. On the other hand, the paragraphs should seldom be as long as those in the typical scholarly treatise. In general, about two hundred words should be the maximum limit for paragraphs in a report, and the average ought to be considerably less.

6. The development of the details within the paragraph must be orderly. The "logical" paragraph plan consists of a summarizing topic sentence, placed first, with a series of details enlarging upon that sentence. These details may be a reiteration of the general idea, presenting substantially the same thought in different ways. They may furnish evidence in support of one of the writer's contentions. They may be specific examples illustrating the main statement. This "logical" plan of development is more often found in reports than elsewhere, for it is a plan particularly fitted to their direct, matter-of-fact style.

Another plan of development may be termed the chronological. It follows the order of a narrative exposition, beginning with a sentence that points out the direction of the development, and proceeding with sentences that explain the steps of a process, an achievement, or a set of directions. As in the second illustration below, this plan is often adopted even when the subject matter is not truly narrative.

The two plans are exemplified in the following paragraphs:

(1)

The *logical* plan:

This manuscript, although in no sense original or constructive, provides excellent material for elementary courses in the subject. It is extremely conservative, but probably in a beginning text that is a merit. It confines itself to essentials, advances no new theories, and sidesteps controversy. It presents the simple facts clearly. Abundant and useful exercise material is a distinct point in its favor. Finally, it is brief enough to find a market among those instructors who are looking for a teachable survey text.

(2)

The *chronological* plan:

Meanwhile RCA was making a start in network broadcasting. In the spring of 1923 RCA acquired sole control of Station WJZ in New York City, and later that year it constructed and started to operate station WRC at Washington. The first network broadcast by RCA occurred in December 1923, and involved only WJZ and the General Electric Co.'s station WGY at Schenectady, N. Y. The connection was made with Western Union telegraph wires.[3]

The subject of a paragraph is always one of the minor divisions of the report. The main divisions, or sections, frequently demand more complete treatment than is possible within a single paragraph. Subdivisions within the section are indicated by proper paragraphing. Every paragraph is a single unit, complete so far as it goes, but dependent upon other units and bearing a close relationship to them and to the whole. Each unit must be compact, orderly, and solid. It must definitely advance the development of the whole subject.

The sentence. Good sentences may not of themselves make good reports, but if a writer's sentences are sound he may have numerous faults in general organization without disgracing himself. Certainly, clear sentences count more than anything else in the production of clear reports.

The student probably has had general training in composition and already writes reasonably correct sentences. If not, he should buy a good handbook of English usage and study it faithfully.

---

[3] *Report on Chain Broadcasting*, Federal Communications Commission, May 1941.

Here it will not be a waste of time, however, to call to his attention, for review and emphasis if for no other purpose, a few qualities that have an important bearing upon successful report writing.

1. **Objectivity.** From laboratory experience, most students have learned to avoid such forms as these:

Fill a test tube with water.
I filled a test tube with water.
Filled a test tube with water.

Instead of any of these sentences, the laboratory student writes:

A test tube was filled with water.

Why the insistence upon this particular form? The answer is that, in scientific and technical work, emphasis is placed upon objective facts, not upon the personality; upon the experiment, not upon the experimenter. In many kinds of reports the same construction is desirable. Let the writer decide whether his assignment calls for impersonal emphasis upon what *has been done*, or for a personal expression of what *I have done*. Usually it is the former.

2. **Completeness.** The carefully prepared report avoids incompleteness in sentence structure just as it avoids incompleteness in its treatment of the whole subject. Of course, if the hurried notes jotted down at the end of the day are to form a report for a reader who is accustomed to abbreviated and hastily constructed forms, then the writer need not worry much about rigid rhetorical principles. But if the report is to serve an important function as information or as a permanent record, it should be written in complete, well-planned sentences. In such a report, the following examples are indefensible:

Have just been to factory.
Object of tests to determine efficiency of boilers.
Temperature and heat input measurements made every ten minutes.
Was found work could not be finished today.

All these sentences have important omissions. If nothing worse, they give an impression of careless writing, and some of them are far from clear. Written correctly, they will read:

I have just been to the factory (or *The factory has just been visited*).
The object of these tests was to determine the efficiency of the boilers.
Temperature and heat input measurements were made every ten minutes.
It was found that the work could not be finished today.

A complete statement is read more easily and more quickly than a partial statement. To omit articles, connectives, a subject or a verb, may save a little time for the writer; it never saves any for the reader.

3. **Consistency.** It is well known that reports, particularly those of a technical nature, commonly employ the passive voice in preference to the active. It is essential to good writing, however, that the author hold to the form with which he begins. If he starts with the active voice, let him continue it. If he starts with the passive, let him be consistent. An awkward mixing of voices is one of the most common faults of report writing:

> Having made the necessary preparations, the work was started.
> Comparing the several methods, it must be remembered that there is a similarity of plan and procedure.
> Knowing the market, production may be regulated accordingly.

In each of these sentences the main clause is written in the passive voice, the subordinate construction in the active. To be consistent and grammatically correct, one must write them as follows:

> The necessary preparations having been made, the work was started.
> When the several methods are compared, it must be remembered that there is a similarity of plan and procedure.
> If the market is known, production may be regulated accordingly.

Another form of inconsistency in sentence structure is in the failure to maintain parallel construction for parts of a sentence that are similar in thought:

> Having established the new department, and since more men were now employed, the cost mounted.
> This so-called "efficiency" plan made the workmen dissatisfied, work listlessly, demanding more wages.
> The salesmen were told the value of this product, and how to stimulate interest in it.

Consistency, kept by parallel construction, calls for a different expression:

> Since the new department had been established and more men were now employed, the costs mounted.
> This so-called "efficiency" plan made the workmen dissatisfied, listless in their work, and insistent in their demands for more wages.
> The salesmen were told the value of this product and the way to stimulate interest in it.

4. **Restraint.** Reports should seldom use the vivid language of advertising and publicity. Opinions, conclusions, and recommen-

dations especially must be free from exaggeration. Enthusiasm must not be too apparent. Understatement is preferable. The following sentences, for example, have no place in most reports:

The engineering plans are extraordinarily practicable.
This site was found to be ideal in every way for both immediate and future uses.
The installation will unquestionably pay for itself in less than a year.

The writer showing "scientific restraint" would write those sentences as follows:

The engineering plans appear to be entirely practicable.
The site seems to be satisfactory in all important respects for both immediate and future uses.
In the light of this study there is reason to believe that the installation may pay for itself in less than a year.

5. **Length of sentences.** Short sentences are usually preferable in a report. Often they are easier to grasp, more emphatic, and less likely to be incoherent. Related ideas, however, must be brought together, and complex sentences often save words. Childishly simple sentences must be avoided. Variety of length is a desirable quality.

Punctuation. Punctuation, as every writer knows, is intended primarily to make the sense more evident to the reader. Too much punctuation, therefore, is fully as bad a fault as too little, and inconsistent punctuation very often leads to a reader's confusion. The best practice is to punctuate only where you can see a sound reason for punctuating.

Bad punctuation often accompanies complex and involved sentence structure. The solution, therefore, may be to employ simpler sentences rather than to attempt correct punctuation of constructions that are needlessly difficult. If the sentence is long, rambling, and incoherent, punctuation is difficult. If it is unified and clear, the problem is seldom very troublesome. For the sake of review, study the following fundamental rules:

Use the comma:

1. To separate independent clauses connected by the coordinating conjunctions (*and, but, or,* and *for*):

No work has been done on the problem, but a number of companies have indicated a willingness to cooperate.
It is his job to operate the filters, and it is yours to see that a sufficient vacuum is maintained.

NOTE 1: The comma is often omitted between short clauses:

We can take it with us or we can buy it there.

NOTE 2: The comma must not be used to separate two independent clauses which are not connected by a coordinating conjunction:

Wrong: This is your job, this is his.

2. To separate introductory phrases or clauses from the rest of the sentence:

In the underground gasification of coal, the basic problem is . . .
Since the contractor agreed to all the changes in specifications, the contract was signed.
After the forming operation has been completed, the green carbon blocks are allowed to cool to room temperature.

NOTE. Short phrases are often used without the comma:

At present there is no need for more men.

3. To set off non-restrictive elements:

Mr. Kenneth Houp, *one of our carpenters,* . . . .
The main plant, *situated seven miles to the north,* . . . .
These mines, *which have belonged to the company a long time,* . . . .

But, commas must not be used when the elements are restrictive, when the meaning of the sentence would be lost or changed if the elements were removed:

The American *Barney Ewell* won the race. (This sentence means that more than one American raced; with *Barney Ewell* set off in commas it would mean that only one American raced, and he is identifiable by the word *American.*)
Give it to the man *operating the second lathe.* (This sentence wouldn't be very meaningful without the participial phrase if there were two or more men in the shop.)
During fueling, never open any of the valves *whose handles are painted red.*
The company refuses to hire any man *who has not had this kind of experience.*

4. To set off parenthetical, interrupting, or displaced expressions:

This plan, *if it has done nothing else,* has succeeded in revealing the possibilities of expansion.
Another plan, *however,* may prove more feasible.
That the light metals are suitable, we recognize.
Nothing has been done, *according to the literature,* to reduce these hazards.

5. To separate the items (three or more) of a series:

Everyone seems to agree that the system has been *complicated, inefficient,* and *costly.*

They are used in *drill presses, jigs,* and *lathes* in order to *cut down shafts,* to *cut threads,* and *to perform countless other operations.*

6. To separate the parts of a date, the parts of an address, a name from a title, or inverted parts of a name:

May 17, 1949   222 Beaver Avenue, Tyrone, Ohio
Hugh Pyle, General Manager   Beard, Charles A.

7. To separate adjacent numbers:

In 1952, 4343 houses will have been built in the area.

8. To separate a quotation from the rest of the sentence:

He asked, "When are you beginning operations?"

9. Whenever its use will avoid confusion:

Whatever type this is, is it practical?
More material, not labor, is required.
In drilling, the core is kept separate.
In the process of transplanting, the seedlings are. . . .
To begin with, this does not belong to us.

Use the semicolon:

1. To separate two independent clauses not connected by a coordinating conjunction:

Every reasonable demand has been met promptly; as a result these customers are enthusiastic about our service.

2. To separate any long coordinate clauses that contain commas:

All the planets, as we have noted, are in the same plane as the sun; but in the atom the electrons outside the nuclear center are not confined in their motions to a single plane.

3. Similarly, to separate members of a series when one or more of them contain commas:

The investigation revealed three things: that, as we had expected, labor is scarce in the area; that transportation facilities are inadequate; and that the local taxes, so far as industry is concerned, are exorbitant.

Use the colon:

1. To indicate a following enumeration or explanation:

These conclusions seem evident: first, . . . ; second, . . . ; third, . . . ; and fourth, . . .

2. **To introduce a long quotation.**
3. **After the salutation of a letter.**

Use a dash:

1. **Seldom in technical writing.**
2. **To indicate a sharp break in thought and construction:**

When these companies finally entered into an agreement—failure to agree would have meant suicide to most of them—they were all satisfied they had found the best solution.

3. **To set off expressions that demand unusual emphasis:**

If their estimate is low enough—and that means substantially lower than these other bids—we should consider it seriously.

Use quotation marks:

1. **To mark off the words of another writer or speaker when they are exactly reproduced.**

NOTE 1: Long quoted passages are usually introduced by a colon, unmarked by quotation marks, indented and either reduced in type size or single-spaced—as has been the practice in this text.

NOTE 2: Indirect statements do *not* employ quotation marks:

The manager said that he would be here.

2. **Around the name of a magazine article** (see Bibliography, page 149).

3. **To enclose technical words or words used in unusual senses if the reader is not expected to understand them. Their meaning should, of course, be immediately given.**

NOTE 3: The simplest rule for placement of the quotation marks follows:

Always place the period or the comma within a closing quotation mark; and always place a colon and semicolon outside the closing quote. The question mark (and exclamation point) is placed where it will indicate how much of the sentence it controls —if only the quotation is a question, then the question mark goes within; if the whole sentence is a question, it goes outside:

It is not a question of "expediency."
"They are," he said, "known as 'glauber salts.'"
They asked, "What are these men doing?"
What reason have they to say, "This is unsatisfactory"?

Correct usage: It is beyond the scope of this text to touch on all
the problems of grammar and diction. However, a few of those
that have been found most troublesome to technical writers are
discussed in the following glossary:

a, an	*A* is used before all words beginning with a consonant sound, including *h*:

a hotel	an hour	a hydraulic press
a history	an ending	an *n*th root

above	Avoid using this word as a noun.
above-mentioned	Overworked and awkward. Preferably repeat the subject or use a synonym.
accept,	*Accept* means "to receive" or "to approve":
except	They *accepted* the shipment.
	Except (as a verb) means "to leave out":
	We *excepted* those who had poor vision.
affect,	*Affect* is always a verb; it means "to influence"
effect	or, in a different usage, "to simulate":
	The explosion did not *affect* our work.
	The foreman *affected* a gruff manner.
	Effect is usually a noun, meaning "result":
	These are the *effects* of the war.
	But *effect* is occasionally used as a verb in the sense of "to bring about":
	This action *effected* a complete change in labor legislation.
agree,	*Agree with* a person, *agree to* a thing.
agreement	In any clause, the verb must agree in number with its subject. Two special cases are worth noting:
	(1) In the pattern *one of those who, one of the plans which, one of those methods that,* the verb of the subordinate clause is plural:
	This is *one of those plans that look* good on paper.
	(2) The verb in an *either-or* or a *neither-nor* sentence agrees with the nearer subject:
	Either his plan or the plans we have already discussed *are* suitable.
	Either the plans we have already discussed or his plan *is* suitable.
amount,	*Amount* is used for things in bulk or mass:
number	a large *amount of potash*

Number is used for things that are countable:

a large *number* of machines

and, etc.

If *etc.* (*et cetera*, meaning "and others") must be used, omit the redundant *and.*

and/or

Most authorities, including the American Standards Association, condemn its use. Rewrite:

welding and/or riveting
welding, riveting, or both

and,
  to

Do not use *and* for *to*:

Try *to* do it. Not: Try *and* do it.

as,
  like

Conservative usage does not use the preposition *like* for the conjunction *as* to introduce a clause of comparison containing a verb:

This operates *as* the other does.
But: This operated *like* that one.

as per

Meaningless. Use *according to* or a synonym.

as,
  since

Avoid the weak (and often ambiguous) use of *as* for *since* or *because*:

Not: The power was cut, *as* men were working on the line.

bad,
  badly

Be sure that you mean the adverb when you use it, especially after verbs like *seem, appear, taste, smell,* and *feel*:

He feels bad. (He is unhappy physically or mentally.)
He feels badly. (His sense of touch is poor.)

balance,
  remainder,
  rest

Balance is used in the sense of equilibrium. Do not use it for "rest" or "remainder."

beside,
  besides

Beside means "next to"; *besides* means "in addition to."

blame on

The verb *blame* is not followed by *on*:
Blame us for it. Not: *Blame* it *on* us.

can, may

Can denotes ability; *may,* permission or possibility.

capacity,
  rating

These words should not be used interchangeably. A motor's *rating*, for example, may be lower than its *capacity.*

claim

Do not use *claim* for "assert" or "maintain."
Claim should be used in the sense of "to demand as being due":

The foreman *maintains* (not *claims*) that they did not do their work.

continual, continuous	*Continual* means "repeated frequently"; *continuous* means "repeated without interruption."
data	Usage still demands that *data* be considered a plural: These *data* are convincing.
different than	*Different from* is the correct form.
discover, invent	*Discover* something that already exists; *invent* something that did not previously exist.
double prepositions	The use of consecutive prepositions should be avoided when possible: Get off (of) the filter bay. They are (over) at the office.
due to	The chief objection to *due to* is that it is overworked, particularly in technical writing. But it is incorrect grammatically to use it as an adverb in place of *because of*: Wrong: It expanded *due to* a rise in temperature. Right: It expanded *because of* a rise in temperature. Right: The expansion is *due to* the rise in temperature. Thus, *due to* may be used correctly in the sense of *assignable to*.
economic, economical	*Economic* means "having to do with economics"; *economical* means "avoiding waste, thrifty."
electric, electrical	Practically interchangeable, except in the figurative sense: The response to the announcement was *electrical*.
enthuse	Avoid as colloquial.
factor	Webster defines *factor* as "one of the elements that contribute to produce a result." It should not be used for "consideration" or "part." Wrong: Financing is an important *factor* in industry. Right: Good financing is an important *factor* in the successful promotion of new enterprise.
farther, further	Preferably, *farther* is used for physical distance; *further*, for other comparisons.
in, into	Generally, *in* locates and *into* directs: The trouble is *in* the supercharger. The men will have to go *into* the mud drums.
inside of, within	*Inside of* should not be used for *within* in the time relationship: The job must be completed *within* a year.
irregardless	A redundant corruption of *regardless*.

less, fewer	*Less* refers to amount; *fewer* refers to number: *less* potash *fewer* sacks of potash
liquid, fluid	Not always interchangeable: all fluids are not liquids.
many, much	*Many* is used for countable quantities; *much,* for quantities in bulk or mass. *much* potash *many* bags of potash
maximum, optimum (adj.)	Webster defines *maximum* as "the greatest in quantity or value attainable in a given case," and *optimum* as "most favorable or conducive to a certain end." The distinction is sometimes important; for example, the *maximum* speed of a motor is seldom its *optimum* speed.
most, almost	*Most* indicates either the superlative degree or "the greater part of"; it should not be used for *almost* in the sense of "nearly."
a number, the number	A *number* generally refers to several persons or things, therefore requiring a plural verb; *the number* generally refers to a total and takes a singular verb. A number of plans *are* here. The number of men *has* increased.
only, just	Occasionally, misunderstanding will result from improper placement of these words in the word order. Better emphasis is obtained, and occasionally misunderstanding avoided, by placing these words next to the word they describe: The mill only turned out 20 tons of salt cake. Better: The mill turned out only 20 tons of salt cake. Different meanings: The mill just turned out 20 tons of salt cake. The mill turned out just 20 tons of salt cake.
percent, percentage	*Percent* (now acceptably written as one word) is used only with a number; *percentage* is never used with a number: 99.44 percent a small percentage
plurals of foreign words	Technical and scientific writing has exhibited a reluctance to follow the trend of Americanizing plural endings of foreign words. The following list indicates the status of the more common ones in technical usage:

Singular	Preferred Plural	Optional Plural
addendum	addenda	——
alumna	alumnae	——
alumnus	alumni	——
analysis	analyses	——
apparatus	same	apparatuses
appendix	appendixes	appendices
axis	axes	——
bacillus	bacilli	——
basis	bases	——
crisis	crises	——
criterion	criteria	criterions
curriculum	curricula	curriculums
datum	data	——
diagnosis	diagnoses	——
formula	formulas	formulae
focus	foci	focuses
fungus	fungi	funguses
hypothesis	hypotheses	——
index	indexes	indices
locus	loci	——
medium	media	mediums
memorandum	memoranda	memorandums
nebula	nebulae	nebulas
neurosis	neuroses	——
nucleus	nuclei	nucleuses
ovum	ova	——
parenthesis	parentheses	——
phenomenon	phenomena	phenomenons
radius	radii	radiuses
series	same	——
species	same	——
stadium	stadia	stadiums
stimulus	stimuli	——
stratum	strata	stratums
syllabus	syllabuses	syllabi
synopsis	synopses	——
synthesis	syntheses	——
terminus	termini	terminuses
thesis	theses	——
vertebra	vertebrae	vertebras
vertex	vertices	vertexes
vortex	vortexes	vortices

possessive case   The following rule for forming the possessive case generally applies. It should be remembered that the possessive of an inanimate object is rarely approved, in technical writing especially.

If the word to be made possessive does not end in *s*, add *'s*; if the word does end in *s*, add only the apostrophe:

man	man's	* curves	curves'
men	men's	* analysis	analysis'
child	child's	* analyses	analyses'
children	children's	Wiggins	Wiggins'
horse	horse's	horses	horses'
year	year's	years	years'
month	month's	months	months'

* These would almost invariably be written: *of the curves, of the analysis,* etc.

practicable, practical

Practicable is applied only to something that is capable of being put into practice. *Practical,* opposed to *theoretical,* means "sensible" when applied to persons, "efficient" when applied to things:

> The building of a bridge across a large body of water might be *practicable* (it could be done), but it wouldn't be *practical* unless it were the most efficient method of connecting the two shores.

principle, principal

Principle is always a noun meaning "a general truth" or "a fixed rule." *Principal,* as either noun or adjective, always conveys the idea of "chief."

> The *principle* of this machine is . . .
> The *principal* method for obtaining ammonia . . .

reason is because

Awkward and redundant

> Not: The reason the motor failed was because . . .
> But: The reason the motor failed was that . . .
> Or: The motor failed because . . .

seasonable, seasonal

Seasonable means "suitable to the season"; *seasonal* means "pertaining to or dependent upon the seasons of the year":

> Bitter winds are not *seasonable* in May.
> Most *seasonal* work is performed by migrant workers.

singular nouns

The following nouns regularly require a singular verb:

ceramics	anybody	none
economics	each (pron.)	no one
ethics	every	nothing
hydraulics	everybody	public
mathematics	everyone	someone
physics	news	series
politics, etc.	nobody	whereabouts

so

So is overworked and awkwardly ineffective as a conjunction:

Poor: The mill ran out of steel; so it shut down.
Better: Since the mill ran out of steel, it shut down.
Or: Having run out of steel, the mill shut down.

**some,
somewhat**

Formal usage does not permit the use of the adjective *some* for the adverb *somewhat*:

This method is *somewhat* (not *some*) less expensive.

**split
infinitive**

There is no longer any objection to splitting an infinitive if the resultant construction is clearer and less awkward:

In order *to better acquaint* the public . . . (clear)
In order *better to acquaint* the public . . . (awkward)
The Germans had failed seriously to affect the Allied offensive. (ambiguous)
The Germans had failed *to seriously affect* the Allied offensive. (clear)
Entries are sufficiently informative to frequently obviate the necessity of going to the files. (illogical)
Entries are often sufficiently informative *to obviate* the necessity of going to the files. (clear)

**verbal,
oral**

Strictly, *verbal* means "in words, written or spoken"; *oral* means "spoken."

**while,
and,
though**

While should be used to express time relationships. Its use for *though* is weak and for *and,* inaccurate:

Right: The machinery should not be oiled *while* it is running.
Weak: Welding is best, *while* riveting is nearly as good.
Poor: Their work is completed, *while* ours is yet to be done.

Capitalization. Among some writers there is a tendency to capitalize important words indiscriminately and without real justification. Such writers tell of *many large Industrial Concerns which have President and Directors who can be depended upon for Efficiency.* Wholesale capitalization of this sort cannot be defended. It costs money and wastes time. The following rules will answer most questions concerning capitalization. The illustrations represent correct practice.

Capitalize:

1. **The first word in a sentence.**
2. **The first word in a quotation when it begins a sentence.**
3. **The first word following a colon when it begins a sentence.**

4. The first word in parentheses when it begins a sentence.

5. Official titles of organizations:

General Electric Company
Mellon Institute

Prentice-Hall, Inc.
Ohio State University

6. Geographical, political, and racial proper names:

Hudson River
Crater Lake
Rocky Mountains
Great Lakes
the French

Texas
the state of Texas
Central Park
France
Negroes

7. Points of the compass *only when identifying specific areas:*

the Pacific Northwest
the Far East

North vs. South
the Middle West

8. Important historical events:

the War of 1812
Louisiana Purchase

Battle of the Bulge
Yalta Conference

9. Titles *preceding* a name:

General Marshall
Chairman of the Board Jones

Professor Smith
Curator Harlow

10. Titles used in place of specific proper names:

the Senator (a specific one)
the Mayor (of Pittsburgh)
the Secretary of State

11. All the principal words (always including the first and last) in the titles of publications:

The Theory of the Leisure Class
A Report on the Uses of Low-Carbon Steel

12. Abbreviations of academic degrees and similar distinctions:

M.D.
M.E.
Ph.D.
F.R.S.

doctor of medicine
mechanical engineer
doctor of philosophy
Fellow of the Royal Society

13. *Fig., Table, No.,* and *Vol.* when they appear either in the text or under cuts and tables.

Do not capitalize:

1. Names of the seasons.

2. Points of the compass unless identifying a specific area:

four miles east of here
northeastern Ohio

east wind
facing south

3. Words derived from proper nouns but no longer associated with them:

babbitt	diesel [4]	paris green
boycott	macadam	pasteurize
china	ohm	plaster of paris
volt		

Numbers. In technical and business writing of all kinds, figures are used freely. For purposes of clearness, they are usually preferred to written numbers. A few rules, followed generally, will simplify the problem of determining when figures should be employed in report writing.

Use figures for:

1. Dates and times of day:

October 1949   8:30 p.m.
September 22, 1959   2:14 a.m.

2. Street numbers:

221 Woodland Drive

3. Numbered objects:

Table No. 3   Page 44   Boiler No. 4
Fig. 8   Vol. 5   Site 4

4. Numbers containing decimals:

3.1416   0.4321   99.44

5. Numbers which are partly fractional:

1½   4¾   66⅔

6. Numbers over nine:

10   4300   1722   10,444

7. All numbers appearing in connected groups:

The 87 new stations include 14 in New England, 18 in Greater New York, 12 in Pennsylvania, 9 in Illinois, and 7 farther west.

8. In exact dimensions and unit modifiers:

2 by 4 in.   60-cycle motor
2- by 4-in. plank   4-wheel drive

---

[4] Diesel is still commonly, but inconsistently, capitalized.

9. For percentages:

| 99.44% | 0.64% | 75% | 4½% |

Do not use figures:

1. At the beginning of a sentence. Write out, or, better, revise the sentence:

> Wrong: 1948 was a good year for business.
> Right: For business, 1948 was a good year.
> Or: The year 1948 was a good one for business.

2. For numbers one through nine, unless they occur in connected groups where figures make comparisons easier.

3. For round-number estimates or approximations:

> about two hundred tons
> one or two thousand

4. For fractions standing alone:

> three-fourths of an inch
> one half of the distance

Miscellaneous:

1. Omit the comma in numbers of four figures:

| 1951 | 4334 | 1003 | *but* 34,156 |

2. In decimal numbers having no units, always place a cipher before the decimal point:

> 0.5632   *not* .5632

3. When one number follows another without punctuation, spell out either the first or the shorter:

> thirty 4-in. bolts   240 seven-hour days

4. In expressing an amount of money, do not add unnecessary ciphers or decimal points:

> $1500   *not* $1500.00

5. Except in legal documents, do not repeat a written number in figures. Use only figures:

> $75,000   (*not*) seventy-five thousand dollars ($75,000)

Abbreviations. Abbreviations, even in reports, should be used sparingly. Since the best business and professional writers try to maintain dignity of expression, they regard too frequent short cuts as likely to give an impression of slovenliness. Nevertheless, in many routine reports, and especially in those that are definitely technical, the writer is allowed considerably more freedom in this respect than he is in general composition. Recognized abbreviations often save as much time for the reader as for the writer. When this is true, that is, when a reader is known to be in the habit of thinking in abbreviations, the writer should employ them with judgment.

The report writer will do well to use few abbreviations rather than many; when he has any doubt, it is always safe to write the terms in full. Take no chances. Be sure that your meaning is clear to your reader, and that the report appears carefully written and "professional." Some rules for abbreviating follow:

1. Never abbreviate words that are not regularly abbreviated.[5] Do not write *h-p cylinders* for *high pressure cylinders;* or *this prod.* for *this product.* The following terms are among those that should always be written in full when they appear alone:

acre	mile
boiler pressure	million
coulomb	month
day	ohm (or Ω)
frequency	potential
grains	rod
lira	ton
mass	ton-mile
megacycle	week

2. Use most abbreviations in the singular only:

14 in., *not* 14 ins.
24 lb, *not* 24 lbs
12 cm, *not* 12 cms

Among the exceptions are: pp., pages; vols., volumes; Figs., figures; Nos., numbers; mfrs., manufacturers.

3. In technical and scientific writing omit the period after an abbreviation except when the omission would result in confusion.

24 hr	a-c system
60 hp	250 kwhr
27 in.	20 qt

---

[5] The American Standards Association *Abbreviations for Scientific and Engineering Terms* is included in Appendix C.

4. Abbreviate titles only when they precede a proper name, and then only when initials or the given name follows:

Wrong: Pres. Jones
  It seemed advisable to go to the Supt.
  He visited the Gov.
  The engr. looked over the work.
Right: Pres. A. K. Jones
  Supt. Thomas E. Forbes
  It seemed advisable to go to the Superintendent.
  He visited the Governor.
  The engineer looked over the work.

5. Never abbreviate the name of a city:

> Philadelphia, *not* Phila.
> New York City, *not* N. Y. C.
> Chicago, *not* Chi.
> Los Angeles, *not* L. A.

6. Spell out all names of months when the day is not given:

January, 1940   Jan. 16, 1942

7. Employ lower case (no capitals) for all abbreviations, except when the word abbreviated is normally spelled with a capital:

> lb, *not* Lb
> hp, *not* H.P. (horsepower)
> Btu, *not* B.T.U. (British thermal units)

8. Use such signs as (') for *feet*, (") for *inches*, and @ for *at* only in tables and figures where they are needed for saving space. The sign for *percent* (%) is now often used. The following examples are correct:

> 27 lb (*not* 27#)
> 47%
> 16 ft 7 in.
> 40 lb per cu ft (*not* 40 # /cu ft)

Hyphenation. The condensation of report-writing style often results in considerable confusion unless the writer adopts artificial methods to make his meaning clear. One characteristic of technical writing, often abused, is the abundant use of compound words. Despite the objections of some critics to such condensed expressions as business and technical writers employ, these compounds cannot be very severely condemned. An iron-furnace is surely a better form than *furnace employed for smelting iron ore.* *Fuel-saving device* is better than *device designed to save fuel.*

Save words, by all means, when the meaning can be made as clear with a shorter expression.

Observe the following rules:

1. Hyphenate all adjective compounds in the report. This rule is simple and logical:

> 10-hour day
> weather-stripped doors
> home-service test
> internal-combustion engine

Such a rule provides a definite separation of the compound attributive adjective from its noun and in that way prevents possible ambiguity. "Ten hour shifts" may mean ten shifts of one hour each or ten-hour shifts. A hyphen simplifies and makes the meaning unmistakable.

2. In general, do not hyphenate noun compounds:

> air chamber   pig iron
> gas engine   force pump

Frequently, however, the compound forms a single word:

> horsepower   roadbed
> framework   workmen

Only when there is possibility of confusion with a preceding adjective, or when the combination of words has two different meanings, should the hyphen be employed. For example, a *bent rod* simply means a rod that is bent; but a *bent-rod* is a technical term in engineering construction. Usually the first member of a hyphenated noun indicates the *use* to which a thing is put. An *iron-furnace* is a furnace used for smelting iron ore. A *burning-oil* is an oil used for burning.

The technical writer will find in Appendix D a list of inseparable compounds, separable compounds, and hyphenated words, which will be useful for reference. There is also (in Appendix C) a list of abbreviations approved by American Standards Association which are permissible in technical reports.

Exercises

1. Rewrite the following paragraph in an objective, impersonal style:

Our committee went to work at once. We organized the foremen into groups of twelve and suggested that they meet once a week with a member of our committee as chairman. We decided that it is impractical to have less than ten or more than sixteen in a group, and we believe that the most satisfactory number is twelve. In contrast with the methods that we followed in earlier foreman-training projects, we have induced the conference leaders not to follow the lecture plan. Instead, we bring out our ideas by means of suggestive questions and illustrative examples. We get everybody to talk. We committee members introduce the subjects and guide discussions so that irrelevant argument will not consume too much time, but we make the foreman do most of the talking.

2. Prepare an analysis of an imaginary reader of one of your reports. Consider his education, training, interests, needs, and desires.

3. Rewrite this paragraph, according to the principles of effective report style:

Many of the men are at great distances from the home office. They have information that may be valuable to the company. Important losses sometimes occurred. Heretofore there was no regular system of getting information from these men. In 1948 such a failure to record an important situation with the home office resulted in a loss to the company of several thousand dollars. It is for these reasons that the system of regular monthly reports has been adopted. These reports are presented on forms prepared by this office. They are due on or before the tenth day of each month. They will be a great aid to efficiency, and no mistake was made in putting this plan into operation.

4. Rewrite the following paragraph in more condensed style:

It should be kept constantly and permanently in mind that the great steel business is one thing that has for an extremely long period of years been governed almost entirely by .precedent. Even in this advanced and progressive age in which we are now living the steel business, that gigantic and fundamental industry, continues to look to the past. There was one plant that for years had been on the convertor operation. The management determined to institute a change. They compelled the shutdown of the convertor and the consequent installation of a modern and up-to-date electric furnace. After it had been installed for a certain length of time, the personnel of the plant was entirely unanimous in making complaints of all kinds and descriptions, and in finding fault with its practice. These troubles continued and increased until such a time as the management finally directed that a change be made to the convertors once more. Since there appeared to be no decrease of consequence in the trouble that had been experienced heretofore with the electric furnace, after a period of two months during which the convertor was used, the electric furnace was again put into operation and has continued up to the present day. The operating force, it will be seen readily enough, simply had convinced themselves unreasonably that the electric furnace would not be satisfactory to them, and hence found numerous faults which were not really important in any sense of the word.

5. Write a paragraph on one of the following subjects, attempting to make it as concrete as possible:

A pure water supply, or water purification
Gas-turbine locomotives
Televising an outdoor event

Jet propulsion
The United Nations

6. Develop by the "logical" plan a paragraph on one of the following subjects:

Success of a photograph
Engineering
Advances in development of the grasses
Results of the final examinations
Athletic record of a year

7. Develop by the "chronological" plan a paragraph on one of these topics:

How to sell boats
A manufacturing process
Finding a job
Campaigning for funds
Organizing a flying club

8. Rewrite the following sentences correctly and effectively:

(1) Purpose of this report is to tell results of experiment carried on during last week.

(2) Before purchasing this pump many different devices for raising water was employed.

(3) Due to the present need there were purchased two large engines of considerable H.P.

(4) 27 men reported this week but 7 left before Sunday, that was a serious handicap.

(5) The Officers and Foremen met to determine the results of the plan of Pres. Randall but due to very heavy orders the meeting was cut short.

(6) In loading a plate holder great care must be taken usually.

(7) The heavy oil engine did good work although never working so efficient as we hoped.

(8) Due to the present need there were purchased two large engines.

(9) This forty H.p. motor runs at 535 R.p.m.

(10) It was found that an analysis of accidents showed two hundreds and five casualties.

(11) Using this formula, the coefficient of heat transmission can be found.

(12) The Marmon river runs through this district, at Southington it widens.

(13) He had once been a Foreman but he rose rapidly and was Vice-President before he died in Aug., 1940.

(14) The system was installed hurriedly that is; first there were not enough men employed, second it was necessary to hire unskilled workmen, third the short time remaining to finish it.

(15) We can give no more details at present as the results are still uncertain.

(16) It is not claimed that this is perfect, what is claimed is that the balance of the work will be small indeed.

(17) One factor in the management is office personnel of high quality, which, due to high wages demanded, and etc., is not easy to get.

(18) We never had less complaints than we have now.

(19) Your favor at hand and referring to same find that you want to know why we have such a small per cent. of changes; in regards to that we can give a full account.

(20) In fig. twenty-two you will find a diagram of this machine.

(21) We need about 5,000 4-in. bolts now.

(22) .68% is the error.

(23) We ordered about 27 lbs. in May, 30 lbs. in July, and 35 lbs. in Sept., that is enough for several months.

(24) The electric furnace chamber was the same size as the oil furnace, 13'2" long by 2'9" wide, while the height of the spring of the arch was 2'10".

(25) A rather large variety of castings have been made by this company for wear resisting purposes, ranging in section from ½" to 8" and include, in the main, equipment for steel plants, such as; rolling mill plugs, piercing dies and plungers, pig machine wheels, etc.

(26) Much interest was shown by Operators of Foundries, and others.

(27) The ideal type of furnace would be a sphere which has the minimum amount of surface exposed to radiation per cubic in. of content, having the minimum amount of refractory surface exposed to wear per cu. in. of the content, and provides absolutely equal distribution of the heat from the arc throughout the charge.

(28) Elec. furnace castings, however, in 1925, amounted to 22 per cent. of the entire out-put.

(29) During the past 5 yrs. construction expenditures for additions, bettering conditions or the replacement of equipment have amounted to about $1,000,000.

(30) About one-fifth of the Customers complained of this kind of Service to us.

9. Make brief transcriptions, devoid of technicalities, of several patents as described in the *Patent Office Gazette.*

10. From a laboratory manual, copy verbatim the technical description of a chemical experiment, using abbreviations and technical terms as given. Then write an exposition of the same experiment for a non-technical reader.

CHAPTER 5

GATHERING FACTS

The Variety of "Facts"

WITHOUT FACTS there can be no real report. Ideas, opinions, and judgments must grow out of facts. Thus, long before the writer begins to organize and construct his report, he must take the first step of gathering and assembling his data.

The facts of reports are of many varieties. For convenience, we may classify reports roughly as follows:

I. Reports based on routine records:
   A. Periodic—accounts of the activities of an organization or division, such as a company, department, agency, office, foundation, society, bureau, or association.
   B. Progress—accounts of work done on definite projects, such as works of construction, development, survey, reorganization, or extended research.
II. Reports based on new investigations:
   A. Examination—accounts of inspections, experiments, tests, surveys, and studies of published sources.
   B. Recommendation—accounts of investigations that result in proposals affecting policy.

Gathering the facts, then, involves many different kinds of activity for different problems and different reports.

Facts in Progress and Periodic Reports

Progress and periodic reports present information already in the writer's possession or, at least, readily available in records. Such reports call for no special investigation. The writer does not initiate the activities that he reports, usually, but merely *records* them as they occur in the natural order of events. For example, the weekly report of an engineering department, the monthly report of a sales manager, and the annual report of a corporation are all "periodic" reports which record the activities of organizations for a period of time. The regular reports of an engineer during the construction of a dam, of a supervisor of a city survey, and of the research scientist engaged in a long and complex study are all "progress" reports which provide information about work done on specific projects.

If the writer has had intimate contact with every phase of the activities reported, he relies entirely upon his own records and his own memory. Records, represented by notes or memoranda, are obviously more reliable than memory. If the writer must report activities with which he has had no direct contact, then he relies upon letters, memoranda, accounts, and subordinate reports of other persons for the facts to be incorporated in his own periodic or progress report.

Facts in Examination and Recommendation Reports

Examination and recommendation reports are alike in the nature of the facts upon which they rely: both present *new* facts, the results of special investigations. Hence it is unnecessary to make distinctions here about the kinds of material needed in each.

The investigator must begin with the questions that he wants to answer. Sometimes he finds these questions specifically stated in a preliminary letter of instructions; sometimes he must determine them himself from the nature of his general problem.

The investigator is always guided by the principles of his own job or profession. The usefulness of a chemist's report depends upon his reliability as a chemist. The mining engineer's reports can be no better than the mining engineer.

The investigator must be open-minded. There is the danger of forming opinions before he has finished his studies, and hence of finding only what he *expects* to find. Unless he can rid himself of his preconceptions, or, at least, keep his eyes open to new developments, his usefulness will be seriously impaired. The two requirements for investigation are perspective and objectivity.

Defining object and scope of investigation. Investigation starts, not with answers, but with questions. Those questions determine the scope of the study. Suppose we take a few examples.

The problem is "to inspect the safety equipment in Plant No. 3." The investigator knows, then, that he is to be responsible for determining the dependability and adequacy of all equipment in Plant No. 3 that was installed to reduce safety hazards. He lists all such equipment. Then he checks and tests each item, asking, "What is it devised to do? How well does it do it?" Of course, each piece of equipment is measured by its own standards.

The problem is "to determine the best site for the new factory." The investigator, through previous studies, has limited the choice to five different sites located in three different cities. He has learned the requirements of his company. He must find answers to these questions:

Accessibility:	How near markets? How near raw materials? What transportation facilities?
Labor:	How much skilled labor in the community? Unskilled? What wages and hours are customary? What unions are there?
Utilities: .	What rates and sources of water? Of power and light? Of fire protection? Sanitation?
Governmental influences:	What taxes? What restrictions? What police protection?
Costs:	Cost of property? Of grading? Of improvements?

Of course, most of these questions might suggest numerous subsidiary questions.

Every investigator has his own questions to answer, and his own techniques for getting the answers. The chemist, the biologist, the geologist, and the mechanical and industrial engineer—each uses scientific or technical methods that he has learned well. This chapter discusses certain procedures not commonly included in technical courses.

Deciding on the method of attack. The method and the scope of attack are determined largely from these sources:

1. The earlier experience of the investigator
2. The experiences of others who have conducted similar studies (generally published)
3. The adaptability of known methods to the immediate situation.

Even the most experienced investigator is always ready to make use of the expert knowledge of others, and especially to profit by earlier investigations of the same or similar problems.

Obtaining the facts. From reading, interviewing, and questionnaires he reaches other persons for help.

Reading. The investigator's reading may be confined entirely to the files of his own organization—to the unpublished reports, records, contracts, and specifications that have been kept for just such reference as this. If all earlier reports have been clearly labeled and dated, and the filing system is a modern one, the investigator will have little trouble in finding everything that has previously been done by his colleagues or predecessors in the same organization.

In libraries the investigator may find the published reports of federal, state, and municipal bureaus and agencies; the bulletins of experiment stations; and a good many reports published by individuals, universities, and privately endowed foundations. The investigator should be familiar with the indexes in his own profession, such as the *Engineering Index* and the *Agricultural Index,* and he should learn how to use them economically. The services of the Engineering Societies Library are available to members of the cooperating societies; this library can make any reasonable search, check references, and compile bibliographies. Inquiries may be addressed to the Director, Engineering Societies Library, 29 West 39th Street, New York, N. Y.

The questionnaire. When other means of obtaining the necessary information are available, the investigator should not rely upon a questionnaire. Even under the most favorable circumstances, replies can be expected from only a fraction of those to whom copies are sent. Nevertheless, the questionnaire is obviously necessary in many investigations. The problem, then, is to prepare it in such a way as to produce the maximum number of answers, and to make it simple and clear enough so that the results can be easily tabulated.

A few rules for the preparation of questionnaires are in order:

1. Explain briefly the purposes of the questionnaire and emphasize all possible benefits to those who cooperate in answering the questions.

2. Make it as short as possible. Combine questions of similar nature; condense; reject every question that you can do without.

3. Avoid ambiguity. Test each question for clarity. Be sure that only one interpretation is possible.

4. Avoid questions that suggest the answer (Do you oppose the Government's extravagant spending policies? Do you agree that there is need in our modern world for the spreading of educational

opportunities to more persons?). Unless the questionnaire is a device for propaganda purposes (and such questionnaires have little relationship to reports), questions may mislead.

5. Usually avoid questions that call for very general opinions. If possible, ask only for specific facts. If some opinions are desirable, ask for opinions only on specific points.

6. Frame questions, when possible, so that they can be answered by a check in a yes-no or a multiple-choice arrangement:

> Do you use color film?　　　Yes ( )　　No ( )
> If so, how many pictures do you take each month?
> 　　　　　　　　　Less than 20　　( )
> 　　　　　　　　　20–100　　　　( )
> 　　　　　　　　　More than 100 ( )

7. Be careful to mention factors (of cost, weight, and so forth) which are likely to influence the answer:

> Not: Would you like an overdrive in your car?
> But: Would you like an overdrive in your car *at an added cost of $150?*

Usually, a short but tactful letter must accompany a questionnaire. Such a letter would make a courteous request for help and at the same time emphasize the possible gain for those who cooperate. Study the following example:

THE CARSON CHEMICAL CO.

324 Shore Road
Wichita, Kansas

Dear Sir:

The Carson Chemical Company has perfected an apparatus for generating oxygen and acetylene by chemical means. We are designing a portable oxyacetylene welding unit using this apparatus to generate the gases as needed. Our generator has several advantages over the conventional cylinders. The cost of chemicals, including shipping, will be about 80% of that for cylinders of the same gas content. The chemicals will occupy only about one-sixth the storage space of cylinders. The danger of cylinder leakage in transit is eliminated.

As such an apparatus can be made in many sizes and capacities to suit different uses, we are interested in knowing what industry wants. On the reverse side you will find a questionnaire which will aid us in this manner. We will appreciate any suggestions you have.

> Yours truly,
>
> *Arthur L. Larkin*
> Arthur L. Larkin, Secretary

ALL:ACK　　　　　　　THE CARSON CHEMICAL CO.

1. Which of these units would you prefer?

	Weight of generator	Cu. ft. gas per charge	Minimum time per charge	Cost of generator	
Unit (1)	20 lb	400	½ hr	$50	( )
Unit (2)	50 lb	800	1 hr	$100	( )
Unit (3)	150 lb	1600	2 hr	$200	( )

2. What size torch is generally used?

Heavy	( )
Medium	( )
Light	( )

3. On what type of terrain do you usually operate?

Smooth	( )
Rough	( )

4. What method of transportation do you use to get equipment to the job site?

Push by hand	( )
Tow by auto	( )
Carry on truck	( )

5. Remarks:

The interview. The interview is a frequently important method of securing essential information for reports. Sometimes it is desirable to question colleagues who have knowledge that will eliminate the requirement of extensive personal study. Sometimes it is helpful to talk with specialists in related fields. Again, it may be necessary to ask questions of the workers in a plant, the dealers who handle the company's products, prospective customers, or persons who are living in a tenement district that is being investigated.

The best interview, of course, is the one that gets the pertinent information in the shortest time and with the least friction. That means definite planning. It is clearly unwise to approach a person with a vague general question and then "hope" that specific information will be secured. The interviewer must know exactly what questions he wants answered. He must plan the most effective order of presenting those questions. He must give attention to the wording, too, so that he will avoid all incitements to suspicion or fear.

If possible, the interviewer should talk informally without taking notes. Of course, there are times when exactness demands immediate note-taking; but if the answers can be remembered for half an hour, it is always better to wait till later to record them. Some people become very self-conscious when they see their words being taken down, and the result may be a lack of complete frankness.

The results of the interview, however, should be recorded on paper immediately after it is over. It is unwise to place too much faith in memory.

A plan for a typical interviewing program may be illustrated. First, the manager of a company writes a short letter of instructions to the investigator:

Mr. Wilde:

Will you please interview the sales engineer of the Stamped Steel Company and members of our own staff concerned, to help me decide whether we should consider replacing our own cast-iron stands for hot-water tanks by stamped-steel stands made by the Stamped Steel Company?

I should like the information by tomorrow noon, when you may bring your notes to me.

C. L. Doran, Manager

Now the investigator sketches a plan. He decides in what order he should see the men whom he will interview. He determines the best possible approach to each man. Perhaps he realizes that a full explanation of his purpose might, in some instances, cause suspicion or resentment. He may decide that the preliminary inquiry had better be "blind." He may jot down the following plan:

Questions to Be Asked of the Sales Engineer:

Has your company ever handled a job of this sort? What article and firms?

What advantages are there in stamped steel over castings?

What is your off-hand estimate of cost on the minimum quantity that it pays to manufacture by your method?

What price on subsequent orders?

What deliveries may we expect on first orders? Subsequent orders?

Questions to Be Asked of Department Heads:

Foundry:

What do cast-iron stands cost us?

What is the percentage of defects which would cause scrapping?

Have we reached capacity with present equipment and labor force?

What is the life of a pattern?

Shipping and adjustment department:

What breakage is there of cast-iron stands?

What is the total amount of claims for adjustment on account of breakage for various periods?

What does freight cost on these stands?

Pattern shop:

What is the cost of a stand pattern?

What is the life of a pattern?

Machine shop:

Have you any information on the making of stamped-steel products? Without making any lengthy study of the subject, will you state what additional equipment and labor would be necessary to make steel stands for hot-water tanks instead of our present cast-iron type?

Sales:

What do you think of stamped-steel stands, as compared with our cast-iron ones?

Of course, the final questions may not be presented in exactly these words. This is only a plan. Nevertheless, it tends to guarantee that every important item of information will be available for the manager's use.

Sampling. A very large proportion of the conclusions found in examination reports are based upon the process known as "sampling." The principle is simple enough: a representative *part* is assumed to be indicative of the characteristics of the *whole*. With a homogeneous product, such as a strand of wire, a rod, or a rail, which may have been produced in hundred-ton lots, called "heats," a test of a small piece taken anywhere from the finished product will serve as a test of the whole product. With heterogeneous subjects, such as the voters of the United States, a larger sample must be taken, and often special methods must be used to guarantee its reliability. The Gallup and *Fortune* polls of "public opinion," for example, are conducted according to a very complex plan.

The proper methods of sampling coal, metals, oil, soil, cement, and similar materials are known to every specialist who has had technical training for his work. There is no need to explain them here.

The sampling of *persons*, however, is somewhat different. Perhaps the investigator wants to know what the employees in a plant think of the group-insurance plan just introduced. If there are thousands of employees, he may reasonably decide that a "sample" of opinion will be more quickly secured and may be almost as accurate as a poll of all employees. How shall he pick his sample? Or perhaps he wants to know what the people of Lyscom Valley prefer as the route for the prospective highway between Lyscom and Aaronsville. How shall he select a "sample" of these citizens for questioning?

Following the modern practice, the investigator will try to

make his sample representative by making sure that he has in it
the right proportions of every significant element. For example,
his sample of employees would include the right percentage of all
wage and salary groups (those earning $35 a week, those earning
$75 a week, and so on—in the right proportions); the right per-
centage of all national groups (Italians, Slovaks, Poles, native
Americans); the right proportion from every department; and
perhaps the right proportions according to years of employment
with the company. The sample of Lyscom County citizens would
include the right proportions from each city, village, and district;
the right proportions in each important occupation (farmers, mill
workers, executives); and especially, of course, the right proportion of car owners and non-car owners.

Recording the data. The experienced report writer learns early
in his career that he must be systematic and consistent in recording the data for his report. Even the retentive mind should not
rely on the memory alone. Very often it is essential that original
records be kept for future reference by others, or for obtaining
and maintaining patents. The research worker especially, with
these considerations in mind, must be careful to record his data
in permanent form. His data should be entered *as taken* in a
bound notebook, and in ink. Each page and each entry should be
dated and, in some companies, signed or initialed—even when the
material is later compiled or tabulated in the same book. Errors
should be neatly crossed out, not erased; and minimum space
should be left between entries.

Such meticulousness is not always necessary outside the laboratory or the field, but the writer must determine the value of permanently recording his original observations and ideas, whether
or not they are eventually included in his report. But all report
writers should work from written notes. If the report is a short
one, or a routine one, one page may prove sufficient for jotting
down the necessary information. From this sheet the writer can
transcribe the data to his report with less danger of omission and
with the advantage of logical arrangement. Most reports, however, require a more elaborate method.

Note-taking. The method of note-taking found to be most economical of time and labor and yet most efficient in the long run
is the "loose-card" system. Preparatory to taking notes, and even
to attacking the problem on which he is reporting, the writer

should draw up a preliminary outline. This outline may or may not resemble the one that he will eventually use for arranging the material in his report. But at least it will supply him with a crude system for classifying his data as he acquires them. If, for example, his problem is to investigate the possible methods of increasing the water supply of a given city, he might arbitrarily divide the problem into the following sections—even before he begins his investigation:

First (Preliminary) Outline

1. Analysis of present system
2. Present and future demands
3. Possibility A (enlarging present reservoir)
4. Possibility B (building additional reservoir)
5. Possibility C (drilling series of wells)
6. Possibility D (consolidation with near-by system)
7. Possibility X (some solution not yet thought of)
8. Miscellaneous information

Admittedly such an outline is crude, and admittedly there is overlapping, but it does provide the basis for a filing system which will divide an unwieldy mass of ideas and observations into eight reasonably homogeneous categories.

Now, the loose cards.[1] Preferably they should be lined, and at least three by five inches in size. If obtainable, cards in eight different colors would be very helpful. Suppose that the first information the writer uncovers has to do with the city's present consumption of water. Glancing at his preliminary outline, he records his findings thus:

```
                                              2    ← INDEX TO
                                                     OUTLINE
        Water Consumption                             NUMBERS

   Pres ave.   consump:  1,755,000  g/day
        min.             1,465,000
        max              2,150,000

   Observation: 2/7/49

       Water Authority Records
```

---

[1] For the student, half-sheets of paper are satisfactory.

As his investigation proceeds, he records all his data in the same manner. He must be careful to be consistent: each element should always appear in the same place on the card. He must be accurate: numbers, for example, should not be rounded off if a more specific entry is available and meaningful. He must be complete: all the elements in the illustration, and often others, are necessary. He must not sacrifice clarity for brevity; if others may use his original notes, he must use only standard symbols and standard abbreviations. Finally, he must enter only one central idea on each card. When material is derived from interviews, reading, or, possibly, from questionnaires, the source must be precisely identified:

For material taken from the literature, an abbreviated but complete bibliographical notation should be made.[2]

It is difficult for the novice to believe that the effort consumed by so laborious a procedure is worth while. But a few attempts at organizing unsystematically recorded data into a logically arranged report will be remarkably convincing. As we discuss the remaining steps in the construction of the report, the advantages of such a system of note-taking will become increasingly apparent.

[2] There is no necessity, however, for writing out the complete bibliographical description on each card. A numbered bibliography can be kept separately and the source can then be identified simply by placing the appropriate number on the note card. Thus, if the above interview with City Engineer Jones was the fifth item on the bibliography, the number five could be substituted for the longer identification. For a discussion of bibliographical practice, see pages 149–151.

Exercises

1. Prepare a questionnaire to be sent:

    (1) To farmers on their income from cattle, corn, or wheat
    (2) To fraternities on their methods of rushing
    (3) To contractors on the comparative popularity of stucco, frame, brick, and stone
    (4) To mine operators on the comparative efficiency of safety devices
    (5) To automobile mechanics on the comparative durability of three different cars
    (6) To local employers on their labor policies

2. Prepare an outline for an interview with one of the following men:

    (1) A college president on his attitude toward fraternities
    (2) An athletic coach on the best way for an athlete to spend his vacations
    (3) An engineer on the advantages of his profession
    (4) An employer on his relations with labor unions
    (5) An unskilled workman on his working conditions
    (6) A research scientist on the purposes of his research

3. Submit to the instructor notes gathered from:

    (1) An interview
    (2) Reading on an assigned problem
    (3) Observations made of a construction job

4. Make a complete plan for a sampling of one of the following:

    (1) College students on the merits of fraternity membership
    (2) Grocery clerks on their hours, wages, and working conditions
    (3) Colleges and universities, to determine the nature of their entrance requirements
    (4) Union members, to determine their loyalty to their union
    (5) Owners of mechanical stokers, to determine the fuel costs

CHAPTER 6

PLANNING THE REPORT

Organizing the data. By the time the investigation is completed and the information recorded, it is probable that some sense of the pattern into which the data logically fall has crystallized in the writer's mind. He will have reached certain conclusions. In the example (discussed in the preceding chapter) possibly the investigator will have discovered that (1) population trends indicate a doubling of water requirements within the next decade; (2) the present reservoir cannot be enlarged unless a new dam is constructed; (3) a dam in an adjacent area could impound sufficient water for any predictable requirements, but another city, already amply supplied, owns the watershed; (4) ground water obtained from wells drilled into the limestone would require softening— and so on. Let us say he is satisfied that only a new reservoir (outline item No. 4) and a series of wells (No. 5) offer practical solutions. Now, much as a card player sorts his hand, he pulls out and studies all cards indexed 4 or 5. After study and, perhaps, further investigation (also recorded, of course), he reaches a more specific conclusion: these two possibilities are about equally good solutions to the water-supply problem, and the advantages and disadvantages of each must be presented to the city council for their decision.

At this point he constructs another outline, a trial arrangement of his material as he will present it to the council in report form.

Second Outline[1]

1.0 Introductory material
      1.1 Statement of the problem
      1.2 Purpose of the investigation
      1.3 Scope of the investigation

---

[1] Instead of the decimal system of outlining, the traditional I, A, 1, a, (1), (a) system may be used.

2.0 Possible solutions
    2.1 Elimination of possibilities A, D, & X
    2.2 A new reservoir (possibility B)
        2.21 Possible sites
            2.211 Site N
            2.212 Site O
            2.213 etc.
        2.22 Detailed analysis of best site
            2.221 Available water
            2.222 Geology
            2.223 etc.
        2.23 etc.
    2.3 A series of wells (possibility C)
        2.31 Analysis of existing wells
            2.311 Quantity of water
            2.312 Quality of water
            2.313 Depths
            2.314 etc.
        2.32 Selection of well sites
            2.321
            2.322 etc.
        2.33 Etc.
  3.0 Conclusions
      3.1   ·
      3.2
      3.3   etc.
  4.0 Appendix
      4.1   Exhibits
      4.2   Calculations

This outline completed, the report writer possesses a framework on which he should be able to hang the information in his notes.

His original classification of the data into eight categories now proves useful. For example, everything indexed with a 3, a 6, or a 7 is quickly re-indexed 2.1:

Everything indexed 4 becomes 2.2; 5 becomes 2.3, and so on. Miscellaneous items (first indexed 8) will, of course, be variously placed—if they prove relevant at all. Possibly some of them will be important enough to demand the inclusion of a new major item in the outline.

Once the material is thus brought into rough order, it remains for the writer to arrange the cards in each subsection. This he can do physically, by the trial-and-error method, until the cards present their information in the sequence most logical and effective for reader comprehension. When there are a great many subsections and a great many cards within subsections, some writers reduce the handling problem by combining on larger cards the closely related data making up one subsection. The flexibility of the loose-card method, particularly valuable at this stage, will have proved a tremendous asset all through the process of arranging the material. For, if the writer becomes dissatisfied with his tentative outline (as he often does), he can quickly rearrange the data in any or all of the sections until he is satisfied.

The writer now constructs his final outline. This may closely resemble his second outline except in the supporting facts of the subsections, and except for the addition of the complementary sections required of some types of modern reports. If his second outline, like the preliminary one, was constructed with his own needs primarily in mind, this final outline will differ in a third respect; for the order in which the writer himself acquired his information is rarely the order in which it can be most effectively presented to the reader. The final outline will become the table of contents for the report, and the writer must have his reader or readers in mind when he prepares it.

Potential forms of reports. The form in which the report is to be submitted will belong to one of three classes:

1. Letter reports
2. Short-form reports
3. Long-form reports

1. *Letter reports.* The letter report, it will be recalled, has nothing but its purpose to distinguish it from any business letter. It has heading, date, inside address, salutation, letter text, close, and signature. The letter *is* the report.

2. *Short-form reports.* The short-form report adopts a different make-up. It has none of the mechanics of the letter and none of

its informality. Sometimes it has a title page indicating subject, author, and date—followed directly, without salutation, by the report text. Another common plan to use in heading the report is as follows:

```
Report to ........................
Submitted by .....................
Subject ..........................
Date .............................
```

The sections of the report, usually introduced by subtitles, follow immediately. Sometimes a short text report takes the form of a memorandum:

MEMORANDUM

```
Client ...........................
Project ..........................
Pertaining to ....................
Date .............................
```

The report usually follows such a heading without further introduction.

3. *Long-form reports*. For longer reports, the combined letter and text form is used by a great many companies. It has the advantage of allowing for an informal introduction, with a personal touch, and at the same time maintaining the serious and formal manner of presenting facts and results. The basic parts of such reports are usually arranged in this order:

1. Letter of transmittal
2. Table of contents
3. Introduction
4. Text

The exact make-up of the long-form report varies with the needs of the situation and with the practices of the various companies. The form to be adopted depends upon the type of reader, the subject matter, and the length of the report. The combined form is useful, of course, only when a report extends over five pages or more. In shorter documents the letter of transmittal is a needless addition, unless, as in some governmental reports, it is required to show authorization.

Which of the first two forms is desirable for a short report depends entirely upon the degree of formality desired. The letter report carries a report from person to person, and should usually be informal. The short text report subordinates personalities. It is so written, in most instances, that any part of it can be incorporated without change in another longer or more important report. It is, in other words, objective and formal.

Little attention need be paid here to the so-called "form" report, which is a common and necessary type for reporting or recording the routine business of large organizations. Each organization develops its own forms—tailored to its specific needs—and the presentation of facts on these forms requires little original thought from the writer. Such forms are constructed much in the manner of the questionnaire (see pages 113–115).

Periodic-report plans. Information in the usual periodic report is not gained for special investigations; it concerns the routine activities of a department, agency, company, or other organization. Such reports, especially those covering short periods, are often the easiest to plan because the material comes to hand almost automatically during the course of the day, the week, or the month covered. Very often reports covering equal periods of time will include identical items. For instance, every report of the manager of a factory might be expected to include the headings:

    Condition of the plant
    Record of production
    Personnel
    Cost of production

Daily, weekly, and monthly reports of technicians, subordinate officials, and departments naturally form the basis for the more general semiannual or annual reports. Weekly reports, often derived from the daily reports, may be mere résumés, and may be still further condensed in the main weekly account of the executive who reports for a division. Monthly and yearly reports may recapitulate identical items. These are often cumulative; that is, they present statistics covering similar periods and extending over a considerable time prior to the current report. They may compare a certain item with its counterpart a year ago, a week ago, or last month. They may contain summaries or totals, so that the last monthly report of the year will, in a way, serve as an annual report on a single item or division.

The executive's problem can be illustrated by a concrete example. Suppose that the president of a small corporation, preparing his annual report to the board of directors, has before him such material as this:

A 50-page report from an engineer
A 3-page financial statement from the treasurer
A 5-page report from the sales manager ·
President's reports for the past ten years
His own notes, jotted down during the year

His problem is to organize this material so that the directors can understand the condition, accomplishments, and future outlook of the corporation. He must evaluate, condense, and arrange his facts for the convenience of busy readers. The annual report, then, might be organized as follows:

   I. Condition of the Company (short summary of the year, financial statements, comparison with other years)
  II. Administration (from his own notes)
 III. Sales (from sales manager's report)
 IV. Production (from his notes)
  V. Plant (from engineer's report)
 VI. Forecasts and Recommendations

Most of the material in such a report comes from others; the writer's task here is to select, condense, and proportion the material needed.

Two other examples of periodic-report plans follow:

Annual Report of Manager of a Factory

   I. General summary
  II. Equipment
     Buildings
     Equipment
 III. Organization
     Administrative personnel
     Labor
 IV. Details of operation
     Record of production
     Plant efficiency
     Morale in the organization
     Cost of production
     Return
  V. Statistical data

Annual Report of a Housing Association

   I. Introduction
  II. Sanitary inspection service
 III. Special surveys
     Dwelling construction for the year
     Demolitions
     House rents in the city
 IV. Legislation
  V. Public information
 VI. Financial statement: receipts, contributions, disbursements

Progress-report plans. Progress reports cover the successive developments of a project. A series of such reports will provide a running account of the work related to the project from beginning to end. They are usually periodic in the sense that they are submitted at regular intervals: daily, weekly, monthly, and sometimes even annually. The series ends when the project ends.

The writer's plan for a progress report depends, of course, upon his subject matter. Sometimes it may be almost strictly chronological, merely recording events in the order of their occurrence. Sometimes it proves more useful to divide the subject according to certain factors vital to the work, such as "supervision," "equipment," "materials," and "labor." Except in the briefest reports covering very short periods, it is generally advisable to follow this general plan:

I. Introduction (purpose of the project, summary of work to date)
II. Résumé of earlier progress reported
III. New progress for this period (including obstacles encountered, methods used, personnel employed, and work accomplished)
IV. Forecast (including recommendations essential to future work)

The following detailed outline is an adaptation of such a plan:

. OUTLINE

THIRD PROGRESS REPORT
WESTERN STATE PARKWAY
by
ANSON H. FIELD, CHIEF INSPECTOR OF CONSTRUCTION

Letter of transmittal

I. Summary
　　1. Progress since last report
　　2. Suggestions
　　3. Forecast

II. Introduction
　　1. Description of project
　　2. Summary of earlier progress

III. Details of Progress Since Last Report
　　A. Section I: Taylor–Blairstone
　　　　1. Grading
　　　　　　a. Clearing
　　　　　　b. Cut
　　　　　　　　1. Dirt
　　　　　　　　2. Stone
　　　　　　c. Fill
　　　　　　　　1. Dirt
　　　　　　　　2. Stone

      2. Structures
         a. Bridges
            1. Underpasses
            2. Natural Obstruction
               Single-span
               Russian River
         b. Culverts
         c. Retaining Walls
      3. Surfacing

B. Section II: Blairston–Eastman Crossing
      1. Structures
         a. Bridges
            1. Underpasses
            2. Natural Obstruction
         b. Retaining Walls
         c. Ramses Tunnel
            1. Lining
            2. Ventilating Shafts
      2. Surfacing
         a. Sub-base
         b. Pavement
      3. Clean-up
         a. Construction
            1. Curbing
            2. Island
            3. Guard rail
         b. Landscaping
            1. Borrow pits
            2. Finished grading
            3. Planting

IV. Exterior Considerations
      1. Right-of-way litigation
      2. Intersected traffic
         a. Public
         b. Private
            1. Utilities
            2. Individuals

V. Personnel
    A. Contractors
    B. State Inspectors

VI. Appendix
    A. Costs Itemized
      1. Total to date
      2. Since last report
      3. Prospective
    B. Data

Examination-report plans. No reports, of course, illustrate so wide a variety of plans as those based upon new investigations.

There are so many different situations that any effort to classify them is sure to meet with objections. Nothing illustrates their range and variation so well as representative outlines taken directly from style manuals on the preparation of reports or derived from analyses of actual reports. Consequently, considerable space will be devoted to their examination. It should be stressed that most companies are well aware of the need for breaking the pattern of "standard procedure" when the nature of the material or the requirements of the reader are then better served. Usually, however, standard practice saves the reader time and effort. The outlines:

— 1 —

The Detroit Edison Company

Short-Form Report	*Long-form Report*
Summary	Title page
Detailed results	Table of contents
Discussion	Statement of problem
Procedure	Conclusions and summary of results
[Title, date, authorship, and authorization appear at top of first page]	Procedure
	Results
	Discussion of results
	[Graphs, drawings, etc., included in report body]

— 2 —

Standard Oil of California

Producing Department Short-Form	*Engineering Department Short-Form*	*Engineering Department Long-Form*
Introduction	Brief statement of important conclusions	Title page
Results	Introduction	Synopsis
Conclusions, recommendations	Discussion	Table of contents
Detail	Summary	Introduction
	Detailed computations, graphs, etc., attached	Body
		Conclusions
		Recommendations
		Appendix

— 3 —

Hercules Powder Company Experiment Station

Introduction
Procedure and results
Conclusions and recommendations
Experimental section

— 4 —

The Texas Company

Introduction
Report proper
Conclusions
Recommendations
Future work
Appendix

— 5 —

Owens-Corning Fiberglas Corporation

Title page
Table of contents
Abstract
Statement of problem
Summary of results
Procedure
Test results
Discussion
Appendix

— 6 —

National Bureau of Standards

Abstract
Table of contents
Introduction:
  Scope, objective
Test equipment
Test procedure
Test results
Methods of computing data
Conclusions
References

— 7 —

The Goodyear Tire & Rubber Company

Summary
  Subject
  Statement of problem
  Abstract
Introduction
  More complete statement of
    problem
  Historical background
Test procedure and data
Compilation of results
Conclusions
Proposed future work

— 8 —

The Tennessee Valley Authority

Title page
Letter of transmittal
Table of contents
Summary
Detailed report
  Introduction
  Body of report
  Acknowledgments
  Bibliography
Appendixes
Exhibits

A composite of the elements making up these and other long reports would look something like this:

Composite Outline

Title page
Letter of transmittal
Abstract or summary
Table of contents
Introduction
  Statement of problems
  Purpose
  Scope
  Summary of conclusions
Historical background
Review of the literature
Review of theory
Report text (variously named: *text,
  body, discussion, experimental*)
Conclusions
Recommendations or proposals for
  future work

Representative Outline

Title page
Letter of transmittal
Abstract
Table of contents
Introduction
Itemized conclusions
(Itemized recommendations)
Body of the report
Terminal conclusion
Appendix
Bibliography

Appendixes or exhibits
  Methods of computation
  Calculations
  Tables, curves, photographs, etc.,
    when supplementary
  Bibliography and references

It is difficult to imagine any one report that would need all of the elements in the *composite outline*. The writer must select those that will best present his particular problem to his particular reader. A typical selection for a long-form examination (or recommendation) report would result in an approximation of the *representative outline*.

Recommendation-report plans. The recommendation report is actually an examination report with the addition of a further step: the laying down of a program of action or policy based on the conclusions reached in the investigation.

As in the examination report, the order of investigation may or may not be the order of the written report. If the report is strictly "argumentative," that is, if it aims to influence those who are likely to be reluctant to accept the writer's opinions, then the same order followed in the investigation is psychologically sound for the development of the report. The reader must be led gradually to the same opinion as that held by the writer. The order of the investigation is the natural order in which the mind works in accepting a new idea or opinion, or in reaching a decision to act:

1. Problem
2. Issues
3. Comparisons; advantages and disadvantages, facts
4. Conclusions
5. Decision to act

When, however, as in most situations demanding a report, the writer is not personally concerned with the outcome of his recommendations, and the reader is totally impartial in his attitude toward the question, then a different arrangement is usually preferable. For example, a report on the selection of a type of machinery will usually follow such an order as this:

1. Introductory summary (letter of transmittal):
    Object of the study
    The type selected
    Brief reasons for the selection
    Estimate of cost
2. Object—purpose of the design

3. Scope—standards for selection
4. Advantages and disadvantages of the types studied:
   Type A
   Type B
   Type C
5. Detailed description of the type selected
6. Conclusions

In brief, then, in such reports it is customary to place the recommendations and conclusions at the beginning of the report, since they are the matter of chief interest to the reader.

Another type of recommendation report is that in which the actual recommendations take up most of the discussion. A report on a city plan, for example, may be constructed according to this outline: ,

1. General recommendations
2. Survey of the city
   Conditions
   Probable developments
   Needs
3. Details of the plan

The third part of such a report frequently occupies several times as much space as the first two. The author's reasons for developing his plan are made apparent through his discussion of the conditions and needs of the city, and through explanations and descriptions of the plan. It is essential that these parts provide the necessary defense for the expert's decision.

Specimen Report Outlines

— 1 —

OUTLINE

ANNUAL REPORT OF A LARGE CORPORATION

When one of the large modern corporations is composed of numerous subsidiary organizations, and especially when these subsidiaries are engaged in the manufacture of a variety of products, the annual report will give very little descriptive detail.

Aside from generalizations, much of the matter is in the form of statistics.

I. Condition of the business

   1. Income account for the year
   . 2. Interest and dividends; redemption of bonds
   3. Surplus

II. Operation

    1. Production
    2. Shipments
    3. Maintenance and depreciation

III. Expenditures

    1. Capital
    2. Payroll

IV. Miscellaneous

    1. Pensions, welfare, accident prevention, and relief
    2. Stockholders
    3. Expression of appreciation for services

V. Formal statements and statistics

    1. Consolidated
        A. Auditor's certificate
        B. Consolidated balance sheet
        C. Consolidated accounts
            (a) Property investment
            (b) Consolidated income
            (c) Profit and loss
            (d) Earnings
            (e) Inventories
    2. Of subsidiaries

— 2 —

OUTLINE

ENGINEER'S ANNUAL REPORT OF A POWER PLANT

Letter of transmittal

  I. General summary

 II. Condition of the plant

    1. Tabulations
    2. Diagrams
    3. Discussion

III. Tests

IV. Materials

    1. Materials used
    2. Cost

 V. Labor

    1. Men employed
    2. Wages

VI. Cost per unit of production

— 3 —

OUTLINE

ANNUAL REPORT TO EMPLOYEES

(From Bethlehem Review, "A Bulletin of News for the Employees of the Subsidiary Companies of Bethlehem Steel Corporation")

1941

"Our Imperative Task" (letter from President Grace)
High Spots of Bethlehem's 1940 Operations
Vacation Plan for 1941
Bethlehem Payrolls Up 33% from 1939
Accident Frequency 79% Below 1916 Rate
Bethlehem and the National Defense
Additional Open-Hearth Furnace Capacity to Meet the Needs of the Times
New Facilities Step Up Production of Bethlehem Alloy Steels
Pension Plan (table)
Relief Plan—Operations (table)
$8,977,000 for Social Security in 1940
Cooperation of Bethlehem Employees Strongest Defense Against Sabotage
Consolidated Income Statement (table)

— 4 —

OUTLINE

SECOND PROGRESS REPORT

CONSTRUCTION OF THE PEREZ DAM AT LARRY, MONTANA

I. Summary of work to date

II. General introduction

Purpose
Analysis of problem
Schedule of construction

III. Summary of first progress report

IV. Detailed analysis of progress

Diversion of present stream
Excavation
Construction of cofferdams
Construction of bridges
Preparation of site
Analysis of subgrade
Depth
Seepage
Faults
Provisions for grouting
Seam washing
Materials
Drilling

Personnel
  Availability
  Housing
Materials
  Availability
  Transportation
  Materials inventory

V. Costs

— 5 —

<small>OUTLINE OF FINAL REPORT</small>

A TECHNICAL REVIEW OF THE CHICKAMAUGA PROJECT

Tennessee Valley Authority
Technical Monograph No. 46

February 1940

General Chronology of Construction (condensed)
Brief Description of the Project
  Relation of this project to unified development of Tennessee River System
    Flood control
    Navigation
    Power
  Basic data
    Topographic features
    Geology
    Hydrology
  Chickamauga Dam
    Historical
    Description of completed project
    Design
    Access
    Construction program and river diversion
    Foundation and foundation treatment
    Construction plant and methods
    Construction camp and village
  Reservoir activities
    Land acquisition
    Reservoir clearance and protection
    Highway and railroad relocation
    Other reservoir activities
  Construction personnel
  Bibliography
Statistical Summary and Significant Construction Items
  Statistical summary
    Location of dam
    Stream flow
    Reservoir and water elevations
    Navigation facilities
    Navigation lock

Dam
Power plant
Auxiliary equipment
Construction plant
Average concrete mixes and aggregate grading
Plate I—Construction progress
Construction Photographs
Exhibits—Location and Reservoir Maps and Basic Data
Construction Drawings
Construction Operations

— 6 —

OUTLINE

REPORT ON THE EXAMINATION OF A MINE

Letter of transmittal

I. Summary and Conclusions

II. Location of the Property (names and locations of claim or of different blocks, areas, and titles)

III. History
1. Shipments
2. Profits
3. Difficulties met

IV. Economic Geology
1. Topography
2. Vegetation
3. Climate
4. Transportation facilities
5. Claim and topographical maps

V. Study of the Mineral
1. Sampling methods
2. Tests on character and extractable value of mineral
3. Assured mineral
a. Calculations
b. Amount
4. Prospects and limitations of the property

VI. Present equipment
1. Mine development
2. Underground
3. Methods of working
4. Methods of treatment

VII. Water and power
1. Supply
2. Cost

VIII. Fuel

    1. Supply
    2. Cost

  IX. Timber

    1. Supply
    2. Cost

   X. General Materials

    1. Supply
    2. Cost

  XI. Labor

    1. Supply
    2. Cost

 XII. Market conditions

XIII. Governmental conditions

    1. Taxes
    2. Laws
    3. Illegitimate influences
    4. Police protection

 XIV. Financial condition of the enterprise

  XV. Advice

    1. Development
    2. Scale of operations
    3. Equipment
    4. Capital required

 XVI. Estimated return on the investment

— 7 —

TABLE OF CONTENTS

REPORT ON CHAIN BROADCASTING
Federal Communications Commission
Commission Order No. 37 — Docket No. 5060
May 1941

— 8 —

Outline

REPORT ON SELECTION OF MATERIALS

Letter of transmittal

  I. Recommendations

 II. Needs of the business

III. Sources of supply:

    1. Adams & Company
       Location
       Accessibility
    2. Blankenbiller Corporation
       Location
       Accessibility

IV. Value of supply

    1. Adams & Company
       Service
       Dependability
       Tests of materials
       Experience with materials
    2. Blankenbiller Corporation
       Service
       Dependability

Tests of materials
Experience with materials

V. Costs

1. Comparative costs
2. Probable future costs

VI. Transportation

1. Possible methods
2. Comparison of routes

— 9 —

OUTLINE

RECOMMENDATION REPORT ON NEW METHODS FOR MINING

Letter of transmittal
  I. Introduction: Reasons for the report
 II. Conclusions and recommendations
III. Results of present methods
        1. Present cost of mining
        2. Present price of materials
        3. Profit and loss
 IV. Details of present mining methods and costs
        1. Drilling
        2. Timbering
        3. Development work
        4. Surveying
        5. Powder
        6. Mucking
        7. Tramming
        8. Hoisting
        9. Pumping
       10. Sampling and assaying
       11. Surface expense
       12. General repairs
       13. Superintendence and overhead
       14. Insurance
       15. Amortization
  V. Possibility of cutting costs with present methods
 VI. Details of proposed methods
        1. Drilling
        2. Mucking
        3. Tramming
        4. Hoisting

— 10 —

OUTLINE

REPORT ON A CITY PLAN, BY THE CITY PLANNING BOARD

Introduction
Recommendations on the city plan
Recommendations on the transportation plan

I. The civic survey
    1. Growth of population
        Factory employment
        Office employment
    2. Growth of the city area
    3. Existing conditions
        Summary of needs
        Distribution of population
        Building distribution
        Range in land values
        Public utilities
        Railroad and industrial properties
        Public properties

II. Planning studies
    1. The general plan
    2. The business district
    3. Main thoroughfares
    4. Parks and parkways
    5. Park circuit drives
    6. The civic center
    7. School playgrounds
    8. Zoning
    9. Housing

III. Transportation
    1. General conclusions and recommendations
    2. Railroad track development
    3. Plans for the Union Station
    4. Forecast of the growth of the city
    5. Ultimate transit plans

Exercises

1. Make complete outlines for the following specific reports:

    (1) A periodic report
    (2) A progress report
    (3) An inspection report
    (4) A report comparing alternatives
    (5) A report on the advisability of ———
    (6) A report elaborating a proposed plan

2. If an annual report were to be prepared on the campus activities of your college, short reports by leaders of various groups might be included. Prepare a careful and complete outline of the entire report.

The Actual Process of Writing

BY THE TIME the writer is ready to write, he has already organized his material into its most effective arrangement. Consequently, this step in the construction of the report should be devoted *entirely* to writing. The writing should be done in "blocks of thought." Spelling, punctuation, grammar, and even phrasing may be temporarily disregarded. The writer must concentrate on getting his ideas down on paper, a complete section at a time. He should be occupied with the facts of his subject, not with the symbols with which he records them. His organization is complete; and the revision, editing, and proofreading are to come in the next step. Some writers find it helpful to triple-space their early drafts to allow for revisions and insertions.

If the first steps have been conscientiously performed, the writing should be the easiest step of all. If either the recording or the organizing of the material has been slighted, no amount of effort in the writing will produce a good report.

For the writer who has difficulty in expressing his ideas, a further study of the techniques explained in Chapter 3, "Fundamental Forms of Composition" may prove helpful. For all writers, the means of expressing ideas in symbols other than words, explained in the next chapter, should be carefully considered.

The introduction. By whatever name it is given—*preface, foreword, statement of the problem,* or *introduction*—one of the early sections in every long report must introduce the reader to the report. It must acquaint him with the subject of the report and with its purpose and scope. It may indicate the way in which the subject will be presented. And, if a letter of transmittal or an introductory summary has not already done so, it must tell him how the report came about, what the results of the investigation are, and what, if any, recommendations are being made.

143

Assume the rather typical example illustrated in the *Representative Outline*—in which a letter of transmittal, an abstract, an introduction, and a set of conclusions and recommendations all precede the text of the report. Such a report would, *in the first few pages,* give the reader a brief but complete picture of even a very long report.

The letter of transmittal would give the authorization or origin of the report, would acknowledge any special assistance contributed by persons other than the writer, would state any personal opinion considered relevant, and might comment on the difficulties involved in the investigation.

The abstract, of course, would sketch the content of the report.

The conclusions and recommendations—if in front of the text, as here—would briefly state the results of the investigation and list any proposals derived from them.

The introduction would have to complete the picture. Its function would be to define the subject, purpose, and scope of the investigation. And, although the abstract and the table of contents would have indicated the detailed order in which the material was to be presented, the introduction could usefully suggest the general plan of presentation.

Scope. The scope of an investigation deserves special attention in the report. Particularly to future readers, it is extremely important to know what the limitations of the investigation were. They should be carefully defined: If, for example, a survey were limited to "eastern United States," that area should be exactly identified; if an investigation of "modern" methods of cracking were being reported, "modern" should be identified as meaning the years 1940–1950; if, in an experiment, temperature recorders were accurate only to 1500° C, that fact should be pointed out; if only certain aspects of a problem were considered, that fact, too, should be pointed out—and so on.

Note how the introductions which follow perform the functions mentioned above.

— 1 —

The purpose of this report is to recommend a definite storm-sewer design for the area in the Borough of State College, Pennsylvania which is bounded by Beaver and Fairmount Avenues and Frazier and Gill Streets.

The sewer is to connect to the existing out-fall sewer now located on Cresson Alley and Beaver Avenue, and is designed to accommodate the storm-water drainage of the specified area only. Storm water accumulated in adjacent areas is considered adequately provided for.

The data necessary for tabulating the expected requirements of the sewer have been compiled from the rainfall records of the School of Agriculture of The Pennsylvania State College, from actual surveys of the area involved, and from engineering and economic predictions based upon the successful practices of other communities.

The report will first present the conclusions determined from an investigation of the data, and then the recommended storm-sewer design. The design itself includes the area and profile maps necessary to the construction firms who are to bid on the project. The detailed report will show the methods employed in determining the expected rainfall, the time required to reach the sewer inlets, and the size of the pipes required to carry the flow at the varying grades at which the pipes are to be laid.

— 2 —

The tests reported herein are part of an extensive study of substitute motor fuels conducted by the National Bureau of Standards for the Foreign Economic Administration.* The fuels used in this phase of the study were ethyl alcohol and related compounds, either in their relatively pure state or in blends with water or with each other. Particular attention was given to 190-proof and 200-proof alcohol. The principal objectives of this part of the investigation were to show (1) the comparative performance of various engines and fuels with respect to power and fuel economy, (2) the relation of combustion temperatures to air-fuel mixture ratios, (3) the relative efficiency of mixture distribution with various fuels, and (4) the relation of air-fuel ratio to exhaust-gas composition.[1]

[* A reference to other reports in study.]

Historical background, review of the literature, and review of theory. The necessity for including a section that reviews the historical background of a problem, summarizes what others have already learned about it, or outlines the basic scientific theory necessary to an understanding of it must be determined by the writer. Such a section is usually inserted after the introduction but before the body of the report. Its function, of course, is to bring the reader up to the point where the report itself begins. Consequently, it should be included only when such background information is necessary to reader comprehension of the report itself.

The report proper. The main discussion is divided into sections and subsections according to the outline evolved from the loose-card system of organizing the material. The trend in the modern report is to use smaller and smaller subsections. The advantages of the small section are obvious. In the first place, the

---

[1] From National Bureau of Standards Research Paper RP1681, *Utilization of Nonpetroleum Fuels in Automotive Engines*, December 1945.

reader is not compelled to concentrate on difficult material over long periods of time. Second, a reader wishing to refer to only one part of the report can quickly locate and read the one that concerns him. Third, it provides the basis for a table of contents which in turn enables the reader to gain a rapid but comprehensive view of the report content and its arrangement. To make these things possible, an intelligent system of headings and subheadings is used.

Titles, headings, and subheadings. It should be apparent that in any but the shortest reports some system of identifying headings and subheadings is indispensable. To be efficient, such a system must meet the following specifications:

1. Each heading should clearly indicate the relative importance of the section it heads.

2. Conversely, headings of the same relative importance should be identical in form.

3. Headings should be readily distinguishable from other orders of headings.

4. Headings should be clearly distinguishable from text.

To satisfy these requirements on a typewriter involves careful planning. Distinction on the typed page is obtainable in only two ways: (1) spatially, (2) typographically. Consequently, heads can be differentiated from each other and from the text only by the position they occupy or by reason of some typographical distinction such as capitalization, underlining, or the use of identifying symbols (Roman numerals, single capital letters, and so forth).

If the title of the report appears at the beginning of the text, or above the introduction, it deserves the most prominent treatment:

1.

THEORIES FOR THE PREVENTION OF TOOTH DECAY

or, for a longer title:

2.

THE ADVISABILITY OF
ESTABLISHING A PILOT PLANT FOR THE MANUFACTURE OF
BLOATED SLATE AGGREGATE AND CONCRETE BLOCKS

or, for a short title, when it must be distinguishable from the head of a major section (such as <u>INTRODUCTION</u>) appearing immediately below it:

3.

<u>Q U I C K   F E R M E N T A T I O N</u>

4.

<u>QUICK</u>

<u>FERMENTATION</u>

A suggested method for handling other headings and subheadings is illustrated on the next page.

These three styles of headings are usually sufficient for all the needs of report writing. Main divisions, or sections, are distinguished by centered titles, capitalized, surrounded by white space, and, often, numbered. Next subdivisions are often distinguished by titles on the margins. The other two methods are then available in situations where a further division and classification of material is demanded.

It is always better to show the relationship of points in the report by the position and style of subtitles than to show it by symbols, such as I, A, 1, a, (I), (A), and so on. These symbols certainly detract from the appearance of the report, and they are often more difficult to follow than the simpler methods that have been explained.

More than any other factor, the length of a report determines the number and complexity of the subdivisions. There are, however, other determining conditions. When a very thorough and comprehensive explanation of the subject is demanded, or when the material is logically subdivided, the writer must employ a more complicated system than is necessary under ordinary circumstances.

Unless titles are systematic, reading is made exceedingly difficult. Of particular importance is the arrangement of the parts of the report. Every title found in the table of contents, we have seen, must appear in the text of the report. There must be the same order and the same distinction between the sections, the subdivisions, and the sub-subdivisions. All headings of the same class should introduce subjects of equal rank; and, further, they should agree in their relationship to the whole work. Divisions that are

FIRST-ORDER HEAD

The major, or first-order, head is generally placed in the center of the page at the top. It is capitalized and underlined. If three orders of heads are necessary, the second-order appears against the left-hand margin, also underlined, but in lower-case letters except for the initial ones.

Second-Order Head

Third-order head. The third-order head would then appear indented into the paragraph, underlined, but without capital letters save for the first letter of the first word or of proper names. The head would be followed by a period and two or three spaces, and then by the first sentence. It is never good practice to use any head as part of the sentence which follows it.

Another Second-Order Head

If only two orders of heads are required, the third-order head illustrated here is discarded. More than three orders are seldom necessary. When they are, either appearance or distinction will be sacrificed. For example, a second-level head can be inserted between the first two orders illustrated here by centering on the page and underlining a head typed in lower-case except for initial letters. Heads, or, more often, "attention lines," are sometimes typed in the left-hand margin, a practice often followed by textbooks.

Still Another Second-Order Head

Appearance is improved and the head tied more closely to the section it controls by skipping more space above than below it. Whatever ratio is used, it should be maintained consistently.

Another third-order head. Every head should be underlined. Without the underlining, heads are much less distinguishable.

Fig. 6. Specimen Headings

[148]

given the same prominence in title should not overlap; nor should one title ever be subordinate to another of equal standing.

Conclusions and recommendations. Conclusions and recommendations have already been discussed in Chapter 6. It should be repeated, however, that there is a growing tendency to place the conclusions (and recommendations, if there are any) at the front of the report. They appear either as a separate section or as a "summary of results." As a separate section, they are usually itemized and, regardless of their number, given a page (or pages) to themselves. When they appear before the body of the report, they are briefly stated. No substantiation is necessary. When, however, the conclusions appear at the end, they draw supporting facts from the body of the report, which, presumably, the reader has by that time read.

Appendixes. Appendixes, when they are needed, represent the section into which all material not directly contributory to the reader's understanding of the subject is placed. The writer must decide whether or not tables, charts, maps, curves, photographs, and the like, are sufficiently helpful to reader comprehension to be included in the report text. Sometimes the decision is an easy one. Calculations, for example, are rarely useful in the body of the report—yet they must be available for reference. Tables which are summarized in the text are seldom of use there and should be placed in an appendix. But if the text refers to a table or curve in such a way that the reader must look at it to understand what is being said, then the table should be placed where it will be most convenient to him. Often the reader must refer to a diagram (flow sheet, and so forth) at several places in the report. When this is true, it is probably desirable to put the diagram in the appendix at the end of the report, or, better, to put it on a "pull-out" where it can be referred to continually without search.

Occasionally, by-product or "tangential" information uncovered during an investigation is too valuable to be discarded, yet it is not directly relevant to the purpose of the report. Such material is included in an appendix. Bibliographies are a good example.

Bibliography or references. Strictly, a bibliography is a list of publications dealing with a particular subject; and a reference list is one to which specific reference has been made (as in endnoting) or from which material for the writing of the report was actually drawn. Any report that has derived material from printed sources or from interviews should contain a list of references, regardless of whether footnotes or end-notes are used. A sound practice is to construct the bibliography or reference list as follows:

1. Index and number each article, bulletin, report, or book alphabetically by author.

2. Index all anonymous publications under the author "Anonymous" alphabetically by the first significant word of their titles.

3. For books, the following elements should appear in this order:

(a) Author or authors (exactly as they appear on the title page, but with first surname first):

Gaum, Carl G., Harold F. Graves, and Lyne S. S. Hoffman

In footnotes, more than two authors are seldom listed:

Gaum, Carl G., and others (or: et al.),

(b) When a particular chapter is cited, its title is put in quotation marks:

"Some Matters of Style,"

(c) Title of the book, underlined:

Report Writing,

(d) Edition (or translation), if necessary:

Second Revised Edition,

(e) Place of publication, publisher, and date of publication:

New York: Prentice-Hall, Inc., 1949

4. For articles from periodicals:
(a) Author or authors (as for a book)
(b) Title of the article in quotation marks and with initial letters of all significant words (including first and last) capitalized:

"The Essentials of a Good Report,"

(c) The name of the periodical, in italics (that is, underlined):

Journal of Chemical Education,

(d) The date, and other useful identifying data, *all labeled:*

Vol. 24, No. 3, pp. 129–140, March 1947

5. For reports and bulletins, the procedure is much the same. It is important in listing government publications to give the exact division, bureau, or department which prepared the publication, and exact identifying details.

A bibliography on technical report writing would look like the following sample:

1. Anonymous, American Standard Abbreviations for Use on Drawings, (ASA Z32.13–1046). New York: American Standards Association, December 1946.
2. Anonymous, The Preparation of Engineering Reports for the Tennessee Valley Authority, Technical Monograph No. 21. Knoxville: Tennessee Valley Authority Engineering and Construction Department, September 1942.
3. Anonymous, Style Manual, Revised Edition. Washington: United States Government Printing Office, January 1945.
4. Crane, E. J., "Words and Sentences in Science and Industry," Science, Vol. 86, No. 50, pp. 549–553, December 17, 1937.
5. Jordan, Richard C., and Edwards, Marion J., Aids to Technical Writing, Bulletin No. 21, Vol. 47, No. 24. Minneapolis: University of Minnesota Experiment Station, May 15, 1944.
6. Nelson, J. Raleigh, Writing the Technical Report, New Second Edition. New York: McGraw-Hill Book Company, Inc., 1947.
7. Wall, Florence E., "The Essentials of a Good Report," Journal of Chemical Education, Vol. 24, No. 3, pp. 129–140, March 1947.

Preliminary Parts of the Report

Although the title page, the letter of transmittal, and the table of contents appear first in the report (or, in short reports, not at all), they must usually be composed last.

Title page. In typewritten reports the title page consists of at least four items: (1) a complete title; (2) the name of the person or organization to whom the report is submitted; (3) the name of the writer and his position; (4) the date—the same date as appears on the letter of transmittal. All of this information is of real importance, especially for any later reference that may be made to the report.

The need of a complete title demands great emphasis. In private reports, the value of a "catchy" title is lacking. Conciseness, to be sure, is a merit to be sought, but the title may sometimes be fifty or more words in length if so many are required to convey a complete understanding. In research reports and theses, the long and complete title is especially characteristic. The title, it should always be remembered, must be adequate for later reference as well as for the immediate reader. If a report is filed, its title must be so complete and so clear that it can be immediately identified at any time. The periodic-report title, for example, must always include the period covered by the report, since that is the only item that will inevitably distinguish its title from the titles of all the other reports in the same series:

> Annual Report of the Sales Manager for 1949
> Monthly Report of the Shipping Department for March 1949

The title of a progress report is also one of a series, all of which are alike except for the difference in date:

> Report on the Progress of the Westgate Experiment for May 1950
> Report on the Progress of the Millerstown Bridge Construction from February 25 to April 15, 1950

The progress-report title indicates, by the word "progress," the nature of the report. An examination-report title usually includes no date in the title, but sometimes it should distinguish a "preliminary" from a "final" investigation. It is also possible to distinguish between an examination and a recommendation report. Examples of examination-report titles:

> Report on the Preliminary Survey of Manufacturing Methods in the Shoe Factories of Brockton
> Report on a Study of Wage Payment Systems Suitable for the Barron Biscuit Company

The title of a recommendation report is usually distinguished by the inclusion of such a term as "advisability" or "proposed":

> Report on the Advisability of Adopting a Task and Bonus System for the Ashcom-Cooper Company
> Report on a Proposed Plan of Re-routing in the Bacon Shops

Specimens of typed title pages appear on pages 153 and 154.

Abstract or summary. The *Abstract* and the *Summary* have already been discussed in earlier chapters. It should be pointed out, however, that practically no modern report of any length fails to include at least one of these elements either as a separate section of itemized conclusions and recommendations, or incorporated in the letter of transmittal. The summary in some form or other has

A PROPOSED DESIGN FOR THE ILLUMINATION

OF THE MUNICIPAL AIRPORT

DALEWILD, NEW YORK

––––––––––––––––––

Submitted to
Mr. Q. T. Webster
Head, Design Department
City of New York

––––––––––––––––––

By

Randall H. Rice
Head, Illumination Division
Lumen Corporation

––––––––––––––––––

May 17, 1948

FIG. 7. Specimen Title Page (Recommendation Report)

SOCONY–VACUUM LABORATORIES
(A Division of Socony–Vacuum Oil Co., Inc.)
Research and Development Department
Paulsboro, N. J.

PROCESS DEVELOPMENT DIVISION

PROJECT NO.

930

REPORT NO.

48.1–DM

JANUARY 12, 1948

REACTIVATION CHARACTERISTICS OF X/Y DESICCANT AND
EFFECT OF *——————— CONTENT ON DESICCANT STABILITY

Report by: Work by:

A. Frickson   R. C. Noyes
C. H. Thaler   A. B. Schwar
                                              A. Frickson

Approvals:

FIG. 8. Specimen Title Page (Research Report)

[154]

proved so efficient a time-saver that the executive who must read a great variety and number of reports demands it.

The letter of transmittal. The letter of transmittal performs about the same function in the report that the preface performs in a book. It tells what the report is about. But, as prefaces differ, so do letters of transmittal. Some consist of but a single sentence; others cover pages. Some tell the reader only the subject of the report or the authorization for it. Others tend to increase his interest and confidence; to supply him with a summary of results, conclusions, or recommendations; to explain how the report is prepared; or to call his attention to particular points that need special emphasis. Since the possible uses are so many, it is hardly wise to generalize too much concerning the function of each letter. The better plan will be to examine specimens of some of the different types.

The simplest form merely indicates the subject and authorization for the report:

— 1 —

BROWN & DAVIS

Consulting Engineers
Carmel 3, New York

January 4, 1949

George T. Deck, Inc.
400 Fifth Avenue
New York 22, N. Y.

Attention Mr. William Keeler

Gentlemen:

In accordance with your instructions of December 14, we are submitting the following report on "The Operating Characteristics of Fluorescent Lamps and Auxiliaries."

Yours truly,

The customary letter of transmittal in a public report is not essentially different. Invariably, however, the authorization for the report is of particular importance. The following letter of transmittal by Dr. Vannevar Bush also, of course, introduces the report[2] requested in President Roosevelt's letter of instructions (pages 20, 21).

---

[2] Bush, Vannevar, *Science, The Endless Frontier*. Washington: The U. S. Government Printing Office, 1945.

— 2 —

LETTER OF TRANSMITTAL

Office of Scientific Research and Development
1530 P Street, NW.
Washington 25, D.C.

July 5, 1945

Dear Mr. President:

In a letter dated November 17, 1944, President Roosevelt requested my recommendations on the following points:

(1) What can be done, consistent with military security, and with the prior approval of the military authorities, to make known to the world as soon as possible the contributions which have been made during our war effort to scientific knowledge?

(2) With particular reference to the war of science against disease, what can be done now to organize a program for continuing in the future the work which has been done in medicine and related sciences?

(3) What can the Government do now and in the future to aid research activities by public and private organizations?

(4) Can an effective program be proposed for discovering and developing scientific talent in American youth so that the continuing future of scientific research in this country may be assured on a level comparable to what has been done during the war?

It is clear from President Roosevelt's letter that in speaking of science he had in mind the natural sciences, including biology and medicine, and I have so interpreted his questions. Progress in other fields, such as the social sciences and the humanities, is likewise important; but the program for science presented in my report warrants immediate attention.

In seeking answers to President Roosevelt's questions I have had the assistance of distinguished committees specially qualified to advise in respect to these subjects. The committees have given these matters the serious attention they deserve; indeed, they have regarded this as an opportunity to participate in shaping the policy of the country with reference to scientific research. They have had many meetings and have submitted formal reports. I have been in close touch with the work of the committees and with their members throughout. I have examined all the data they assembled and the suggestions they submitted on the points raised in President Roosevelt's letter.

Although the report which I submit herewith is my own, the facts, conclusions, and recommendations are based on the findings of the committees which have studied these questions. Since my report is necessarily brief, I am including as appendices the full reports of the committees.

A single mechanism for implementing the recommendations of the several committees is essential. In proposing such a mechanism I have departed somewhat from the specific recommendations of the committees, but I have since been assured that the plan I am proposing is fully acceptable to the committee members.

The pioneer spirit is still vigorous within this nation. Science offers a largely unexplored hinterland for the pioneer who has the tools for his task. The rewards of such exploration both for the Nation and the individual are great. Scientific progress is one essential key to our security as a nation, to our better health, to more jobs, to a higher standard of living, and to our cultural progress.

Respectfully yours,
(s) V. Bush, Director

The President of the United States
The White House
Washington, D.C.

Since it is desirable to keep the text of the report impersonal and objective, a writer is often prompted to express something of his own personality and his own opinions directly in the letter of transmittal. Here he may write in the more informal style of business correspondence. It is possible for him thus to increase the interest of his reader, to furnish information that will lead to greater confidence in the facts and conclusions of the report text— in brief, to increase respect for both writer and report.

— 3 —

Box 201
Freeport, Michigan
December 30, 1949

Mr. N. B. Ewell, President
Olympic Corporation
Lancaster, Pennsylvania

Dear Mr. Ewell:

My ideas for the establishment of a by-products mill at Freeport are incorporated in the following report, which you requested in your letter of November 15. I hope that the information meets your requirements.

Though I am a native of Freeport, I believe you will find the report objective. However, I should like to express the personal opinion that it will be advisable to choose the Industrial Relations Department in the new mill carefully. Labor, as I have pointed out in Section V of the report, is plentiful, but has always received much better than average treatment from the local employers. No "outside" industry has ever come into the town and I am convinced that strong-arm methods would prove very embarrassing.

Mr. McFalls, from the Chicago office, has been invaluable in obtaining the data for Section IX. It is noteworthy, I think, that he agrees with my opinion about the local labor situation.

Respectfully yours,

Another possible function of the letter of transmittal is to summarize the report, so that the executive or the layman may know immediately the results of an investigation and the conclusions reached by the writer. The plan of placing a summary at the beginning of the report is now the most common practice, and the letter of transmittal is very often a good place for it.

— 4 —

ACME STEEL TUBING CORPORATION

South Pittsburgh
Pennsylvania

February 3, 1950

Mr. Ralph J. Stacy
General Sales Manager
Acme Steel Tubing Corp.
75 Pine Street
New York 5, N. Y.

Dear Mr. Stacy:

In accordance with your instructions of October 10, 1949, I am submitting herewith my report on the results of the tests to which our #345-H seamless steel tubing was subjected in order to determine its suitability for use in high-temperature oil-cracking systems.

The report first considers various types of high-temperature applications in such a system, and then discusses the various tests to which the tubing in question was subjected to determine its suitability for each type of service.

In discussing these applications, it has been shown that in addition to strength the tubing must possess surface and structural stability, must be free from temper embrittlement, must be able to retain its original properties during service, and must maintain good hot-ductility to render the best service.

The merits of this tubing with regard to these qualities have been discussed and a set of five graphs is included in the appendix to provide a clear picture of the results at a glance.

The tests placed special emphasis on creep and stress-rupture characteristics. The short-time tests for indicating load-carrying ability are not discussed because the information they yield is not pertinent to the question.

The tests used in determining these characteristics are among the most valid in the field of metallurgy and are wholly endorsed by the American Society for Metals. In view of this, together with the positive results obtained, we recommend our #345-H seamless steel tubing for high-temperature oil-cracking systems.

Respectfully yours,
Signature
Luke A. Yerkovich
Research Engineer

Letters of transmittal may be intended for *one, several,* or *all* of the following ends:

1. To make reference to the assignment of the report, the letter

of instructions, or the custom which makes the report necessary.

2. To "motivate" the writer himself; that is, to prove (indirectly, of course) his fitness, ability, or seriousness, and to indicate how much time and thought he has given to the report. In other words, the writer recognizes that the attention given to the report depends in part upon the amount of confidence that the reader places in him, and by means of his letter of transmittal he tries to increase that confidence.

3. To "motivate" the report itself; that is, to suggest the possible values or uses of the report—to give the reader a "motive" for reading it carefully and considering it intelligently.

4. To summarize the report. Usually, of course, such a summary is a mere epitome, emphasizing the chief conclusion reached or presenting one or two important recommendations.

5. To point the reader's attention to specific sections of the report which the writer especially wants him to read.

The position of the letter of transmittal in the report make-up is considered more fully in Chapter 6. Normally, if it is closely related to the report, it appears in the position of a preface—immediately after the title page and before the table of contents. If, however, the same report is to be sent to more than one person, each with interests of his own, separate letters may be sent to each reader. When that is the situation, each letter of transmittal is different and each usually emphasizes the fifth purpose—to point out specific sections of the report that will be of interest to the individual reader.

The table of contents. If the report is more than a few pages long, and if numerous subtitles are employed, the reader needs some sort of index to guide him to those points that have particular worth and interest for him. A table of contents is the method most commonly used.

In the preparation of a table of contents, these rules should be observed:

1. List in the table of contents every title and heading that is to appear in the text of the report; on the other hand, list no titles that are not to be found in the text. Use identical phraseology in both places.

2. Use Roman numerals to distinguish the main sectional headings, but do not use numbers or letters for the other subheadings unless there is some real need for an elaborate outline. In the table of contents never use symbols that are not also used in the text.

3. Show the relationship of headings in the table of contents by indentation.

4. List by number and title all tables and figures—including sketches, maps, graphs, photographs, and so on—separately, at the end of the table of contents.

TABLE OF CONTENTS

Editing the Manuscript

The last step in the construction of the report is the editing of the manuscript for submittal. In this step both the content and the presentation must be checked—and checked carefully. Footnotes, bibliography, physical layout, and typing must be completed. Since this work is likely to be tedious, the young writer is tempted to minimize its importance. But carelessness or neglect here will cripple the report.

The content should be checked first. Inaccuracies, irrelevancies, and omissions must be discovered and corrected. The process is deceptively time-consuming, but it is essential.

For the inexperienced writer, the process of editing and revising the presentation may prove even more time-consuming. The ideas which were set down rapidly in blocks of thought must be examined for the accuracy and effectiveness of their expression. When his revision is complete, the writer must be able to answer positively the following questions:

1. Are the ideas expressed in language the reader can understand?

2. Are the ideas expressed so clearly that the reader cannot *misunderstand*?

3. Are the important ideas properly emphasized and the unimportant ones subordinated?

4. Is the writing concise? Have graphic time-savers been used when they would be helpful?

5. Is the tone objective and the language restrained?

6. Are the rules of paragraphing, sentence structure, grammar, punctuation, and spelling adhered to?

7. Do the abbreviations, symbols, numbers, tables, curves, and the like, conform to the practices discussed in this text or advocated by authoritative style manuals such as those of the American Standards Association?

In general, when checking either content or presentation, apply the rule: *When in doubt, save the reader's time, not yours.*

Once the writer is satisfied that the content and presentation of his report meet the requirements, only two things remain for him to do. He must acknowledge any help received from others; and he must plan the physical layout and construction of the report.

Acknowledging contributions of others. The writer of a report is often indebted for much of his material to other investigators or writers. Unless he is summarizing the information pertaining to an organization or a division for which he is personally responsible, he must be careful to give credit for every fact or statement that he borrows. Even the executive often finds it good practice to mention those subordinates who have helped him.

The preface or letter of transmittal sometimes mentions the

writer's indebtedness to individuals, but that general acknowledgment is seldom enough. When the writer uses words or facts furnished by another, his reader has a right to know it. Every quotation, therefore, must be so set off from the text that its nature is unmistakable. If it is more than a few lines in length, the margin of the quoted matter should be five to ten spaces to the right of the margin of the text proper. A word of introduction or a footnote must indicate the exact source of the quotation. Sufficient space must separate the quoted matter from the main text; and, unless quotation marks are employed, and the quotation is very short, all such material should be single-spaced.

Acknowledgment of borrowed materials is essential for two very good reasons. In the first place, it is common honesty. When you are aided by the work of another, you must admit that help. An unacknowledged quotation becomes a theft. Plagiarism in reports is no less despicable than plagiarism elsewhere. In the second place, it is possible to add weight to the discussion and the conclusions of a report by presenting the sources of information. Data and opinions are of worth to a reader only when he knows who is responsible for them. He has a right to know the source of every fact. If the writer has been careful in his investigations, he may add considerable strength to his conclusions by making certain that every source is listed.

Footnotes. Footnotes are employed to supply the exact source of quotations from books, periodicals, or other reports; to acknowledge the contribution of a set of data; to point to further substantiation of a statement in the text; or to give supplementary information. In general, they are used only when the information noted would interrupt the trend of the reader's thought if inserted in the text.

With the convenience of the reader, not of the writer, in mind, the most satisfactory system of footnoting is as follows:

1. Footnotes are placed at the bottom of the page on which the point of reference occurs. Exception: In referring to a table or an item in a table, the footnote is placed at the bottom of the table.

2. Footnotes are numbered consecutively from the beginning of the report to the end. Exception: Some systems number only a page at a time, others only a section.

3. Arabic numerals are used in the text for indexes to the notes. Except for the asterisk (*), other symbols of reference are not

available on the standard keyboard. In tables, the asterisk (*), and double (**), or lower-case letters (a, b, c) are used as indexes to avoid confusion.

4. The index number is placed at the point in the text at which the reader naturally questions the source:

. . . according to the Jones theory,[6] no oxygen . . .

5. Since most typewritten reports are double-spaced, there is usually sufficient space to permit the use of full-size numerals as superior figures. If, in single-spaced copy, this method proves undesirable, the number can be placed in virgules /36/ on the same line as the typing:

Commissioner of Patents Ooms[36] has said . . .
Commissioner of Patents Ooms /36/ has said . . .

6. Footnotes are separated from the text by two spaces, a line, and another space. The line begins at the left margin and extends about a third of the way, or all the way to the right margin.

References to published material are entered as described in the next section of this text. The Latin abbreviation *ibid.* ("in the same place") is used only when the reference being cited is identical with the one cited immediately above it except for the change in page numbers. The abbreviation *op. cit.* ("in the work cited") is preceded by the author's name and followed by the new page number.

7. Footnotes are always single-spaced.

In other words, if these were the last lines on a report page possessing five footnote references, the bottom of the page would resemble the following:

18. Also known as a *Konimeter.*
19. Weischlaus, L. J., "Dust Collection with Filters," *Chemical Engineering,* August 1947, Vol. 54, No. 8, pp. 113–116.
20. *Ibid.,* p. 131.
21. Bubar, H. H., *Dust Problems,* Third Edition. New York: Ellison and Son, 1946.
22. Weischlaus, *op. cit.,* p. 67.

End-notes. A few reports, and many technical journals, substitute end-notes for footnotes, placing all notes in one place at the end of the report or article. Except in articles or short reports, this system is inconvenient for the reader, though simpler for the typist and the printer. End-notes usually follow the same order as would footnotes and use *ibid., op. cit., idem,* and so on. A simplified system uses index numbers in the text to refer to a numbered and alphabetized bibliography at the end of the report. Thus, if *Weischlaus* were the thirtieth author listed alphabetically in the bibliography, every reference to his article would be indexed in the text with a "30."

Layout and Typing of the Report

Importance of appearance. Clean and attractive copy adds to the effectiveness of a report almost as much as it adds to the effectiveness of an important letter or advertisement. Even in interdepartmental work of a thoroughly routine nature, the writer has something to gain by giving his readers a favorable impression. Good make-up cannot fail to play its part in attracting favorable attention to the report.

A few of the advertiser's more conventional devices may be used very effectively in reports. The advertiser, it is true, goes to extremes in his efforts to force attention from an uninterested reader. His make-up includes all kinds of devices: pictures, varieties of print style, borders, lines, and arrows. It is not expected that the report writer will use many of the unique devices of the advertiser. His reader already has some interest before he begins to read. But, for example, an unusual amount of white space on a page occasionally throws emphasis upon a small group of exceptionally important points or statements. A table or diagram may be attractively "framed." Sectional headings or subtitles may be so placed on the page that they catch the eye. These are all legitimate, perhaps essential, methods in good make-up.

The chief object in planning the display of a report is, of course, to make it possible for the reader to refer to any section with little time and trouble. Every means adopted must have value as an aid either to the understanding or to the convenience of the reader.

How reports are bound. If the report is printed, the writer is usually not directly concerned with the manner in which it is to be bound. If it is typed, however, he must often decide for himself the kind of binding that will be most suitable.

The most common form of binding for typed reports is a stiff Manila folder slightly larger than the paper on which the report is written. On this cover should be recorded the full title, the name

THE STANDARD OIL COMPANY (OHIO)

MANUFACTURING DEPARTMENT
GENERAL ENGINEERING DIVISION

GED NO.--------

TITLE

SURVEY OF MECHANICAL CONDITION
API WASTE WATER SEPARATORS
NO. 1 REFINERY

DATE: September 4, 1947   **REPORT BY:** T. A. Mullett

FIG. 9. Specimen Cover Make-up

of the author, the date, and any other information needed for identification (in some companies, a report serial number, for example). A student with average ability in lettering can create a better cover with a pen than with a typewriter. The Sohio cover, which is reproduced in Fig. 9, could be used as a guide. Incidentally, this cover is blue, to denote its source as the General Engineering. Division; Sohio uses buff covers for its Technical Service Division. This type of cover is never folded, of course.

Another binding consists only of a backing of heavy paper, which laps over the title page on the first sheet of the report, and is fastened at the top with paper staples or an equally good substitute. The report and jacket are folded twice—one-third the distance from the top, and one-third from the bottom. The title and other important information are typed across the back of the central fold, so that the report may be found and recognized without unfolding it. In this form it fits into the "legal" filing cabinet.

With either type, the pages should be fastened to the binding, preferably by semipermanent fasteners. In a Manila folder, the report is always fastened at the left side of the page so that it can be read like a book.

Unless the report is mailed, or is in the form of a letter, it should usually be submitted flat, never folded or rolled. When a long, Manila-covered report is mailed, it too is either wrapped flat or enclosed in a very large envelope. When a report of five or ten pages is to be mailed, it is bound in a jacket and folded twice, as for filing. Such a report may usually be enclosed in the ordinary long envelope.

Some companies make it a custom to bind their most important reports in cloth or leather, to insure their permanence.

The paper. Reports are submitted on paper of standard size— 8½ by 11 inches. The report then fits conveniently into Manila folders, can be fastened at the side for easy reading, and can be filed in standard files.

Reports should be written on white paper of good quality: since they frequently have a permanent value, the paper must last as long as the report is to be useful. In some large organizations, various colors of paper serve to distinguish communications from different departments, or on different subjects; but white paper is conventional.

Standards for margins and spacing. Good make-up for the text of a report approaches the appearance of the printed page. There should be uniform margins and spacing, and a generous amount of white space on every page.

The left-hand margin is, of course, even. Since the margins after binding should appear to be about equal, it is usually necessary to allow half an inch more margin at the left than is needed at the right. Margins at the top and bottom of the page must be at least an inch in depth. An attractive page can be achieved with a top margin of 1¼ inches, a left of 1½ inches, a right of ¾ inch, and a bottom of 1 inch. The wider left margin allows for binding.

If the report is consistent and neat in make-up, the choice between single and double spacing is not of great importance. There are, however, conditions that have weight in determining a decision between the two. When corrections, changes, or minor additions are required in the finished copy, the report must be double-spaced to allow sufficient room for these changes. Furthermore, if numerous quotations are to be included, they are more readily distinguishable when spaced differently from the text proper—as, for example, when they are single-spaced in the body of double-spaced text. The advantage of single spacing under normal conditions is, nevertheless, considerable. Much more can be put on a single page. The report is less bulky. Tables and figures may be referred to more readily, since the explanations regarding them need not cover so much space. All references, in fact, are likely to be made with greater speed and ease.

An indented quotation, and, unless it is very short, the letter of transmittal, should always be single-spaced to allow for rapid reading and to give an impression of brevity and conciseness.

It is not good judgment to save space by sacrificing either appearance or reader-convenience. Very few typed reports use more than one side of the paper. Headings for major sections are customarily placed at the top of the page, regardless of where on the previous page the last section ended. No heading or subheading should be placed at the bottom of the page without text below it. Similarly, a paragraph should not be begun on the last line of the page. Liberal white space should be allowed for all headings, more for the major heading than for the minor. Figures, tables, and graphic devices of other kinds should not be crowded. Quotations over two lines in length should be indented from both margins from six to eight spaces. A few companies include fly-leaves at the beginning and end and between major sections of the report; most do not, regarding them as unnecessary bulk.

Page numbering. Beginning with the first page of the report itself, every page must be numbered. Since the place first seen by most readers is the upper right-hand corner, most writers place the number there. When the title appears at the top of the first page, it is standard practice to simply omit the number. It is also standard practice to number the pages preceding the text with lower-case Roman numerals (*ii*, *vii*, and so forth). The numbering in the appendix should be a continuation of that in the text.

Submitting the manuscript to the printer. A manuscript submitted to the printer must be legible beyond possibility of error. The chief requisite is, of course, to give full directions for all matters that are to be decided by the writer, and to leave other matters to the good judgment of the printer.

However, it must be remembered that the average printer will follow copy rather literally in such matters as indentions of quoted material, paragraphing, italicizing, capitalization of headings, use of boldface type, and so forth. For instance, if the author of the report wishes a certain heading to be set in boldface, that is, heavy type, he should underscore it with a wavy line. If he wishes it italicized, he should use a straight underscore. Before composition is started, it is always wise to have a personal conference with the printer for the purpose of deciding all details of style.

All illustrations, charts, photographs, and other cuts should be submitted separately, since they are not handled by typesetters. To insure that these will be all properly placed in the printed report, the author should mark the position of each in the text with a number corresponding to that found on the illustration.

REPRESENTATIVE REPORT MAKE-UP

On the following right-hand pages appears a typewritten recommendation report. It is presented here as an example of plan and make-up, but analyze each part of it for function and content also.

Letter of Instructions

In what way does the letter differ from standard practice?

Since it has no salutation, is the complimentary close necessary?

Is space well-utilized?

Does the letter state its purpose clearly? If you received this letter, would you know exactly what Mr. Smith wanted?

Is the tone discourteous? too courteous?

Can you shorten the letter without omitting valuable information?

JONES MANUFACTURING COMPANY
Philadelphia, Pennsylvania

May 15, 1950

To: Mr. C. R. Parce
     Production Department
     General Offices

From: Mr. H. B. Smith

Subject: Production at Plant No. 6, Scranton, Pa.

At our Scranton plant, production for the last two years has cost 6 percent more than the general average for all the plants. The general condition of business will not permit this to continue, and we are therefore asking you to go to Scranton at once, make an investigation, and let us have your recommendations for the lowering of their production costs to compare more favorably with the general average.

We suggest that your investigation be conducted and recommendations made with these three divisions in mind:

    1. Plant
    2. Personnel
    3. Methods

Will you please let us have this report as soon as possible. It should be in our hands by June 5 at the latest.

                        Yours truly,

                        (*Signature*)

                        H. B. Smith
                        General Manager

[171]

Title Page

Are all necessary elements included on this title page?

Does the title indicate the purpose, nature, and content of the report satisfactorily?

Is the appearance (spacing, etc.) good?

Report on

PROPOSALS TO IMPROVE PRODUCTION CONDITIONS

at

PLANT NO. 6, SCRANTON, PA.

Submitted to

Mr. H. B. Smith

General Manager

By

C. R. Parce

Production Department

May 29, 1950

Letter of Transmittal

What functions does this letter fulfill?

How much of the letter is fact? How much personal opinion?

Is the last paragraph useful?

Is the shift from active to passive voice excusable?

JONES MANUFACTURING COMPANY

Philadelphia, Pennsylvania

May 29, 1950

To: Mr. H. B. Smith, General Manager

From: Mr. C. R. Parce
       Production Department
       General Offices

Subject: Production at Plant No. 6, Scranton, Pa.

As requested in your letter of May 15, I have made
an investigation of the production work at our
Scranton plant. A report on it is now submitted.

I arrived in Scranton on the 17th and remained there
ten days. Most of the time was spent in the inspection of the plant property and machinery, and
in the determining of a few sample standards in an
effort to get an idea of the general efficiency.
Some time was also spent in conference with the
Superintendent, Mr. Sullivan, and other employees.

Most of the employees with whom I came in contact
were very willing to cooperate. This was particularly true of Mr. Sullivan, and I believe he will
do what he can to carry out any orders you may care
to give.

I trust that this report will satisfy your requirements.

                Yours truly,

                (*Signature*)

                C. R. Parce

Table of Contents

Is the appearance attractive?

What do the indentations show?

Do the entries agree in wording and position with their counterpart headings in the text?

Will a few moments' study of this page give the reader a quick comprehension of the content of the report and the relative importance of the various sections?

Is there any necessity for listing page numbers for the subsections?

Should these particular tables be listed separately in the table of contents?

TABLE OF CONTENTS

Subject	Page

Introduction

Is this section important enough to demand a separate page?

How does this Introduction differ from the letter of transmittal?

Is the problem clearly stated?

Does the Introduction define the scope of the report adequately?

Why is the last paragraph useful?

Summary of Recommendations

Will this section, with the Introduction, enable the reader to grasp all the essentials of the report?

Is the classification of the recommendations into three divisions efficient?

Is there good reason for separate itemization of each recommendation, or does it waste space?

Why are the recommendations unsupported?

INTRODUCTION

This report covers the investigation of production in the Scranton plant, No. 6, which was directed by the General Manager in a letter of May 15, 1949. Because production costs in this plant have been six percent higher than the general average of all plants, the aim of the study has been to find means of reducing expense and increasing efficiency.

The investigation was carried on between May 17 and May 29. It included inspection of plant and machinery, observations of plant operations, and conferences with Superintendent Sullivan and various employees.

This report begins with a summary of recommendations, then makes detailed suggestions regarding Plant, Personnel, and Methods.

SUMMARY OF RECOMMENDATIONS

It is estimated that production may be increased about five percent, and costs correspondingly reduced by five to six percent, if the following recommendations are carried out:

Plant

All equipment should be inspected weekly.

A system of regular lubrication for all machines should be set up.

Individual lighting is recommended for the milling machines.

For proper ventilation, oscillating electric fans should be placed at 50-ft intervals along the side walls of both floors of the factory building, with the exception of the shipping and store rooms.

Obsolete and worn-out machines should be junked and replaced as proposed in Table 1.

Examine the system of headings and subheadings. Can the reader see at once exactly what each heading controls?

Should the recommendations be scattered throughout the report?

Are the recommendations sufficiently supported by evidence, by facts?

Is there good reason for giving "Boiler House" and "Garage" separate sections?

Is the paragraphing efficient?

How much of the discussion is personal opinion? How much is fact?

Why are one-story *and* steel-frame *hyphenated?*

Is the use of numbers inconsistent?

Personnel

    After production standards have been estab-
lished, it is recommended that the working force be
reduced by 20. Inefficient workers, as determined
from production records, should be gradually weeded
out. Table 2 indicates where reductions in personnel are advisable.

Methods — arap.

    It is recommended that standards be set for
all repetitive jobs, and wages determined accordingly.

    A system of production control, such as Gantt
charts, is advised.

    The storeroom material should be rearranged
and a perpetual inventory system adopted.

    The stock in the shipping room should be re-
arranged.

PLANT

    The Scranton plant, No. 6, manufacturing wash-
ing machines, consists of a factory building, a
boiler house, and a garage. The factory building
and boiler house are fifteen years old; the garage,
five. The factory building, constructed of rein-
forced concrete, has two stories and about 10,000
sq ft of floor space. The boiler house is a small,
one-story brick building which contains a boiler
used for heating the factory and an air compressor
which supplies compressed air for various processes.
The garage is of steel-frame construction with
stalls for eight cars or trucks; a small room at
one end contains oil, grease, and a small assort-
ment of tools.

Boiler House

    No changes are recommended for the boiler
house.

Can you find a misspelled word on the opposite page?
Should "Table 1" be identified by title?

No changes are recommended for the garage.

Factory Building

Heating. Though there was no heat in the building at the time of the investigation, Superintendent Sullivan states that the system works efficiently.

Lighting. Except for requirements of the milling machines, the lighting is generally satisfactory. Electric lamps hanging from the ceiling are enclosed in translucent globes. Walls and ceilings are painted white.

Because of the highly accurate work required, each milling machine should be individually lighted.

Ventilation. Excessive heat at times results in complaints and a perceptible slackening in production. Ventilation is provided by windows and by ventilators in the roof, but at the time of the inspection the temperature was 80°—too high for efficient work.

This situation should be relieved by the installation of oscillating electric fans on the side walls at intervals of 50 ft, except in the store room and shipping room, where the temperature is normal.

Power. Power is supplied by the local electric company. No changes are recommended.

Machinery. Though most machinery was found to be in serviceable condition, some replacements are needed. Table 1, which follows, indicates machines that should be junked and the number needed to replace them.

Could the information in Table No. 1 be conveyed more simply in words?

Does the make-up of the tables seem good? (See Chap. 8)

Would the whole section "Maintenance" be more effective if written as a single paragraph?

Can you write a topic sentence for the paragraph under "Present Working Force"?

Table No. 1

Machinery Recommended to be Junked		
Machines	No. to be Junked	No. to be Replaced
Brown & Sharpe Grinder	2	1
Cleveland Drill Press	1	1
South Bend Lathe	2	1

Where the table shows fewer replacements than machines to be junked, a time study has indicated that production would not be decreased as a result of partial replacements.

Maintenance. No regular systems of inspection and lubrication are in force. The maintenance force gave attention only to actual breakages. Lubrication seems to be done without regard to the special requirements of different machines.

It is recommended that a system of weekly inspections of each piece of equipment be installed.

It is also recommended that a definite lubrication schedule be established with attention given to the specific requirements of each machine.

These precautionary measures, which should decrease breakages and replacement costs, are possible without adding to the present maintenance force.

PERSONNEL

Present Working Force

The working force at the Scranton plant totals 520, of whom 50 are women. About half may be classified as skilled. In general, labor relations have been satisfactory and turnover has been somewhat lower than in other plants. Table 2 shows distribution by departments.

Would reader-comprehension be improved by the use of capitals in the table?

Possible Reductions

By applying more efficient methods, as discussed in the section on "Production Standards,"
it should be possible to reduce the working force
as shown in the following table:

Table No. 2

Possible Reductions in Working Force		
Department	Present Force	Reduced Force
Stores	8	7
Shipping	10	9
Machine	100	95
Stamping	25	23
Pressing	50	48
Painting	10	10
Inspection	75	70
Assembly	150	146
Testing	40	40
Maintenance	5	5
Tool	15	15
Engineering	2	2
Office	15	15
Transportation	15	15
Total	520	500
Reduction		20

It is also recommended that the management
undertake to weed out gradually all workers whose
production records for a period of six months do
not reach 60% of the standard set for the particular jobs they are doing.

What is the difference between the recommendations in the text and those in the summary at the beginning of the report?

Is the title of Table No. 3 adequate?

Are "fair standards" defined? (Read "Production Standards.")

In paragraph below Table No. 3, how is the "five percent" increase arrived at?

Does the writer assume too much knowledge on the part of the reader?

How much faith must the reader have in the writer's expertness?

METHODS

Production Standards

Time studies indicate that a substantial increase in production is possible if fair standards are set. These time studies were made of workers selected by their foremen as about the average. The following table shows the differences between the standard times set and the actual working times during the study:

Table No. 3

Standard Times		
Job	Actual Time	Standard Time
Cutting ring gear	7 min.	5 min.
Turning drive shaft	12 "	10 "
Painting washer frames	3 "	2½ "
Testing wringer drive	8 "	6 "
Assembling drive gears	10 "	7 "

Table 3 seems to indicate that there is sufficient room for improvement to justify a more extensive program of standard-setting. An increase of five per cent in production should be a fair estimate of the results.

It was on the basis of the results shown in Table 3 that the schedule of possible reductions in working force shown in Table 2 was devised.

Wage Payments

All employees, except office and storeroom workers and executives above the grade of foreman, were found to be paid on a piece-rate basis.

With the establishment of standard times for most jobs, it is recommended that employees now on piece rate be placed on a bonus system, since such a change ought to stimulate production.

Would a final summary be useful in this report?

Are the conclusions in this report supported by sufficient evidence?

Production Control

At present the lack of production control leaves the management out of touch with much that goes on in the factory. It is not possible to know at all times how work is progressing or why delays occur.

It is recommended that a system similar to the Gantt chart be installed.

Storage

Considerable inefficiency was apparent in handling material in the storeroom.

It is recommended, first, that after the stores have been arranged so that those articles most needed will be easiest to secure, then a chart should be prepared showing the location of each kind of material.

A perpetual inventory system is recommended in which maximum and minimum quantities are shown. The storekeeper will then know the number on hand, the most he should have at any one time, and the least he should have.

Shipping

Conditions in the shipping room were found to be similar to those in the storeroom.

The recommendations for "Storage" apply equally to the shipping room.

Exercises

1. Prepare, from library indexes, a bibliography on one of the following subjects:

Slum clearance	Flood control
Sanitary chemistry	Forest-fire protection
Regional planning	Textile chemistry
Diesel-engine developments	Concrete-road construction
Airplane motors	

2. Find all the library indexes that are related to your own field.
List the name, the publisher, and the total period of publication for
each.

3. Develop and write a periodic or a progress report on one of the
subjects suggested in the Exercise at the end of Chapter 1, pp. 8–9.

4. With the following information as your foundation, write the
annual report of the directors of a corporation to the stockholders:

Gross earnings	$156,734.20
Expenses	$138,264.15
Net earnings	$ 18,470.05
Capital stock	$300,000.00

Net earnings per share available for dividends:

1940	1.0	1945	5.0
1941	1.2	1946	4.8
1942	2.0	1947	5.4
1943	3.0	1948	6.0
1944	4.5	1949	6.1

Total sales increased 12 percent; total expenses increased 10 percent.

Advertising was increased greatly during the year. Seven additional
salesmen were employed, and new territory was opened up in the South-
west. Competition has been especially keen. New products that we put on
the market were not nearly so successful as standard lines. No new plant
construction, but almost $100,000 was spent for new equipment and repairs.
A new bonus system was established, in which 70 percent of the workmen
participated. Labor turnover decreased by about 10 percent, although wages
were not increased. A new health service was established for employees,
and an educational campaign for reduction of accidents inaugurated. Time
lost on account of sickness and injury was cut down substantially. A fire
protection system was installed. Restaurant, established for employees, paid
expenses. An apprenticeship course was established. No strikes or threats
of strikes.

5. Write a letter to a dean, telling him the progress you have made
during the past month in a course of study.

6. As the assistant coach of an athletic team, write a letter to the
head coach, who is sick in a hospital, telling him the progress made by
the team in practice during the week.

7. With the following information as your foundation, write a formal progress report:

This is the fifth week of work on the heating plant. Three reports of progress were made previously. During the week, boiler settings were completed; boiler accessories put in place and adjusted; feed pump started and boiler subjected to 200-lb pressure; slow fire started under No. 1 boiler to dry side walls and flues. Bricklayers were dismissed today, riggers dismissed yesterday. Rockland Steam Boiler Company will send inspector this week. We expect you to visit the plant next week.

8. With the following information as your basis, write an informal progress report:

Reorganization of branch office was started last week under my direction as new office manager. New filing system installed eliminates need of one girl. Sales conference ordered for Friday. Two salesmen, unsuccessful, dismissed yesterday. Too many employees in office for the amount of work; my intention to dismiss at least two stenographers and possibly one clerk. Salary of Riley raised to $65. Orders received during week slightly less than for last year; salesmen reporting poor business conditions and increased competition. New advertising started in local papers.

9. Select a subject from the list of examination-report topics at the end of Chapter 1. Write a report, from 1200 to 2000 words in length, on that subject.

10. Develop and write a recommendation report on one of the subjects suggested in the Exercise at the end of Chapter 1, p. 10.

11. Select some location in a town with which you are intimately acquainted and write a short report setting forth its qualifications as a site for one of the following buildings:

An apartment house	A department store
A motion picture theater	A chain store
A community market house	A factory for heavy machinery

Develop this report according to the following pattern:

SITE FOR THE GREENOUGH APARTMENTS

Statement of the problem: The Greenough Apartment Building is to provide up-to-date and attractive accommodations for families of the best type. The architect's preliminary plans are for a building of five stories with a frontage of from 100 ft to 125 ft on two streets. It is essential to choose a site that will appeal to desirable tenants both because of is surroundings and because of its accessibility. To be a profitable investment, the total cost of land and building cannot much exceed a million dollars.

Recommendation: The lot on the corner of Lamont and Bernard Streets, with a frontage of 120 ft on Lamont and 145 ft on Bernard, is recommended for this purpose. Such a site satisfies every reasonable requirement from the standpoint of surroundings and accessibility, the price of $215,500 is a fair one, and the estimated total cost for land and building of $1,040,600 will make it possible to realize a good return.

Location: The site, in what is known as West Lambert, is at the intersection of three prominent thoroughfares. It is in one of the best residential sections of the city, and only one block from Rankin Boulevard, the principal automobile thoroughfare to the downtown district.

Surroundings: Directly opposite this site, on Bernard Street, is a small park. Two excellent apartment houses and many well-kept and distinctive homes are in the vicinity. No manufacturing of any sort is found in the neighborhood.

Accessibility: The site is five minutes' walk from the Randolph Railroad Station, two blocks from the street-car line on Maxwell Street, three blocks from the car line on Prospect Street. It is within easy walking distance of the West Lambert shopping and theater districts, and within quick access by automobile or motor bus to the downtown section.

Within a radius of about half a mile are located the Manchester Athletic Club, the University Club, the Westminster Library, St. Paul's Cathedral, and the West Lambert School. A little more than a mile away, at the end of Lamont Street, is the campus of Manchester College.

Cost: Ground values in this section are advancing rapidly. The importance of this corner location is recognized. Hence, the price of $215,500 cannot be considered exorbitant. A reasonable estimate of the total expense follows:

Land	$ 215,500
Building	825,100
Total cost	$1,040,600

The estimation for the building is based upon the architect's preliminary plans and general specifications.

12. The following material should furnish the basis for a recommendation report. These directions are given:

1. Address a report to the president of the company.

2. Write one letter of transmittal, to be bound in with the report, presenting epitome, conclusion, and recommendation.

3. Include title page and table of contents.

4. Add slight imaginary details if you wish.

5. Length: Present all essential data as concisely as possible.

PROBLEM FOR RECOMMENDATION REPORT

The Waterville Street Railway Company furnishes local transportation to a population of about 250,000. One of the heaviest traffic routes extends 1¾ miles from center of city along Third Avenue (wide, paved street) to Denby Square. From Denby Square, 5 lines run to suburbs. Inbound Third Avenue cars make a loop at center of city to return.

17 inbound, 17 outbound cars per hr over Third Avenue for suburb service; 2 or 3 extra cars during rush hours.

5 of 17 cars carry only through passengers, run express from Denby Square to center; remaining 12 cars carry both through passengers and short-haul.

Running time of locals, 15 minutes; express cars scheduled for 12 minutes but usually take 14 minutes.

Third Avenue cars carry average of 12,500 daily, about 60% through passengers.

Suburban residents make frequent complaints about number of stops.

Local passengers make frequent complaints because they must stand.

Transportation Department, therefore, is asked to devise plan for separating through and local traffic and increasing speed of both services.

Plan 1: Construct passing tracks (turnouts) at 2 points between center and Denby Sq. to permit locals and expresses to pass. Company uses this plan on 2 other lines; on one, running time for expresses cut from 27 to 18 minutes. Traffic Dept. estimates that this plan will reduce time of expresses to 11 minutes.

Plan 2: Begin bus service to replace locals. All cars to run express from Denby Sq. to center, stopping inbound only to discharge, outbound only to receive passengers. Locate outbound bus terminal not at Denby Sq., but 1000 ft short of it. Traffic Dept. estimates local traffic will require buses on 5-min. headways during off-peak hours, on 2½-min. headways during rush hours. Requires buses. State law requires seats for all bus passengers. Plan will permit reducing number of cars using Third Ave. tracks from 17 to 11 per hr. Traffic Dept. estimates reduction of running time for expresses from 14 to 10 minutes. Transportation Dept. suggests no change in fares.

Estimated expense:
    track turnout & overhead construction: $16,000 to $20,000
    buses: $52,000

Average net expense for bus operation: 24.5 cents per m
    "   "   "   " car   "   32.9 cents per m

Seating capacity of buses: 25
    "   "   " cars: 44

Bus requires one man to operate
Car requires 2 men to operate
Labor is the largest single operating expense

Tables and Charts:

    1. Make table comparing costs.
    2. Make map, showing 2 proposals.

CHAPTER 8

MECHANICAL AIDS

MOST REPORTS make use of tables, photographs, diagrams, graphs, or other such mechanical aids to present material more quickly, exactly, and clearly than is possible in written composition alone. But these aids are never desirable as mere embellishments. For, though they often add interest and make the report more attractive to a reader, the real reason for their inclusion is the very practical one of making the subject more understandable. Mechanical aids are divided into two classes, tables and figures.

Tables. Since statistics often are valuable in reports, the writer must study the best methods of presenting them to his reader. To put many numbers in the text itself is needlessly confusing, as every experienced writer realizes. The tabulated form is, therefore, widely found in reports of all kinds. A statement of earnings from day to day, from week to week, or from year to year may advantageously be shown in column arrangement. Parallel columns give the reader opportunity for comparison of different periods or of different conditions.

A well-prepared table does more than make comparisons easy for the reader. It emphasizes tendencies, saves useless repetition in the text, aids the eye by eliminating everything but the important data, and often enables the reader to draw immediate and accurate conclusions.

The effectiveness of a table depends a great deal upon its make-up. The following rules should be observed in the construction of tables:

1. Give every table a clear title. Make it easy for the reader to find the data he wants without reference to the text.

2. Be absolutely sure that the units in which the data are tabulated are specified at the top of each column. Also be certain that factors having important bearing on the data are mentioned. For example, in giving the volume of a flow of liquid through a pipe,

the diameter of the pipe must be indicated. It is essential too, in this respect, that comparisons be made on the same basis. That is, if Jones uses two-inch lines in testing pump A and Smith uses four-inch lines in testing pump B, the data must not be directly compared.

3. Number tables consecutively throughout the report, using arabic numerals: Table 1, Table 2, and so on.

4. "Frame" every table. That is, box in the whole table, and use lines to set off column headings, perpendicular lines to set off columns, and so on.

5. Use headings for each column. Be sure that they are clear. If they must be long, they can be set vertically.

6. Use only standard abbreviations and symbols.

7. Avoid breaking tables. If a table is so large that it must be continued from one page to the next, then

(a) Mark the first part of the table *continued on next page;* and mark the second part *continued from preceding page.* Use exactly the same form and dimensions for the continuation of the table. Repeat every column heading whether or not any data appear below it.

(b) Better, if possible, use a summary table to recapitulate the major points. When this is done, the large table is placed in the appendix and referred to in the text.

8. When a great many tables are necessary, they should be placed in the appendix and referred to and, if possible, summarized in the text.

9. Whenever a reference to a table is made in the text, give both table number and page number.

10. Use decimals for column data unless the units are more commonly measured in fractions (pipe sizes, for example).

11. Align the vertical columns on the decimal points, or on the right-hand digits.

12. Use lower-case letters (a, b, c, and so forth) for footnoting within a table.

Figures. *Photographs.* In a report which is severely technical, a photograph is not always useful. The photograph provides only a knowledge of the appearance of a mechanism or development. It covers only externals, and, to the reader who is primarily interested in technical relationships and principles, it may sometimes appear more confusing than enlightening.

Nevertheless, photographs play an important part in many reports. They are naturally more vivid and interesting than diagrams. They provide a much more exact impression of the actual appearance than can any other device. They often serve as substantiation and proof of statements in the text, and hence are often valuable as evidence, as well as for illustration and explanation. The rule, then, is to use photographs when you want your reader to visualize something which the camera can accurately catch.

TABLE 10.—*Effect of imperfect distribution of fuel on engine performance at 1500 rpm, full throttle*[1]

Fuel	1942 Chevrolet		1940 Ford V-8		1942 Plymouth, No. 4		1942 Plymouth, No. 1	
	Power, percentage of theoretical maximum[a]	Mixture enriched at maximum power	Power, percentage of theoretical maximum[a]	Mixture enriched at maximum power	Power, percentage of theoretical maximum[a]	Mixture enriched at maximum power	Power, percentage of theoretical maximum[a]	Mixture enriched at maximum power
		%[b]		%[b]		%[b]		%[b]
Gasoline.............	99.90	0.2	99.83	0.7	99.82	0.6	99.84	0.6
Acetone.............	99.80	.4	99.70	1.1	99.92	.4	....	....
Butanol.............	97.00	11.0	98.60	6.7	99.00	6.7	....	....
190-proof alcohol....	98.86	5.7	99.07	5.0	97.83	10.7	99.08	5.1
200-proof alcohol....	99.02	4.0	99.34	3.7	98.86	5.5	99.29	4.2
No. 1 Blend........	99.79	1.0	99.51	3.1	99.69	2.1	99.26	3.7
No. 2 Blend........	99.62	2.3	99.08	5.1	99.52	2.4	99.19	4.6
No. 3 Blend, intake riser normal......	99.63	1.9	99.14	5.0	99.39	2.8	98.69	6.5
No. 3 Blend, heat added...........	....	....	....	....	....	....	98.55	7.8
No. 3 Blend, full heat on manifold..	....	....	....	....	....	....	99.52	2.5

[a] Maximum power based on perfect distribution and tests of a single-cylinder engine.
[b] Percentage enriched above maximum power mixture for single-cylinder engine.

Diagrams and maps. In routine and technical reports, diagrams and maps are usually more valuable than photographs. For example, the map of a property gives a more nearly exact impression of dimensions and relative positions than a photograph can. In the same way, a diagram of a machine shows the relationship of parts and makes it possible for the reader to understand the working principle. Better than either photograph or diagram, however, is the possible combination of both. What the camera misses or misrepresents may be caught by the sketch, and what might be misleading in the sketch alone is rectified by the photograph.

[1] From *Utilization of Nonpetroleum Fuels in Automotive Engines,* by Jesse T. Duck and Clarence S. Bruce. National Bureau of Standards Research Paper RP1681, December 1945.

All illustrations, of whatever kind, must be allotted plenty of space on the page. Adequate white space should surround them. Every diagram, map, or photograph requires an explanatory title, placed directly below the figure. Every figure should be placed as near as possible to that part of the text which it is meant to illustrate.

Graphical presentation of statistics. While statistics in tabular form are exceedingly useful in presenting information accurately and concisely, the table lacks the impressiveness and interest of graphical methods. (See Figure 11, page 200.)

Graphical charts in all forms have the important advantage of permitting, almost of enforcing, comparisons between two or more sets of statistics presented side by side. A single point on a given curve shows at once two items of information, such as a date and an output, a date and a price, or numerous other similarly related facts.

The chart or graph presents statistics by means of straight or curved lines, bars, and blocks. In the simplest form of chart, vertical and horizontal lines are ruled off at specified intervals to represent the number of units used. Thus, in a simple chart, a rectangular figure may have equal spaces to represent days of the week marked off on its base; and the left end may be similarly marked at equal intervals to represent units of output in a factory.

Figure 10, page 200 shows the method. Points are "spotted," or plotted, to show daily production, and then connected by straight lines to make a "Production Graph."

Here we have a striking visualization of production, enabling us to see one day's output compared with another's. When, as in Figure 12, page 201, two or more curves are shown for the same period, we can quickly make comparisons between sets of statistics, as well as compare the variations in one set.

Curved-line charts are made from abundant data simply by plotting points so closely together that they join in a smooth curve. Such charts show trends or, in the case of some engineering data, enable us to predict future performances under analogous conditions.

As the American Standards Association points out in its *Engineering and Scientific Graphs for Publications:*[2]

---

[2] American Standard Z15.3–1943. This informative manual, too long for reproduction here, can be obtained at a nominal charge by writing the Association at 70 East Forty-fifth Street, New York 17.

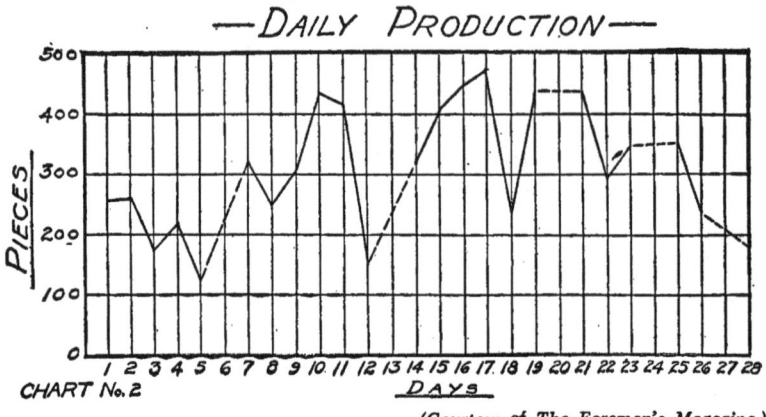

(Courtesy of The Foreman's Magazine.)

Fig. 10. Single-Line Graph

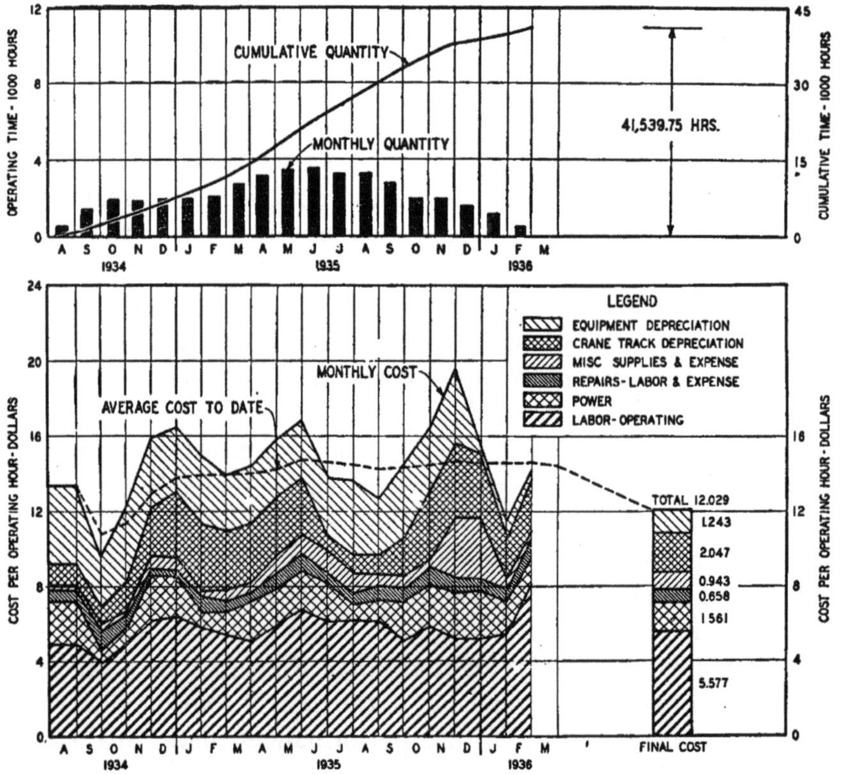

Courtesy Tennessee Valley Authority

Fig. 11. Illustration of a Bar Chart and a Cross-hatched Area Chart. From a Battery of Curves Showing the Operational Record of a Hydroelectric Plant.

200

The preparation of a graph deserves and usually requires at least as much time as the preparation of its equivalent in text. To obtain effective design and layout, it is good practice to make a preliminary freehand sketch roughly to scale. It is often helpful to submit such a sketch to others, preferably typical of the intended readers, for their reaction.

The effectiveness of the graph, like that of the table, depends on the care with which it is made up. The following rules should be observed in its construction:

1. Give every graph a clear title.
2. Clearly identify every unit, every scale, and every curve.
3. In writing the scale caption, indicate both the variable measured and the unit of measurement:

VISCOSITY IN CENTISTOKES

4. Use only standard abbreviations and symbols.
5. Point out when an area rather than a line is significant. The use of color or cross-hatching (see Figure 11, page 200) is useful in this respect.
6. Select the most efficient scale for your purpose. For example,

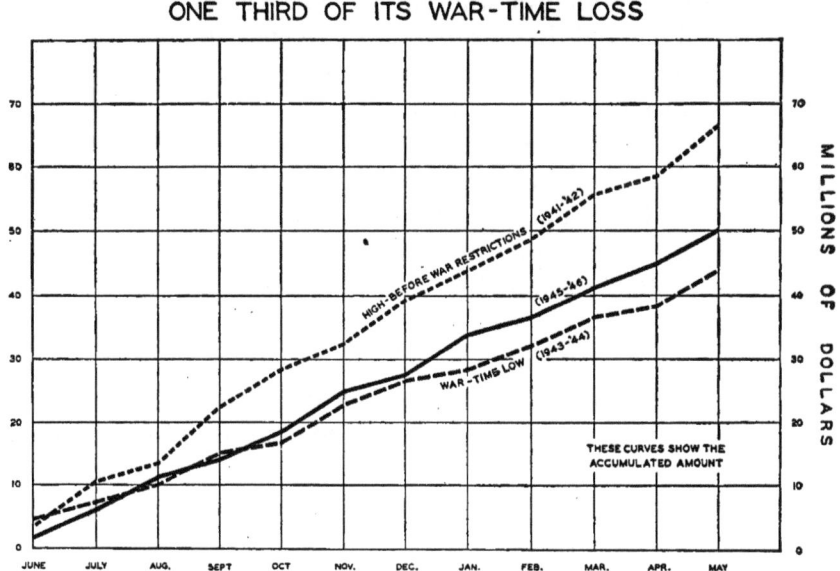

Fig. 12. Multiple-Line Graph

"when it is desired to show whether the rate of change of the dependent variable is increasing, constant, or decreasing, a logarithmic vertical scale should be used in conjunction with an arithmetic horizontal scale."[3]

7. Do not present more than three curves on the same graph unless they are similar in shape and clearly separated. (See Figure 12, page 201.)

8. When two or more curves appear in the same graph, distinguish them by using different types or different widths of lines. See Figure 12, page 201. Furthermore, clearly label each curve within the graph or designate it by a key in the legend.

In helping nontechnical audiences to visualize statistics for advertising purposes, or in reaching the general public with data on such popular topics as health, wealth, earnings, and so on, the graph takes the form of heavy bars or rectangular figures. The comparative sizes of such figures illustrate the growth and decline of the subject investigated. (See Figure 13, pages 204, 205.)

Even more striking is the picturization of some suggestive object. Thus, the Bell Telephone Company printed a series of progressively larger telephones showing the increase in telephone connections. A row of successively taller men will show the increase in a company's personnel, an insurance company's policyholders, or the number of students attending a college.

It should be noted that we may run into constructive falsehoods if we use a figure that is possible of misinterpretation. Thus, if we present two shares for comparison, the second twice the size of the first, the visual impression is that the value of the second is four times that of the first; the *area*, therefore, produces a false picture of the facts. The right to use figures in this way becomes, of course, an ethical question. In any case, the numerical data should be available somewhere near the graph, so that the careful and intelligent reader need not go astray.

A popular form of graph, which, nevertheless, is not the most accurate presentation of the facts, is the "pie" diagram. A circle is divided into segments representing the quantities to be studied. This form is widely used for showing proportional expenditures from income, the sources of government taxes, and similar data. (See Figure 14, page 206.)

---

[3] *Ibid.*, page 11.

Most persons are familiar with the shaded map. It is used to show the density of population, the comparative output or consumption of a commodity, the various "zones" in a modern city, or similar information. To give varying degrees of density or concentration, it is possible to use different shades of the same color, or to employ several styles of cross-hatching. Geographical distribution of data is also frequently shown by the use of "dot" maps in which each dot represents a given number of units.

The report writer should realize that tabular statistics are naturally more accurate than any method of charts that he can adopt. The chart, which is always based upon the data in a table, merely simplifies the facts and makes them graphic. Charts are obviously less significant than tables, therefore, to the reader who is making a thorough study of all aspects of the report. A good rule for the writer is to determine the wants of his reader and to use tables or charts accordingly.

Size of the graph. The size of the graph to be used in a report is determined by the form of the report. To accompany a typed report, the commercial size of cross-section paper may be found ready-made, with rulings of almost any desired unit. The usual form is a 6-by-9-inch plate, ruled on 8½-by-11-inch paper. Long sheets, or rolls, of typewriter-sheet width may also be obtained. These may be folded for binding with the report when a long graph, such as a profile, is required. Firms dealing in drawing supplies furnish standard rulings or will make up special sizes on demand.

Graphs which are to appear in a printed book may be drawn to any size and reduced photographically to the proper page size. In such reproductions, not only are the length and the width of the chart reduced, but the thickness of the lines composing the chart is correspondingly reduced. A fairly heavy line on a large chart will appear very thin and indistinct when very much reduced. Reduction to less than half of the normal size is not generally recommended unless care is taken to make important lines very heavy. It is desirable to have the coordinates lighter than the lines representing the information that the graph is intended to convey.

Organization charts. A special type of chart not based upon statistics is the "organization" chart, on which circles or rectangles (properly labeled) are drawn in such a relation to each other as to indicate the plan of organization of a business or corporation staff.

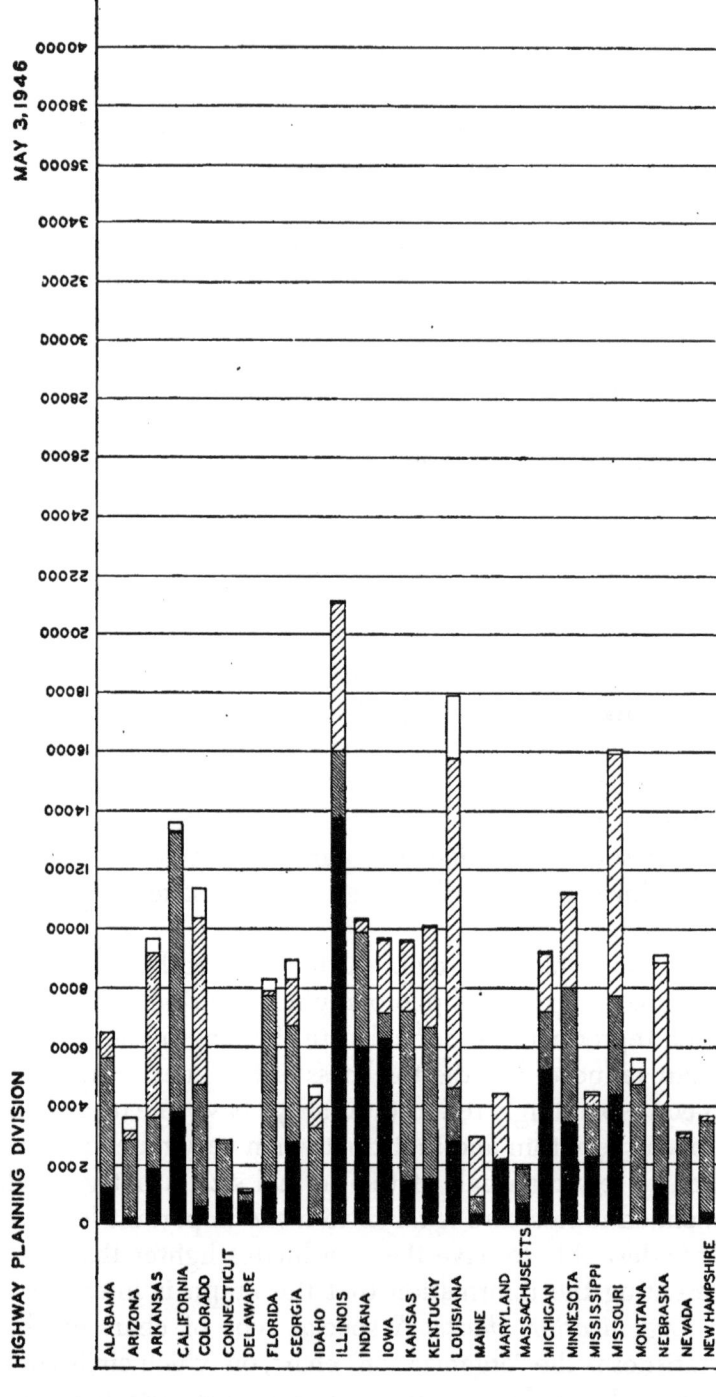

CHART SHOWING ROAD TYPES
ON STATE HIGHWAY SYSTEMS
COMPLETED AND UNDER CONSTRUCTION ON JANUARY 1,1945

HIGHWAY PLANNING DIVISION

MAY 3,1946

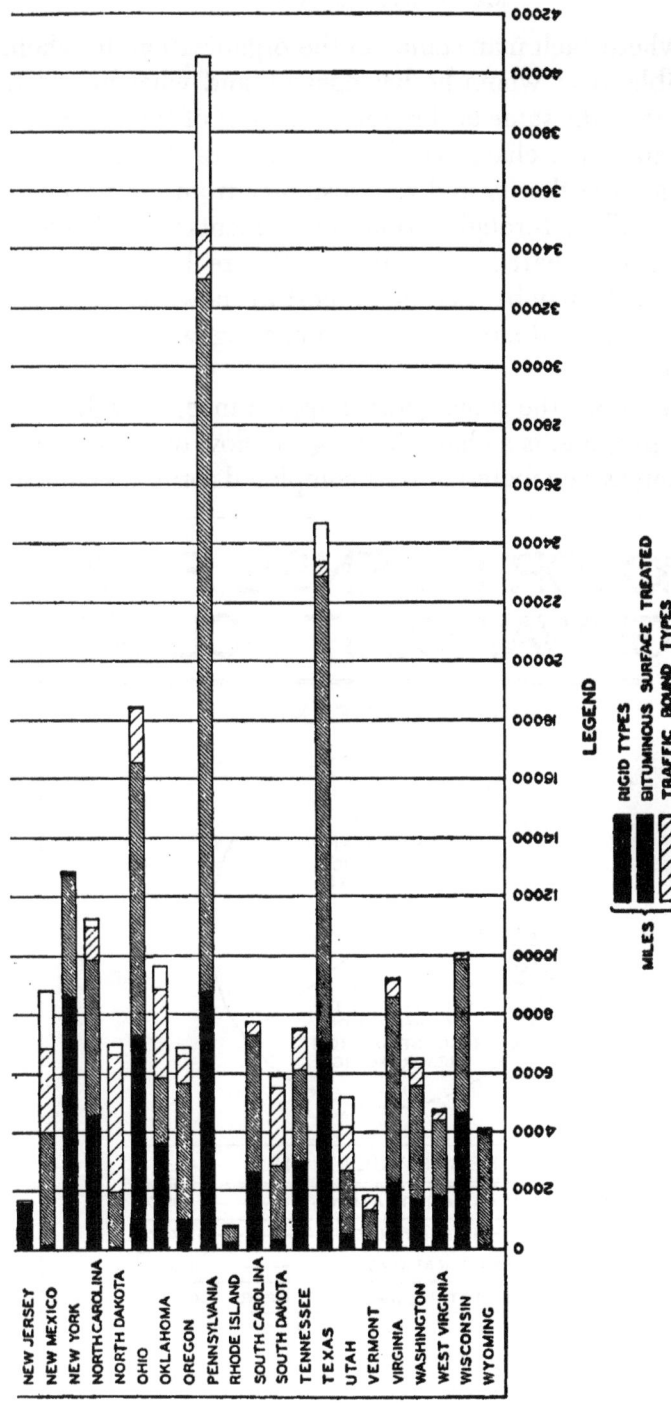

Fig. 13. Bar Chart

It shows where each man stands in the organization, to whom he is responsible, over whom he has control, and what his relations are to others in the same or different branches of the organization.

The organization chart may be so complete that it traces the entire range of authority and responsibility from the president of the company down through various departments to the lowest sub-foreman. Such a chart is illustrated in Figure 15.

Similar charts may be used in a report to show the organization of a field force conducting some engineering work, research, or other project.

Flow sheets. Of the same general appearance, though used for a different purpose, is a chart showing the flow of a product from its beginning as raw material to its completed form. Machines and

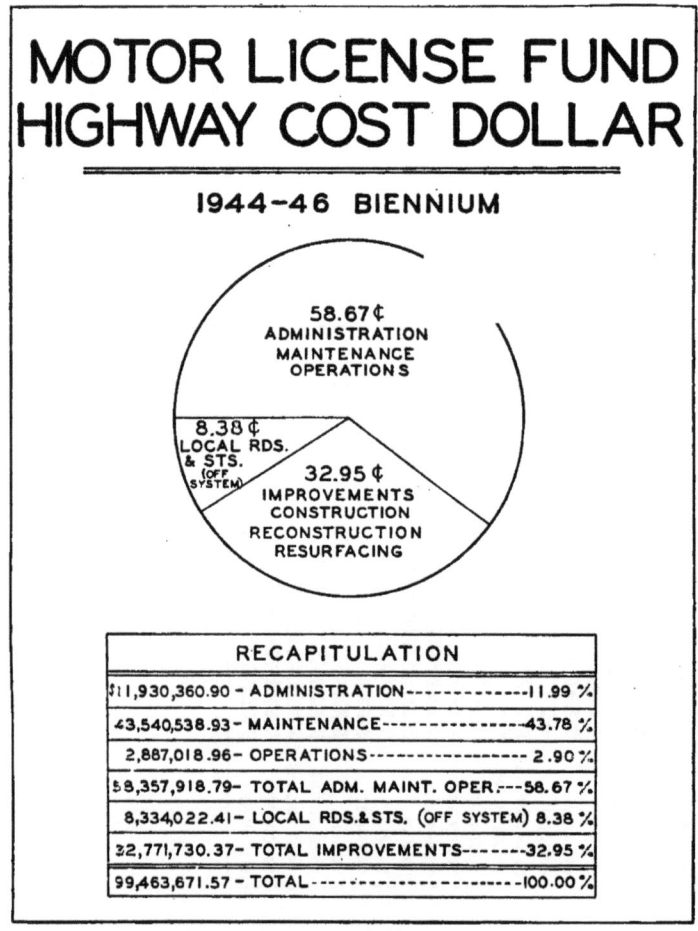

FIG. 14. Pie Chart

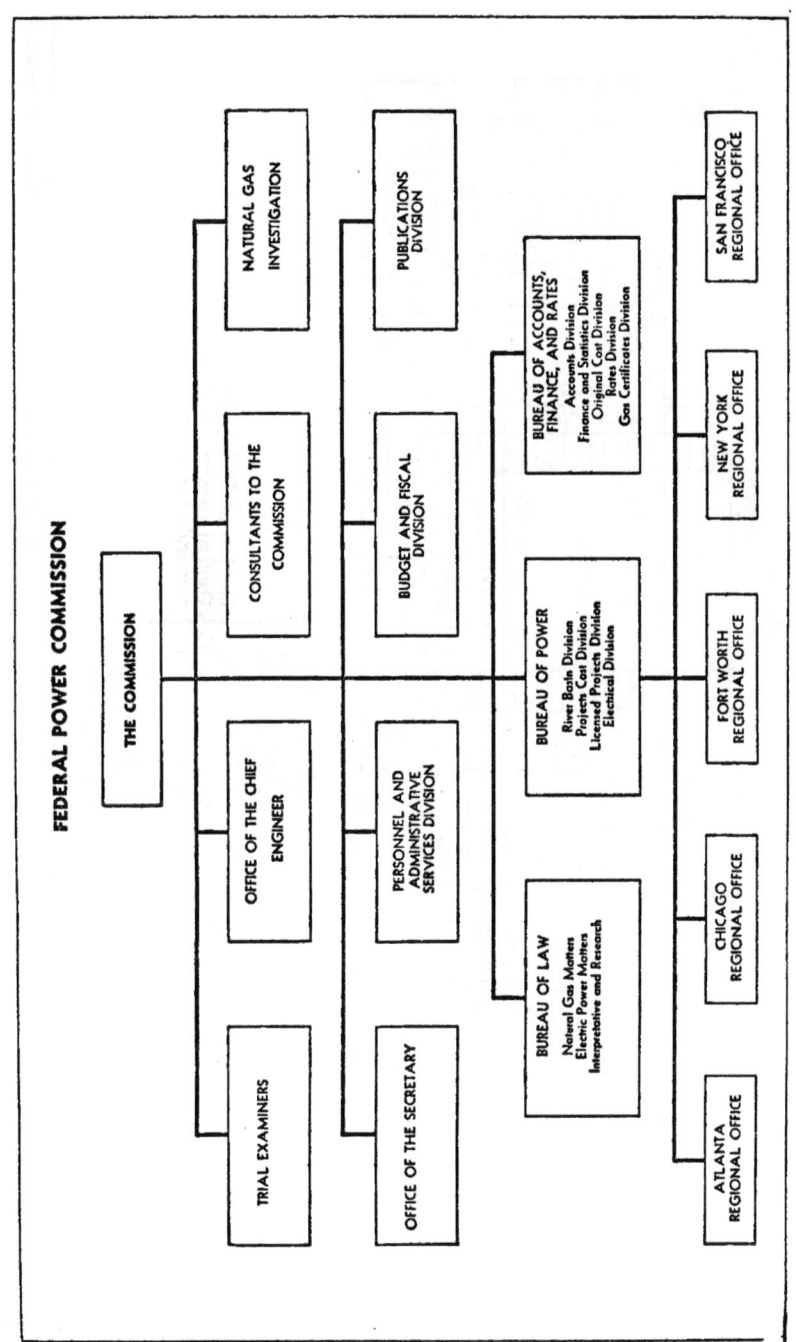

Fig. 15. Organization Chart

207

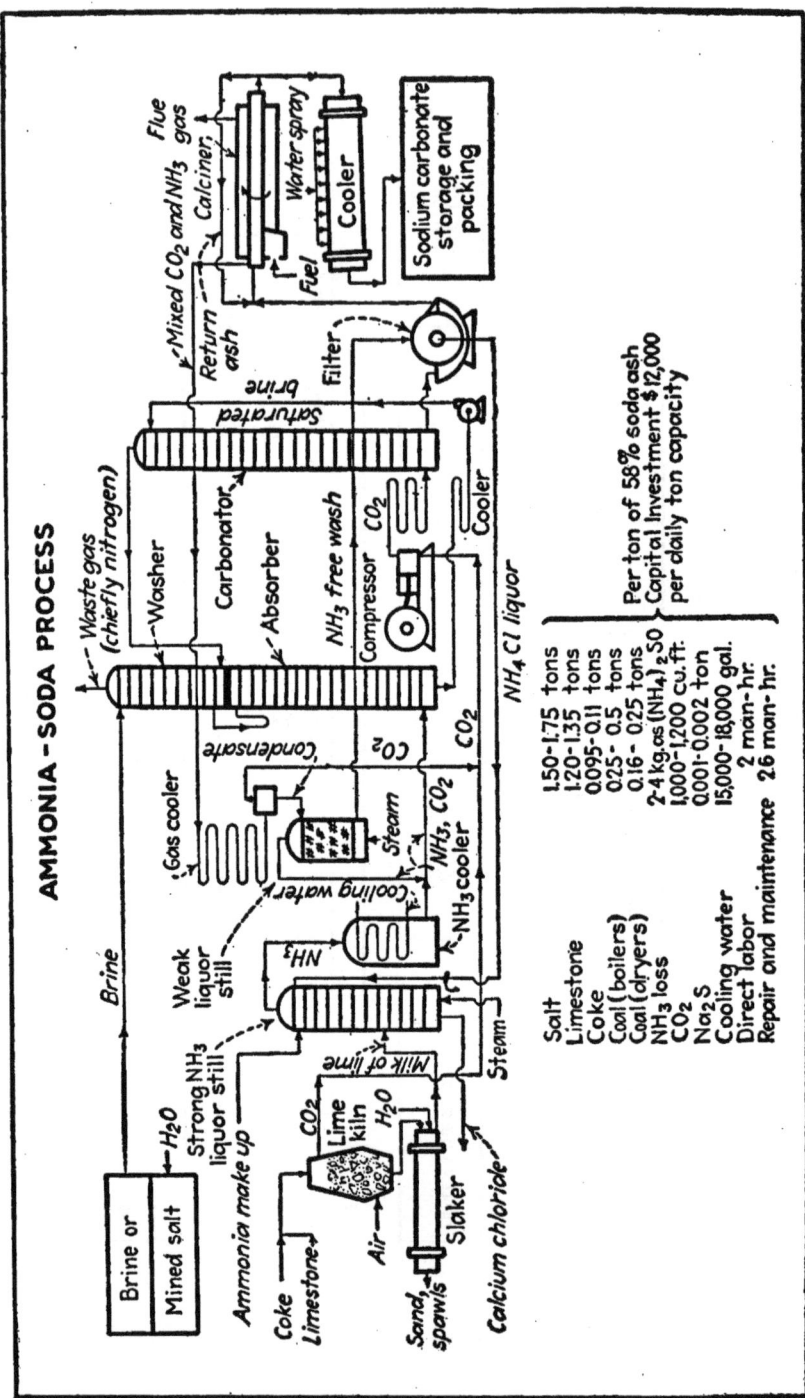

FIG. 16. Specimen Flow Sheet

Courtesy R. W. Mumford, American Potash & Chemical Corporation.

processes are shown conventionalized as rectangles or circles; these are joined by arrowheaded lines indicating the direction in which the product moves.

Position of mechanical aids. Photographs, tables, maps, and charts may appear either in the text or at the end of the report. Their position is determined by the reader's convenience. If they take up little space and are closely connected to the text, they should be placed at the spot nearest that part of the text which relates to them. For example, if a section of the report refers to "Fig. 8, page 11," it is naturally desirable to place Figure 8 as near as possible to the reference. On the other hand, if the mechanical elements are on heavier paper, or if they are folded, or if they occupy full pages, it is usually preferable to place them at the end of the report. If the reader knows exactly where he can find them, he can read the text rapidly and still find the charts and tables when he wants them. It is obvious that graphical material which is supplementary should always appear in the appendix.

The use of color. For reports that must be printed or otherwise reproduced in large numbers, the use of color is usually too expensive. Used judiciously, however, color presents certain kinds of data so vividly that the expense is justified. A glance at the graphic presentation frequently appearing in *Fortune Magazine* demonstrates the effectiveness of color applied to maps, charts, curves, and diagrams of all kinds. The use of color is entirely practical when only a few copies of a report are to be made.

We have already pointed out that colored stationery is sometimes used to identify intra-organization correspondence, and colored binders to classify types of reports. Colored tabs are sometimes used to index the major and minor sections of a report; for example, one company, to facilitate reference, always attaches a red tab to the page on which the report summary appears.

There is little doubt that color will become increasingly useful to the report writer. It will improve the appearance and the effectiveness of his report. But it should not be used, even in the student report, unless it is functional, unless it does the job better than would black and white.

Exercises

1. Prepare a table showing the victories, losses, and ties of the athletic teams of a college over a ten-year period.

2. From this table prepare a curve-line chart.

3. Prepare an organization chart for a student-government system or for a college administration.

4. Prepare a flow sheet of some plant in which you have worked or of which you have made an inspection trip.

SPECIMEN REPORTS

The reports, or excerpts from reports, presented in the following pages are intended for critical study. Although they are taken from reports in specialized fields, they are illustrative of general report-writing practices. They are not necessarily models; they should be examined for faults as well as virtues.

The student should also give particular attention to the specimen outlines or tables of contents appearing at the end of Chapter 6, since from them he can learn most about the basic organization of reports.

Though the following periodic report is entirely concerned with chemical engineering, it illustrates the variety of routine writing problems encountered by any engineer. Consider the report from the viewpoint of its intended readers—the plant manager, the director of research, the sales manager, the chief engineer, and so on. Could it have been better presented to save them more time in reading without jeopardizing its value as a record? Would an initial summary be helpful, and, if so, possible? Could the writing be more concise? (The original was 25 pages long.) Are sufficient details included to give the readers a satisfactory understanding of the work done? Can you think of any graphical devices that would have conserved time or space? Is the physical make-up entirely satisfactory?

INTEROFFICE CORRESPONDENCE*
Trona, California
March 9, 1948

To: Copy to:
  Manager's Office   Executive Committee
Attention: Messrs. Mumford
  Mr. A. A. Hoffman   Eason
Subject: Bridgeford
  Monthly Report
  Research and Development
  February 1948

I. PLANT PROBLEMS SECTION
(Problems directly connected with present
operations, minor changes, etc.)

1. Concentration Process
    (a) Study of Heater Corrosion

    _____[Signature]_____
    T. G. Bernhardi

    During the month, the specific rate of con-
densation (steam consumed per operating day per
degree working—temperature drop) showed some improvement over the values of recent months and
approached the peak values obtained last fall.

    (b) Salting of Heater Tubes

    There have been no new developments in con-
nection with this problem during February.

    (c) Liquor Losses from the Heater—Washout Routine

    No time for further sampling of the evapora-
tor heaters was available during the month because of work on the salt—trap classifier.

    (d) Salt—Trap Filter Behavior and Losses

    There are no new developments in connection
with this problem.

    (e) Clarification and Dilution of Concentrated
        Liquor

    The vapors from the third—effect pan of the
No. 3 evaporator unit were noted to undergo a

* Courtesy of the American Potash & Chemical Corporation.

[213]

large pressure drop between the entrance and exit of the entrainment separator. A measurement showed this loss to be equivalent to about one inch of mercury when the absolute pressure on the third-effect pan is 3 inches of mercury. A further study is being made of this.

2. Potash Plant

Considerable work was done this month in the preparation of a report on plant KCl production efficiency for the year 1947.

The study of potash dryer operation is discussed in connection with the development of coarse granular potash in a subsequent section of this report (see item II-7).

3. Borax Plant

(a) Crude Borax Process

A memorandum covering the proposed mother liquor No. 3 leach system was distributed during the month to interested parties. (See last Monthly Research & Development Report.) The Engineering Department has issued shop orders (Nos. 2066-7-8) to have temporary pipe and equipment changes made so that the system can be given a plant trial.

4. Boric Acid Plant

(a) Plant Operation

The production of coarse granular boric acid is discussed in a subsequent section of this report (see item II-3-b).

(b) Caking of Boric Acid

[Signature]
Hunter Nicholson

A quantity of air-classified boric acid, which had stood in a small bin for several months under conditions of moderate humidity for caking tests (see report for August 1947, et seq.) was returned to the main storage pile during the month. This material was slightly caked, but the lumps were soft enough to be broken easily between the fingers. This is additional confirmation for the theory that boric acid may be kept from caking if the atmospheric humidity is kept sufficiently high to prevent surface dehydration to metaboric acid.

5. Pyrobor Plant

No problems connected with the Pyrobor plant required...

6. Soda Products Plant

(a) Plant Operation

The routine compilation of data and...

7. General Plant Problems

(a) Paints, Concrete Preservation, etc.

[*Signature*]

Edward P. Pearson

The routine testing of paints was continued. A few...

(b) Solubility Work on Plant Liquors

No opportunity for continuing this work was found because...

(c) Outside Storages

No further problems regarding the use of outside...

(d) Miscellaneous

As usual, several miscellaneous plant problems and routine subjects of a minor nature were worked upon during the month.

II. PROCESS DEVELOPMENT SECTION

(Problems including possible new developments, major improvements in present processes, etc.)

1. Soda Products Process Modifications

[*Signature*]

L. G. Black

(a) Process Study

Additional data on the present process and proposed modifications were collected during the

month. These developments are discussed in the
following paragraphs under headings similar to
those used in previous reports.

(1) Sal Soda Cooler Capacity

The difficulties experienced with entrainment and salting below the liquor level in the
high–vacuum crystallizer continued, but no further changes were made in operation pending installation of the axial–flow discharge pump.

(2) Glauber Salt Filtrate Production

Experiments on the counter–current dissolu-
tion....

(3) Sal Soda Filter and Evaporator

No time was found available by this...

(4) Foam Removal

This subject is discussed under Lithium
Recovery...

(5) Primary NaCl Crystallizer

[(6), (7), (8), (9), (10) similarly]

2. Light Soda Ash

(a) Dehydration of Sodium Carbonate Hydrates

In line with suggestions from the Los Angeles
Sales Office, no further work was done on this
method of producing light soda ash pending completion of preliminary cost estimates by the
Engineering Department.

(b) Light Ash by Calcination of Trona

[Signature]	[Signature]
C. F. Ritchie	F. H. May

At the end of the month the experimental
equipment for pilot–plant–scale production of
light soda ash by this method was ready to run.
This equipment consists of a carbonating tank of
our own design fed with boiler–flue gas by a Roots
blower, which draws the flue gas from the old
boilers through a modification of the Blaw–Knox
scrubber. It was found that the Roots blower
has to be serviced with a small stream of water

which is subsequently removed in a standard centrifugal separator. Thus, with this hook–up the
flue gas is given two scrubbings prior to being
delivered in the carbonating tank. The object
of the process, as previously reported, is to
convert sodium carbonate or sodium carbonate
monhydrate into trona, which is then filtered off
and calcined to produce light soda ash.

3. Classification Problems

(a) Salt–Trap Salt

_____
      [*Signature*]

T. G. Bernhardi

The salt–trap classifier was operated inter-
mittently...

(b) Coarse Granular Boric Acid   [similarly]
(c) Separation of Potash and Borax by...
                         [similarly]

4. Evaporator Problems
                  [similarly]

5. Water–Treating Problems
                  [similarly]

6. Lithium Recovery

(a) Production

_____
      [*Signature*]

J. Phillips

The quantity of lithium concentrate in process of drying was increased during the month
when prolonged winds caused delays in sacking
material from the exposed solar drying trays.
Only 6.0 tons (dry basis) was sacked.

A shipment of 45.7 tons (dry basis) was made
to the Maywood Chemical Works on February 14,
leaving 5.6 tons in storage at the end of the
month. This shipment contained 6.55 percent moisture owing to the fact that this material was
sacked while still fairly wet. This was done in
order to speed up production and to reduce con-

tamination and loss of lithium concentrate by
wind.

Contamination of the product on the solar
drying trays has become a serious problem since
the start of the windy season. A batch of 82
sacks, recently produced, contained 7.96 percent of acid–insoluble material (mostly sand),
whereas representative production dried under
shelter contained 0.32 percent of acid–insoluble
material.

(b) Process Development

[Signature]	[Signature]
J. Phillips	L. G. Black

Work on the lithium material balance has been
confined to tests and calculations to determine
flow rates at relevant points pending completion
of the analyses of samples of the various plant
liquors and salts involved (see item IV–3).

As noted in previous reports, flotation of
lithium–bearing insolubles from various plant
liquors and from the sewer effluent has met with
partial success. However, in these tests the recovery and concentration both left much to be
desired. In the type of equipment used, it was
noted that a good froth could be generated, but
that the coarse bubbles did not float the lithium–bearing solids selectively. Past experience
in removing suspended matter from burkeite liquor
indicated that finely divided particles could be
trapped on air bubbles by evacuating dissolved
air from the solution. It is planned to investigate this general procedure for the flotation of
lithium phosphate by first dissolving air in the
solution under pressure, then releasing the pressure and collecting the froth.

(c) Lithium Drying Tests   [similarly]

7. Development of New Potash Products

(a) Coarse Granular Muriate

(1) Agglomeration Process

[Signature]

The potash dryers were available for only one muriate agglomeration test during the month. In this test so much difficulty was experienced in controlling the feed to the dryer that little additional information was obtained on the agglomerating characteristics of wet centrifugal cake. However, the crystal size of the wet potash samples taken during this run was considerably smaller than of those obtained previously, which would seem to indicate different conditions of crystal growth in the potash coolers. Since the conditions in the potash plant were reported as "normal" during this period, further study of the process will be made in an effort to determine the factors controlling crystal size.

The effect of humidity upon various muriate samples was further investigated in an effort to set up a comparison of stability to atmospheric changes for the commercial products. It was found that samples of competitive muriate of potash (French, German, and domestic) deliquesce seriously when subjected to a humidity of from 75 to 80 percent. Samples of granular muriate prepared from our regular product by agglomerating and heat-treating, as described in previous reports, were little affected by this humidity.

> (2) Aghi Screening   [similarly]

(b) <u>Potassium Sulphate</u>   [similarly]

(c) <u>Potassium Pentaborate</u>   [similarly]

8. <u>Bromine Recovery and Conversion</u>   [similarly]

III. LAKE SECTION

1. <u>Plant Brine Supply</u>   [similarly]

2. <u>Study of Deposit</u>

(a) <u>Test Holes</u>

Nothing further to report.

(b) <u>Sewage Disposal</u>

There is nothing further to report on this subject at present.

3. <u>Removal of Glauber Salt from Searles Lake Brine</u>

No work was done on this problem this month.

4. Competitor's Wells   [similarly]

IV. CHEMICAL AND ANALYTICAL SECTION

1. Solubility Work

Except for some high-temperature determinations...

2. Tungsten

The suggested process under investigation as a possible means of tungsten recovery follows:...

3. Lithium Analysis

[Signature]
Norman Gunderson

The densitometer for use with the previously constructed spectograph has been completed and found to give fairly good results. As soon as the most satisfactory technique has been worked out and the limits of accuracy have been determined, the apparatus will be used in the analysis of plant liquors in connection with the further development of lithium recovery.

4. Flotation Separation of Borax-KCl Mixtures

[similarly]

5. Deferred Items

(a), (b), etc.   [similarly]

6. Miscellaneous   [similarly]

V. PATENT SECTION

[Signature]
H. T. Nies

1. United States Applications

(a) Our File 48 – Methods of Producing Caustic Borate Products

U. S. Patent No. 2,146,083 was issued to us on February 7 on this application. This patent covers a process not now being used, but protects us in case of future developments involving the

[220]

manufacture of caustic borates by fusion methods.

(b), (c), etc.   [similarly]

2. New Applications

An application has been prepared and submitted to our attorneys covering the manufacture of light soda ash by first forming trona and then calcining it without disruption of the crystals.

Time was also spent during the month on study of the following subjects to determine whether patent applications should be filed:

(a), (b), etc.   [similarly]

The following reports are representative of those which were submitted regularly to the General Manager of the Tennessee Valley Authority by the Department of Regional Studies. Note that the pattern of the first report is repeated in the second. Should these reports be called "progress" reports?

Examine the system of heads and subheads. Are they clearly distinguishable?

Gordon R. Clapp, General Manager
Malcolm J. Rand, Sr., Administrative Assistant
Regional Studies
February 13, 1941

PROGRESS REPORT—DEPARTMENT OF REGIONAL STUDIES—
JANUARY 1941

NAVIGATION, FLOOD CONTROL, AND POWER

KENTUCKY PROJECT

Preservation of Prehistoric Materials

Archaeological operations in the Tennessee
portion of the reservoir continue at the Bridges'
farm. Two additional sites have been discovered on
this property, and will be excavated before the
field crews move. Although work at CCC Camp TVA
P-1 was greatly curtailed by a series of epidemics
among the enrollees, the field crews were able to
further develop the stockade pattern unearthed in
December.

CHICKAMAUGA PROJECT

Color schemes for the exterior and interior
painting of the visitors' building were determined,
and other details of treatment and equipment were
field-checked. Planting and general site improvement now in progress in the vicinity of the dam and
at the malaria base were also reviewed in the field.

WATTS BAR PROJECT

Preliminary Investigations

A general plan was completed and submitted to
the Design Department showing the layout of service
roads, parking areas, and general site improvement
in the vicinity of the dam and steam plant.

Preservation of Prehistoric Materials

A new archaeological excavation technique has resulted in the complete excavation of the burial mound on the Wilson farm in Roane County in about 17 working days. It is believed that the last occupational level is now being worked out on the DeArmond site.

Archaeological excavation on the Hampton farm in Rhea County has been broadened to develop all the stockade pattern about the village site under exploration.

FORT LOUDOUN PROJECT

Design

A field trip was made with representatives of the Reservoir Property Management Department for checking work in progress on facilities being provided for visitors. The proposed location of an REA power line crossing the TVA reservation was also checked in the field.

HIWASSEE PROJECT

Contacts were maintained with interested departments concerning plans for planting and site improvement; also recommendations for disposition of houses in the village and the location of the thirty that are to be retained.

CHEROKEE PROJECT

General Design

Reconnoissance was made of proposed sites for visitor accommodations, boat dock, and other recreation features near the dam, and detailed studies were prepared as a basis for accurate estimates of cost for the design of these developments. Field contact was continued with the Highway Division and other departments, preliminary studies being prepared showing the possible recreational use of the shoreline in the vicinity of the proposed highway relocations.

RELATED PROPERTY OPERATIONS

OPERATION OF RESERVOIR LANDS

Staff assistance to the Department of Reservoir Property Management included a general review of the development and operation of boat dock concessions in the various reservoir areas.

The proposed extension of the license agreement between Hamilton County and the concessionaire at Soddy Marine Park was reviewed and commented upon after conferences with representatives of the Tennessee State Planning Commission and Department of Conservation.

A draft of a proposed general enabling act authorizing the establishment of county park commissions and the development, maintenance, and operation of county park systems, prepared by the Tennessee State Planning Commission, was reviewed at their request.

Maps were prepared to show reservoir—margin lands considered surplus from the standpoint of recreation, and work was begun on the supporting statements, as well as a statement of criteria for permanent ownership of reservoir lands for purposes of protecting the recreation resource.

Compilation of data in connection with the study for the measurement of results from the recreational program included tabulation of attendance records for Wilson, Wheeler, and Pickwick parks and analysis of financial statements of TVA boat dock and other commercial concessions on Wheeler, Guntersville, and Norris lakes, for the purpose of establishing criteria for determining license rates.

In accordance with policies outlined in the letter of understanding between the two departments, field technicians who had been assigned by the Department of Regional Studies to assist Area Managers were transferred to the Department of Reservoir Property Management on January 1, 1941.

Design of Grounds and Buildings

Early in January the Board approved authorizations for the development of ten summer cabin designs as an experimental demonstration project to test out demountable methods of house construction through the use of a cellized type of prefabrication. The units for these cabins are to be prefabricated at a shop set up by the C&M Division for this purpose at Muscle Shoals and are to be erected at Pickwick Park. By the end of the month, the equipping of this shop was well under way, and architectural, plumbing, and electrical working drawings for the cabins were completed. Also, preliminary plot plans were completed and the location of these cabins was field-staked. A preliminary layout of water distribution and sanitary sewer systems was completed.

This demountable principle is being applied to designs for house types being developed in connection with the defense housing project in the Muscle Shoals area. In addition, the Kentucky type AA house is being used as the basis for a fourth house type, which, in order to expedite construction during the initial stages of the project, will be built in the conventional manner. At the same time, preliminary plans have been completed for the general layout of streets and locations, sewer and water lines, for approximately 250 houses. These plans were prepared as a basis for estimating the cost of these improvements.

A revised preliminary sketch has been prepared for the proposed transportation....

DEVELOPMENT OF RECREATIONAL FACILITIES IN RESERVOIR AREAS

Conferences were held.........................

....

Design of Grounds and Buildings

The technical services of the department in connection with the development of..................

DEVELOPMENT ACTIVITIES

GENERAL STUDIES AND SURVEYS

Final adjustments........

Reports

No reports were released by the department during the month.

———————

Gordon R. Clapp, General Manager
Malcolm J. Rand, Sr., Administrative Assistant
Regional Studies
March 12, 1941

PROGRESS REPORT—DEPARTMENT OF REGIONAL STUDIES—
FEBRUARY 1941

NAVIGATION, FLOOD CONTROL, AND POWER

KENTUCKY PROJECT

Preservation of Prehistoric Materials

One small archaeological mound in Benton County, Tenn., was completely excavated during the month. No burials or special features were found, but 208 field specimens, evidencing aboriginal trade from a considerable distance, were recovered. About 400 feet of test trench and 8,000 square feet of excavation have been completed at another site in Benton County.

Detailed archaeological reconnoissance of the Kentucky portion of the reservoir was begun during the month.

CHICKAMAUGA PROJECT

Construction progress was reviewed and the electrical installations inspected in the visitors' and harbor master's buildings in the vicinity of the dam, and at the malaria control base at King's Point.

WATTS BAR PROJECT

Preliminary Investigations

Preliminary plans for site improvement in areas adjacent to the steam plant were completed and submitted to the Design Department. Cost estimates and specifications for planting and soil preparation, called for by this plan, are nearing completion.

Preservation of Prehistoric Materials

Excavations which have been proceeding in Roane County have been completed at two locations, and excavation of one mound at a third site is under way. At one of the two sites excavated in Rhea County during the month, a new architectural type was uncovered—a semisubterranean pit house with a bench around three-fourths of the interior and a platform extending out into the center of the building from the fourth side. Work has commenced at two additional sites.

[The remaining headings of this report are exactly the same as those in the January report.]

Does the following boiler-inspection report provide enough detail for future reference? Could the format be improved? Could any of the sentences be written more concisely?

What improvement could you make in organization and layout for the data items listed on the first page?

Would there be any advantage in placing the conclusions and recommendations first?

Report No. 858   October 4, 1947

JOB NAME: X Baking Company

LOCATION: Philadelphia, Pennsylvania
PLANT:
CONTRACT NO: 6466
EQUIPMENT--NO & TYPE:

BOILER 2 $\frac{14-9}{2-36}$ - 18' -160#

SUPHTR
MILL
STOKER
BURNER - 4 Peabody O. B.
MISC. --
EXPECTED PERFORMANCE--MAX. LOAD:
FUEL - Oil
STEAM LB/HR - 264 H. P. (ea.)
STEAM PRESS - 15#
STEAM TEMP - Sat.
EXCESS AIR -
APPROX. DATE JOB WENT INTO SERVICE:
1908
REQUEST FOR SERVICE DEPT. ACTION:
OR1GIN - Customer
REASON - Inspection (tube failure)

ENGR.: S. L. Morse & Asst.
DATE:
ARRIVAL OF ENGR. - 10-3-47
DEPARTURE OF ENGR. - 10-3-47
EXPECT COMPLETE JOB - Complete
SERVICE MAN--DAYS ON JOB - TOTAL
ENDING SATURDAY, 10-4-47: 1
. . . .

    This job was visited in response to a tele-
phone request from Mr. A. B. Doe, Chief Engineer.
He desired the services of an engineer to check over
this installation and to recommend changes to place
the boilers in satisfactory operating condition.
    Discussion with Mr. Doe and inspection of one
idle boiler revealed the following:

1. Some years ago someone decided to eliminate feeding of water to both steam drums, and a new connection was provided to one drum only, through the hole bumped for a water–column connection. On each boiler this feed was to the drum not equipped with the water column.

2. The internal feed pipe and dry pipes have been removed.

3. Six tubes have been renewed in the bottom row, on the side away from the feed connection. These tubes were blistered and bowed upward, and all showed signs of color, from overheating. Several tubes had failed, failures taking the form of a circumferential split in the middle of each blister.

4. Blistered tubes contained a hard scale, having the appearance of calcium carbonate, and possibly some silica, about 3/8 in. thick on the bottom of the tubes. These tubes also showed some signs of "ghost" marking along the tube centerline. The boiler inspected had already been turbined, but the customer advised that the side on which feedwater is introduced is usually clean, with scale forming toward the bottom of the other section of the boiler.

5. The tubes that were bowed upward, in addition to the six renewed in the bottom row, were the other tube in this row, in this section of the boiler, and the seven tubes immediately above these.

6. Make–up is about 50 per cent, which passes through a Non–Chem water conditioner which consists of a horizontal cylinder reportedly filled with glass or copper balls.

From this information the following conclusions are drawn

1. The immediate cause of tube failures and bowing is scale deposit in the tubes.

2. The reason for localized scale deposit reported by the customer is a result of poor circulation from feeding water to only one drum. Under such an arrangement, water for the section of boiler under the other drum can be obtained only through the common mud drum.

The following recommendations were made:

1. Original feedwater connections should be installed so that water is fed to both drums of each boiler, through internal feed pipes. We advised that we would furnish a sketch showing this pipe.

2. The boiler should be equipped with cross-over downtake circulators. These were found on the job, having been purchased several years ago, but not installed. The customer has retained the services of our Erection Department to install these in both boilers.

3. Water of zero hardness, free of scale-forming properties, should be fed to the boilers. We advised that we had had no previous experience with the type of water conditioner they were using, but the presence of scale in the boiler indicated that it was not accomplishing its purpose, since, regardless of the method of water feed, there should be no scale present anywhere in the boiler. We suggested that water from the conditioner be checked for a period, and if satisfactory results were not obtained, a more conventional method of treatment be resorted to, as could be recommended by any reliable feedwater consultant.

Mr. Doe requested confirmation of our recommendations. Service work is complete.

The Introduction, the Summary, and opening paragraphs of an Aluminum Company of America report follow.

How would you classify it—"progress report"? "examination report"? It is written to the Sales Manager; what use is apparently to be made of it?

How well does the style satisfy demands for "objectivity" and "restraint"? Do the probable uses of the report affect the style?

Aluminum Company of America
Pittsburgh, Pa.

REPORT TO: MR. GEORGE J. STANLEY, V.P. &
         SALES MANAGER

RE: ALUMETTE – EXPERIMENTAL ALUMINUM HULL

After Five Years' Exposure

Ninth Inspection – May 13–14, 1941.
Exposure Since Last Inspection – 13 months
Total Exposure – 5 years, 4 months

INTRODUCTION – The inspection herein reported
marks a milestone in ALUMETTE's service test, which
now amounts to something over five years: Consequently, we are issuing this report bound separately
and in such form that the effect of the five years'
immersion may be readily seen without reference to
prior reports.

The summary, pages 1 to 4, together with the
photographs, presents a good general picture of
ALUMETTE's excellent resistance to the action of sea
water and marine growth.

J. O. Chesley

J. O. CHESLEY

I. SUMMARY – Since January 14, 1936, when ALUMETTE
was first placed in the water at Newport News, Virginia, this experimental hull has been under test
continuously except for brief periods of inspection
and reconditioning. These periods have varied from
1 day to 2 weeks, and altogether total less than 75
days. Thus, the net exposure life of the test hull
is well over five years. It is generally in excellent condition, some areas showing slight to moderate attack.

Having long since performed its initial duty
of proving the adaptability of modern aluminum
alloys to standard shipbuilding practices, ALUMETTE
has now undertaken the task of demonstrating what
life may be expected of aluminum hulls and how they
may be best maintained In this phase of her service she has incidentally become not only the oldest,
but also one of the most "realistic" of aluminum
specimens subject to complete or alternate immersion
in sea water in this country. As such, she effectively supplements the extensive corrosion test program of the Aluminum Research Laboratories by providing an important source of information on the
behavior of aluminum alloys under semi-service conditions at sea.

The following items of information have been
gained from observation of ALUMETTE over the past
five years:

1. Wrought and cast alloys of the aluminum-
magnesium type are entirely suitable for the construction of ships' hulls, both from the standpoint
of fabrication and from the standpoint of resistance
to attack by sea water.

2. Aluminum-magnesium alloys are not affected
by any known type of marine growth, although all
types adhere readily and firmly to surfaces which
have not been protected by anti-fouling paint.

3. Alloys of the type used in ALUMETTE afford
sufficient resistance to attack by sea water, even
when unpainted, to insure the integrity of a hull
for periods far in excess of the usual time between
repainting. (The normal period between dockings for
ships is nine months. Longer periods are occasionally encountered, but are avoided whenever possible
because of excessive fouling of the underbody.)

4. Aluminum hulls must be carefully guarded against electrolytic attack due to mooring with steel cables and to use of metallic pipes or electric cables leading to other vessels or to shore connections.

5. Electrolytic attack due to the presence of indispensable dissimilar metal parts on an aluminum hull can be prevented by proper insulation of the parts, or by the use of protective zincs. A combination of both is preferable.

6. About 90% of the underwater area and all of the topside, including the waterline area, is entirely free from evidence of corrosive attack.

7. Attack which had started on underwater areas (due to electrolytic effect of original steel mooring cable or uninsulated dissimilar metal parts) has been arrested completely by cleaning and painting.

8. The best paint schedule now known for protection of underwater surfaces of aluminum consists of one coat of Zinc Chromate Primer followed by an effective antifouling paint. Intermediate or so called "anti-corrosive" coats are neither necessary nor desirable.

9. No appreciable difference in effectiveness has been observed between the Formula X antifouling paint and Suydam's No. 5043. Both are effective for about four months at Newport News. Each appears to accelerate, very slightly, the normal attack on adjacent unpainted aluminum areas.

10. The best adherence of priming paint on underwater surfaces has been on areas which had been sand-blasted. The next best adherence has been

on areas cleaned by chemical cleaners such as De-oxidine.

11. Aluminum alloy (B-214) valves with slow-rusting steel (Allegheny No. 33) working parts appear to be satisfactory for salt water service.

12. Teak deck planking, laid on heavy paper impregnated with Stockholm pitch and shellac, caulked with cotton and oakum and paved with Alumi-lastic, is apparently satisfactory for weather decks on aluminum hulls.

13. Alumilite coated 17S-T lag screws used for securing teak deck planking were unaffected after five years.

II. NINTH INSPECTION – May 13th, 1941

1. GENERAL CONDITION – ALUMETTE has undergone no unusual experience since the last previous inspection, April 3, 1940. Due to the expansion of facilities at Newport News, it has been necessary to change her mooring from the south side of Pier 1 to the north side of the same pier, near the shore end. Although this is a more sheltered position, the water is just as salt and just as full of marine organisms as it is in the former location.

In view of the fact that the hull was more than five years old at the time of this inspection, considerable interest in its condition was exhibited by the Bureau of Ships, U.S. Coast Guard, and Bureau of Standards, all of which sent representatives. In addition, representatives of the Newport News Shipbuilding & Dry Dock Company and of the Supervisor of Shipbuilding's Office, Newport News, were present. The following................

The following Johns-Manville report discusses an inspection or "survey." For what readers does it seem to be intended? Does it fit the readers' interests and background?

Are headings and subheadings clear?

Can readers get the essentials quickly?

Study matters of style: sentences, abbreviations and signs, figures, and so forth.

ENGINEERING REPORT

Subject

_____CORPORATION

_____CORPORATION

INSULATION SURVEY

Prepared for

_____CORPORATION

A JOHNS-MANVILLE SERVICE TO INDUSTRY

ENGINEERING REPORT

Subject   <u>Insulation Survey</u>

Requested by _____Corporation

The inspection at _____ was made as a
result of a request from _____ company
for our recommendations as to replacing insulation
on various towers that had given trouble. A number
of towers and vessels had been insulated in 1943 and
1944 with #450 Cement, asbestos—Portland cement,
chicken wire and Insulkote. (This material had not
been applied by Johns—Manville.) After a period of
about two years, the chicken wire had deteriorated
to the point where the Insulkote finish and in some
cases the cement started to fall off. This disclosed evidence of considerable moisture in the
insulation, which, in addition to causing failure
of the chicken wire, caused considerable corrosion of the vessels. Attempts were made to repair
some of these vessels with not too good success, and
this, together with the corrosion of the vessels,
indicated the necessity for new insulation which
would stay in place and prevent any further vessel
corrosion.

Mr. _____ recognizes this condition as resulting from the moderate operating temperatures in
these vessels and that such temperatures require an
insulation specification, specifically designed to
meet the condition.

     Persons Interviewed:
       _____, Chief Engineer
       _____, Insulation Superintendent

This report is submitted as a Johns-Manville service to industry. It is based on the most recent and
accurate data available and represents our best estimate of performance. However, due to factors beyond our control, responsibility for performance is not assumed. This report consists of the number of
pages given below.

JOHNS-MANVILLE

DATE March 17, 1947 REPORT NO. GH—1021 NO. OF PAGES 8

LOCATION   22 East 40th Street, New York, N. Y.

APPROVED   G. E. Grimshaw, Mgr., Ind. Ins. Dept.

Vessels Inspected

Pentane Isomerization Tower
Approximate Size – 10' diameter x 120' high
Operating Temperature – Approximately 150F
bottom to 100F top

Insulation
Blocks of laminated indented asbestos paper, galvanized steel bands (support angles every 9'),
mineral wool cement and asbestos cement, galvanized
chicken wire, and mastic.

Stabilizer Reflux Drums
Approximate Size – 6' diameter x 18' long
Operating Temperature – Approximately 120F

Insulation
Magnesia Blocks secured with heavy (approximately
#10) wire, asbestos cement, galvanized chicken wire,
and Insulkote.

Isobutane (Alkylation unit)
Approximate Size – 12' diameter x 80' high
Operating Temperature – Approximately 175F
to 130F top

Insulation
2" total thickness of #450 cement plus asbestos and
asbestos-Portland cement leveling coat finished with
galvanized chicken wire and Insulkote. (Support
angles every approximate 12'.)

Catalyst Storage Towers (Catalytic Unit)
Approximate Size – 25' diameter x 30' high
Operating Temperature – Variable from am-
bient to 750F

Insulation
#450 Cement, asbestos, asbestos-Portland cement
(support angles every approximate 12'), galvanized
chicken wire, and Insulkote.

[241]

The Pentane Isomerization Tower was insulated and put into service in August 1944, operating until August of 1945, when it was shut down due to the ending of the war. As this tower is in a government-owned unit, it is questionable when, if ever, the unit will be operated again; however, the condition of the insulation is of interest.

About six months after the tower was shut down, patches of mastic and chicken wire started loosening and falling off, followed by areas of the laminated asbestos paper. At the time of our examination, practically all of the insulation had fallen off. This was quite evidently a result of corrosion of the metal in the insulation, which was accelerated once the vessel was shut down. The vessel itself showed considerable corrosion on the surface.

The two stabilizer reflux drums were insulated with Magnesia Blocks, etc., in 1940. Four months prior to our inspection, the chicken wire under the Insulkote had corroded to the point where repair was necessary. This repair consisted of new chicken wire and Insulkote applied over the original Insulkote, and the examination showed the new chicken wire to be rusting.

A patch cut from the side of one vessel disclosed the shell to be fairly well rusted, but no scaling was evident. The original wire securing the blocks was rusted but still fairly sound. Another patch cut from the bottom of the vessel showed the same degree of rusting with some fine scaling. The Magnesia Blocks on the bottom only were slightly damp. The Insulkote seemed to be well sealed around the connections and the dampness in the Magnesia Blocks could have been due to shutdown. This apparently occurs five days out of every 60 days, and every 8 months there is a 10-days to two-weeks shutdown. The examination of these drums and subsequent repair resulted from the previous examination of some heat exchangers (2' diameter x 13' long) operating at

the same temperature and also insulated with Magnesia Blocks, cement, chicken wire, and Insulkote.
The insulation on these exchangers had been in service 8 to 9 years, and the shells showed considerable
corrosion and rather bad pitting.

The unit including these vessels is near a large
cooling tower which throws off quite a bit of mist.
In the wintertime, the wind direction quite often
is such that it carries the mist over this unit.
In the summertime, prevailing winds generally carry
the moisture away from the unit. There was fair
evidence of corrosion on exposed metal, which indicates that any insulation on moderate-temperature
vessels which are not adequately sealed should be
subject to considerable moisture penetration.

Small towers in this unit finished with chicken wire
and Insulkote gave evidence of deterioration of the
chicken wire.

The insulation on the Isobutane towers was applied
in July 1943. After two years, the finish and
cement began falling off, and a temporary repair
consisting of new #450 cement applied, where necessary, followed by new chicken wire and Insulkote
over the whole vessel. #16-gauge chicken wire was
intended for the whole vessel; however, there was
only sufficient material of this gauge available for
the top half of the vessel. Regular chicken wire
was used for the remainder.

The new finish subsequently tended to slip and
bulge, and belly bands, consisting of 2/#12 wire
twisted together, were added. In addition, further
patching of the Insulkote was required.

A patch cut from about 15' up on one tower showed
the new chicken wire to be well rusted. The vessel
shell was well rusted, with patches of heavy seals.
We were quite surprised to find the #450 cement
quite dry. This was somewhat puzzling, as normally
under such conditions the insulation has been found
to be wet to damp.

There were two catalyst storage towers which were insulated in the Spring of 1944. Again, as in the case of the Isobutane towers, after two years the finish started to fall, and one was repaired with new chicken wire and Insulkote. The repair of the second had been held up pending a decision on some different specification for complete reinsulation. At the time, the insulation had fallen completely from the top third of the vessel.

These storage towers are normally at ambient temperature except occasionally when a small amount of catalyst may be discharged into them, which then raises the temperature somewhat. Otherwise, it is only during the periodic shutdown of the catalytic cracking unit that they are filled with catalyst at about 750F.

As a result of the corrosion experienced on these vessels, this company is going to institute a plant-wide inspection of vessels in order to determine what, if any, vessels are corroding and, if so, the cause of this corrosion.

These people are looking for help in the way of new insulation specifications plus any other measures which may be necessary to avoid corrosion of the external surface of vessel shells. This applies particularly to vessels in the operating range of 50F to 200F. They, incidentally, consider insulation in this temperature range primarily from the standpoint of processing control rather than heat saving.

It is of interest to learn that mineral wool blankets were outlawed in this plant years ago.

CONCLUSION:

1. Reasons for Failure of Insulation

It is quite evident that the corrosion of the vessel shells and the failure of the Insulkote finish over the insulation was due to the presence of water in the insulation. This water could have and probably did have three sources.

One was the water used in sizing #450 and asbestos-Portland cement. If these cements are not thoroughly dried out before the Insulkote is applied, our experience indicates that it had little chance thereafter to get out.

The second source was rain water entering through any opening between the Insulkote and any manheads or pipe connections, etc., or through any cracks in the Insulkote. While there was no evidence of large openings in the weather finish, there were fair-sized openings in a number of instances.

The third source was water vapor in the air entering through any openings in the weather finish and condensing against the vessel shells during shutdown.

Our experience indicates that, in the case of vessels operating at moderate temperatures (100 to 300F), water getting into the insulation tends to be driven outward. However, the temperature head is not sufficient to drive it readily through the Insulkote, in which case it tends to stay within the insulation back of the Insulkote, and corrosion of metal is the result.

It, therefore, appears necessary to use a specification which includes an insulating material which does not require water for its application, and a weather finish which includes means for preventing the entry of rain water but at the same time allows easy egress of water vapor in the event that water accidentally enters the insulation. A weather-finish construction which would provide an air space between the insulation and the finish would appear to have considerable advantage. In addition to the insulation specification as indicated, it appears necessary to properly protect the vessel shells against corrosion.

In accordance with the above, the following specification is suggested:

2. Specification – (Vertical Vessels 72" or more in diameter)

Preparation of Vessel

Angles supporting rings shall be welded to the vessel every 7'6". To these rings angle clips shall be bolted approximately every 2 or 4', for the attachment of Asbestocite weather finish. The vessel shall be cleaned and painted with corrosion- and heat-resisting paint.

Insulation

On the side walls apply J-M 85% Magnesia Blocks 6" x 36" by banding every 12" with 3/4" x 0.020 stainless-steel bands. On the top of the vessel apply 1/2" greater thickness of blocks than on the side. These blocks shall be secured with stainless steel bands in turn secured with the top angle supporting ring. Point large openings only between blox with hard finish Asbestos Cement.

Weather Finish

On side walls apply 7'6" galvanized 16-gauge steel support battens (see details), approximately every 2 or 4'. These shall be secured to angle clips provided. To these support battens secure 4' x 8' x 3/16" Asbestocite sheets. Sheets shall be lapped 3" horizontally with laps secured by self-tapping screws through the sheet into galvanized sheet-steel backing strips. The centers of the sheets shall be secured to the support battens with stainless-steel self-tapping screws and washers. Vertical joints at the ends of the sheets shall be secured with 4" x 1/4" x 3'9" Transite battens fastened with stainless-steel self-tapping screws and washers. (See details.)

Where a vertical panel includes a line of manheads, prevention of water entry through the weather finish around these manheads shall be provided by flat stainless-steel collars clamped around manheads and flashed through butt joints between Asbestocite sheets. Similar treatment shall be provided around the nozzles and angle supports. (See details.)

On the top of the vessel over the insulation, secure 1" stainless-steel chicken wire. Prime insulation surface and chicken wire with J-M Regal Roof Coating. This shall be followed by a 3-course finish of J-M Aertite, 15# Asphalt-Saturated Asbestos Felt and Aertite. This finish shall be carried 8" down from the top edge of the Asbestocite side wall finish. An additional strip of waterproofing Felt and Aertite shall be applied for corner reinforcements. (See details.)

C. E. ERNST
STAFF ENGINEER
INDUSTRIAL INSULATION DEPT.

— Specimen No. 6 —

For what kind of reader group was the following report intended? What evidences of reader-adaptation can you discover from the table of contents or the sections of the report presented here? The original report contains 59 pages of text, 43 pages of diagrams and photographs, and 156 pages of tabular matter. What problems of arrangement did the author or authors have?

COMMONWEALTH OF PENNSYLVANIA
DEPARTMENT OF HIGHWAYS
PLANNING AND TRAFFIC DIVISION

PARKING SURVEY
OF HARRISBURG

HONORABLE JAMES H. DUFF
Governor

RAY F. SMOCK
Secretary of Highways

E. L. SCHMIDT
Chief Engineer

IN COOPERATION WITH THE
PUBLIC ROADS ADMINISTRATION
FEDERAL WORKS AGENCY

1947

C O N T E N T S

TEXT

HIGHLIGHTS OF THE SURVEY

1. During an eight-hour weekday period, 10 a.m. to 6 p.m., over 34,000 vehicles entered the central business district and over 13,000 parked in the district.

2. Approximately 62 percent of all vehicles entering the central business district passed through the district without parking.

3. There are 1,786 parking spaces, 1,844 parking lot spaces, and 1,135 garage parking spaces in the central business district of the city.

4. In these 4,765 parking spaces, 10,889 vehicles parked at the curb, 3,466 vehicles parked in lots, and 1,226 vehicles parked in garages during an eight-hour weekly period.

5. 3,754 vehicles were parked before 10 a.m., 13,138 vehicles parked between 10 a.m. and 6 p.m., and 1,918 vehicles remained in parking places at 6 p.m.

6. A turnover of 6.1 vehicles (including adjacent illegal parkers) occurred over an eight-hour period of curb parking, a turnover of 1.9 vehicles in lots, and a turnover of 1.1 vehicles in garages.

7. The average time parked by all motorists was 1.1 hours at curbs, 2.9 hours in lots, and 4.3 hours in garages.

8. Approximately 54 percent of the total curb length in the central business district is now used for parking. The remainder of the curb is on streets where parking either is prohibited or is reserved for special purposes – bus stops, fire hydrants, driveways, and other uses.

9. 44 percent of the available curb parking spaces in the central business district are metered.

10. 1.8 percent of the curb parking spaces have a 12-minute limit, 0.6 percent have a 24-minute limit, 9.4 percent have a 45-minute limit, 31.2 percent have a one-hour limit, 10.6 percent have a two-hour limit, 38.9 percent have no restrictions, and 7.5 percent are reserved for special vehicles.

11. A total of 76 percent of all vehicles parked at curbs stayed in their parking spaces only one hour or less, and 48 percent of the vehicles remained in their spaces no more than 18 minutes.

12. Only 28 percent of all parking in the central business district is presently done in off-street facilities.

13. Of the 15,581 motorists interviewed, 17.7 percent gave the reason of their trip as shopping, 36.1 percent as business, 28.5 percent as work, 1.8 percent as recreation, and the remaining 15.8 percent as something else.

14. The trip purpose of approximately 24 percent of all curb parkers during the eight-hour weekday period was work, and those parkers used approximately 51 percent of the total curb parking time.

15. 91 percent of all parkers in the central business district walk no more than two blocks to their destinations.

16. 1,451 motorists wanted to park in Market Square, where there are 49 available curb spaces. Approximately 50 percent of those motorists were shoppers.

17. 4,765 motorists violated parking laws in an eight-hour period: 3,212 by parking in illegal locations, and 1,553 by parking longer than the legal time limit.

18. During the survey, 93 motorists left their vehicles in 12-minute parking spaces from 30 minutes to over six hours. The three cars parked over six hours prevented 87 other motorists from making the maximum legal use of those same spaces.

19. In the eight-hour weekday, 1,311 vehicles parked for an average time of 90 minutes at curbs where all parking is prohibited.

20. 30 percent of all commercial vehicles parked were double-parked.

21. Parking on the major streets in the central business district has reduced the capacity of these streets to one and two lanes of moving traffic.

CONCLUSIONS

1. The parking problem affects the entire community and should be considered a civic problem, requiring the cooperation and active participation of all interests – individual, commercial, and municipal.
2. The parking problem in downtown Harrisburg is critical in the area bounded by Front Street, North Street, Third and Fourth Streets, and Chestnut Street.
3. Parking at curbs, by reducing the area of pavement available for moving traffic and by interfering with moving traffic, is one of the principal factors that contribute to traffic congestion.
4. Curb parking has reached its maximum limit in the entire downtown business district, and the increasing heavy volumes of traffic will soon require the elimination of curb parking from a large portion of the curbs of the principal streets in the critical area.
5. Curb parking reduces the traffic capacity of many of Harrisburg's downtown streets to about 53 percent of their possible capacity.
6. The large number of motorists now parking in prohibited locations is visible proof of the demand for additional parking facilities.
7. The provision of adequate and convenient off-street parking facilities is necessary to eliminate curb parking, and the elimination of curb parking is a necessary step in the solution of the traffic problem.
8. During the average hour of a weekday a total of 203 surplus spaces exists in the entire downtown business district, but 549 additional parking spaces are needed in the critical area.
9. During the peak hour of a weekday, 821 additional parking spaces are needed in the critical area and a net shortage of 201 spaces exists in the entire downtown business district.
10. Parking regulations should be more rigidly enforced.
11. The principal need is for off-street parking facilities adequate for and attractive to short-time parkers.

RECOMMENDATIONS

On the basis of the data obtained in the Harrisburg Parking Survey, it is recommended:

1. That civic, municipal, and business representatives make studies of the locations available for off-street parking facilities in the sectors where the demand is greatest, as indicated in this report, and endeavor to have an adequate number of new off-street parking facilities supplied.
2. That a careful study be made with a view to prohibiting curb parking on the principal streets of the central business section.
3. That the present parking ordinance maximum limit of two-hour curb parking be reduced to a maximum limit of one hour in the central business district between North and Mulberry Streets.
4. That the time limits at presently metered curbs be re-examined in connection with the data included herein and the time limits reduced where the present usage of those spaces warrants.
5. That definite measures be taken to discourage long-time curb parking (over one hour) in the central business district.
6. That an investigation be made of Second, Third, Fourth, Market, Walnut, and Chestnut Streets to determine where it may be possible to effect traffic relief by curb set-backs, eliminations of left turns, readjustment of traffic-signal intervals, and one-way traffic routes.
7. That rigid enforcement of the parking regulations be encouraged.
8. That every effort be made to promote the use of mass transportation in lieu of private automobiles.
9. That a zoning ordinance be provided to require the provision of adequate off-street parking and off-street loading and unloading facilities in plans for new building construction, or when major alterations are made to existing buildings.
10. That an ordinance require existing buildings without off-street loading and unloading facilities to restrict those operations to hours of minimum traffic.

LIST OF PLATES

VOLUMES

AVAILABLE PARKING FACILITIES

    In the preparation of the report, it has been necessary to use some terms that require defining to clarify their meaning. These terms are as follows:

Available
Parking
Space . . . . . . Area of parking spaces in off-street parking facilities and spaces legally provided at curb. See "Supply."

Block . . . . . . Several sectors grouped together to enable comparison of parking in portions of the central business district.

Central Business
District . . . . The principal business district of downtown Harrisburg and the area included within the parking survey boundary line. See Plates 2 and 5.

Commercial Vehi-
cles . . . . . . Trucks and buses.

Cordon Count . . The record of the number of motor vehicles entering and leaving the downtown area as counted at streets crossing the parking survey boundary line.

Cordon Line . . . Parking survey boundary line as shown on Plate 5.

Critical Area .. That portion of the central business district where the parking-space deficiency, the excess of demand over supply, is most acute.

[257]

Demand. . . . . . The total need for parking space as determined by the destinations of the parked motorists, assuming that all motorists parked at prohibited locations parked in the same sector as their destination.

Destination . . . The exact location of the place where motorist went after parking his or her car.

Garage – Lot . . A garage and a lot operated, and interviewed, as a single unit.

Illegal Parking Parking at curb and in alleys at locations other than those provided by city ordinances, or not in compliance with time limit.

HARRISBURG PARKING SURVEY
THE PARKING PROBLEM

A motorist usually has two problems – getting to the place he wants to go, and parking his car when he arrives there. When his destination is downtown, the latter problem becomes his number one headache.

From the motorist's point of view, the ideal parking space is at the curb adjacent to his destination. While the average motorist long ago ceased to expect such convenience in the central business district of a city, he still does not like to pay for a place to park his car unless the fee is low and the location quite near where he wants to go. This is particularly true if he desires to stay for only a short period of time.

The irritation of searching for a parking space each time he enters the business district is an exasperating experience, and it has driven many potential shoppers out of business districts. This has been proven in other cities by the many shoppers who are willing to drive extra miles to outlying business establishments where ample parking space is available and where much traffic congestion is avoided. In those cities there have been definite shifts of business to outlying sections, sometimes even outside the municipalities.

When such a shift of business causes a decline of tax revenue in the business district, then either municipal services must be curtailed or the burden shifted to the homeowner and to the home-renter as well. The latter result has actually occurred in other cities.

A recent publication of the American Automobile Association concerning the parking problem listed 32 cities which have suffered central business district valuation losses ranging up to about 40 percent. Harrisburg was next to the bottom of this list, showing only a 3.5 percent loss between 1930 and 1945.

However, it would be foolhardy to neglect action to safeguard the economic future of Harrisburg simply because the city has not yet been seriously affected in this way.

Street parking is one of the principal factors that contribute to traffic congestion. Not only do vehicles stored at the curb occupy an important portion of the pavement, but vehicles maneuvering into and out of parking spaces interfere with moving traffic. Recent studies have shown that in downtown areas a 40-foot street on which parking is permitted has only about 55 percent of the traffic capacity of the same street with parking banned. A 42-foot street with no parking at the curb has the same capacity for moving traffic as two 40-foot streets on which parking is permitted.

Present conditions are fast approaching the point when traffic volumes on the major streets will require the full width of the street to maintain a smooth flow of traffic. This means that off-street parking facilities will have to be provided to replace the present parking spaces along the curbs.

A street has two purposes – to provide for moving vehicles, and to provide a place for vehicles to stop. When traffic volumes are small, both purposes may be adequately served. However, the primary purpose is to provide for moving traffic, and when the volume of moving traffic is large enough to require the full width of a street for that purpose alone, then the continued use of a portion of the street for parking makes that parking space the most expensive space in the city, contrary to the fact that most of the public tends to look upon street parking space as an inexpensive facility.

Only a few years ago merchants were opposing any effort to restrict curb parking. They were particularly opposed to the removal of parkers from in front of their own stores because merchants and retail property owners believed that the success of business depended primarily on the availability of parking spaces in front of their establishments.

Now, in city after city, merchants have learned from their own experience that unless moving traffic is given a chance to continue to move, and unless parking is removed from the heavier-traffic streets, the business of commercial institutions lining these streets will suffer.

The merchants have also learned that only a small percentage of their customers are curb parkers. In a survey made in Philadelphia in 1945, only 8.4 percent of the shoppers came by automobile, and only 2.2 percent of the shoppers were curb parkers. Twelve percent of the curb parkers interviewed who gave the purpose of their trip as business were store owners.

Another aspect of street parking is its influence on traffic accidents. From the 1945 records of 251 cities, the National Safety Council attributed 14.2 percent of all automobile accidents to vehicles parked, or in the process of entering or leaving parking spaces. From the same source, 8 percent of all fatal pedestrian accidents involved pedestrians killed in the act of coming into the roadway from behind parked cars, and 10 percent of all pedestrians injured were injured under similar conditions.

Harrisburg is the focal point or junction of eight major highway routes, and most of the traffic on those routes passes through the central business district. Twelve of the fifteen streets crossing the traffic-survey cordon line are classed as major traffic arteries, and most of the twelve are sufficiently wide to carry either two lines of moving vehicles and two rows of parked cars, or four lines of moving traffic. However, within the central business district, parking on all but one of the streets has reduced the capacities of these streets to one and two lanes of moving vehicles.

Property development within the business district makes it almost economically impossible to materially widen any street.

Wartime shortages and restrictions created a backlog of building programs. Construction in the immediate future will create further parking problems by reducing the amount of vacant land available and by eliminating some of the vacant land now temporarily used as parking lots. Several parking lots now in operation in the section of the central business district where the parking problem is most acute have been definitely scheduled for building operations. It is also true that not all vacant property in the area is suitable for parking purposes, and those parcels which would be most suitable will probably be the first to be occupied by new buildings.

In a previous traffic analysis, it was conservatively estimated that traffic volume in the Harrisburg area would increase at least 55 percent in the next twenty years, and, while traffic growth is not the only factor affecting parking growth, it is obvious that parking will also increase considerably.

Thus, in addition to providing for the present deficiency in parking space, the area is now faced with the necessity for a further reduction in available curb parking facilities, a dwindling supply of parking lots in the near future, and an over-all increase in parking requirements, all of which constitute an ever-growing pressure for more parking space.

The existing street plan cannot be altered appreciably, and the limit of present curb parking has been reached. The parking problem in Harrisburg is, therefore, the provision of adequate off-street parking facilities.

Before an answer could be developed, it was necessary to obtain adequate factual data concerning the various aspects of parking in the central business district of Harrisburg. To obtain those data, the Planning and Traffic Division of the Pennsylvania Department of Highways conducted the Harrisburg Parking Survey in the fall of 1946 with the cooperation of the Public Roads Administration and the City of Harrisburg.

The scope of this survey was to obtain complete information about the location, type, and capacity of all existing parking facilities, to obtain the picture of the way those facilities were being used, the extent to which they met the parking needs, and to determine from the trips of each motorist the type, capacity, and location of the parking facilities required to best satisfy the parking need.

OPERATION OF THE SURVEY

The parking survey was conducted in accordance with methods developed by the Public Roads Administration and consisted of three major phases:

1. Inventory of available parking facilities.
2. Cordon count of traffic entering or leaving the survey area.
3. Interviewing of motorists parked within the survey area.

Data obtained represented an average 8-hour (10 a.m. to 6 p.m.) weekday during the period of the survey (August, September, and October of 1946).

In the INVENTORY, the location, size, capacity, and rates were obtained for each public or private parking lot or garage within the area. Additional data were also secured from the facility-owners or operators as to the peak time period, the peak usage, and the average usage of each lot or garage.

All curbs within the survey area were investigated, and the location, linear feet, and time limits of curb available for parking were obtained, as well as a record of curbs at which parking was prohibited or restricted and the reasons for the restriction.

In addition to these data, supplementary information pertinent to the parking problem was collected concerning parking meters, property valuations, automobile registrations, local population distribution, traffic regulations, and so forth.

In the CORDON COUNT, survey personnel counted the vehicles entering or leaving the survey area at each of the streets crossing the survey boundary line. These counts classified vehicles by type and direction for each hour period between 10 a.m. and 6 p.m. for a minimum of three weekdays at each of the twelve major streets crossing the boundary line (traffic control points) and for one day at each of three minor streets (traffic stations). In addition to the manual counts, automatic traffic recorders were used for a minimum of four full (24-hour) days at each traffic control point and traffic station.

In the INTERVIEWING, trained interviewers questioned the driver of each vehicle entering or leaving a parking lot, a garage, or a curb parking space where parking is permitted by ordinance. Each driver was asked his or her home address and destination and the purpose of the trip. The interviewer also recorded the parking location, type of vehicle, the time parked, and the time of departure from the parking space.

In the survey, drivers of both automobiles and commercial vehicles were interviewed in the same manner.

Vehicles parked in restricted or prohibited spaces at curbs where legal parking was permitted within the same block were interviewed in the same manner, and the type of curb restriction noted. Vehicles parked at curbs where parking was prohibited along the entire block were not interviewed but a record of that parking was obtained by noting, at half-hour intervals, the license numbers of vehicles parked at prohibited curbs.

In all cases, interviewing covered an 8-hour period, 10 a.m. to 6 p.m., on a weekday, Monday through Friday.

The SURVEY AREA was the major portion of downtown Harrisburg, extending from the Susquehanna River to the Pennsylvania Railroad tracks (beyond Seventh Street), and from Forster Street south to Mulberry Street. This survey area or "Central Business District" is shown on the aerial photograph and on Plate 2.

To facilitate the operation of the survey, the survey area was divided into five "Map Areas," and these map areas were further subdivided into sectors. Each sector generally consisted of one city block or part of a city block. Whenever the limits of a sector did not fall in the center of a street or alley, the actual limit used has been indicated on the various maps with a dash line or, as in the case of Market Square, with arrows showing the extent of the sector. Each sector has been given a 5-digit identifying number, and each parking facility (curb, lot, or garage) has been given a 1-digit "facility number" to identify that facility on both the maps and the tables presented in this report. For example, Facility 041212 is the Market Street curb (Facility 2) of Sector 04121. All facilities, sectors, and the map areas are shown on Plate 5.

To permit proper comparisons in the analysis of the parking supply, use, and demand in the portion of the survey area where the parking problem is most critical, some sectors were grouped together and termed "Blocks." These blocks and the sectors which they included are also shown on Page 5. The "Critical Area" within which the blocks were used is explained later in the text.

— Specimen No. 7 —

This is a complete routine "test" report.

Study the heading data. Is the arrangement clear and convenient?

Are the introductory paragraphs direct, concise, and clear?

Could the table be simplified? Can you suggest better make-up and arrangement?

HARBISON-WALKER REFRACTORIES CO.
LABORATORY REPORT

DATE __Jan. 19, 1948__

SUBJECT: Silica Brick Mix – Ours   LAB. No. __D 6727__

Testing of Moistmeter   cc: ETH REB

H. W. Dietert Company   J. B. Campbell, Hays

J. W. Craig (2)

Hays Lab.

File (2)

Samples of power–pressed and hand–made silica brick mix from Hays Works were forwarded to the Harry W. Dietert Company, 9330 Roselawn Ave., Detroit (4), Michigan, to be used in testing a Moistmeter for its suitability as a portable meter for determining quickly the moisture content of silica brick mixes.

The Research Department has had considerable correspondence with other manufacturers regarding similar instruments, none of which proved of any value. The makers of this particular instrument apparently have overcome the lengthy procedure previously required to obtain a reading. The accuracy obtained by the Dietert Company on these samples is satisfactory with one exception, where one reading out of four was in error by 10%. Since 18 out of 19 readings made had a maximum error of 3%, this apparatus would be satisfactory for control laboratories if it can be readily used as the claims show. This would enable a control man to check the moistures of all pans three or four times a day and also to keep a very close check on special mixes which require close tolerances on moisture content. It would be possible to determine the moisture in the pan so that it could be adjusted immediately. By eliminating the lag which now exists, less unsatisfactory material would be put through the brick–making system.

[267]

One of the instruments has been ordered for Hays Laboratory and further investigation will be made at the works.

R. E. Birch

(Cont'd.)

HARBISON-WALKER REFRACTORIES CO.

LABORATORY REPORT

DATE Jan. 19, 1948

SUBJECT: Silica Brick Mix – Ours

LAB. No. D 6727

DETAILED LABORATORY DATA

	Moisture By Hays Lab.	Moisture Reported by H. W. Dietert Co.	
		By Moisture Teller	By Moistmeter
Sample #1 P.P. Brick Mix	7.1%	6.7%	6.6, 6.7, 6.9, 6.6, 6.8, 6.7%
Sample #2 H.M. Brick Mix	9.1%	8.8%	8.8, 8.9, 8.8, 8.8%
Sample #3 P.P. Brick Mix	6.7%	6.0%	6.6, 6.0, 6.1, 6.0%.
Sample #4 H.M. Brick Mix	10.0%	8.6%	8.6, 8.6, 8.6, 8.7, 8.6%.

Screen Analysis:	Sample #1	Sample #2	Sample #3	Sample #4
Held on 6 Mesh	tr.	tr.	tr.	tr.
8	4%	4%	4%	4%
10	11 15%	10 14%	11 15%	11 15%
14	8	9	9	8
20	7	5	6	5
28	5 20	4 18	3 18	4 17
35	3	4	3	3
48	5	4	4	3
65	7 15	7 15	7 14	6 12
100	8	10	7	7
150	5	8	7	7
Pass 150	37 50	35 53	39 53	42 56

Compare this laboratory report with the Harbison-Walker report (No. 7).

Does this give quickly the full information needed by the purchasing department?

STANDARDS TESTING LABORATORY

CLUETT, PEABODY & CO., INC.,
TROY, NEW YORK

TO:

MR. WM. FLINT (2)

SUBJECT:	REPORT NUMBER
ANALYSIS OF WHITE COT-TON THREAD FROM THE X THREAD COMPANY	47-3315

REQUESTED BY:	ON:
MR. WM. FLINT (PUR-CHASING DEPT.)	10-7-47

PURPOSE:— The purpose of this test was to compare cotton thread from the X Thread Company with the standard specifications for thread now used for manufacturing.

RESULTS:— Results of this test indicate that the X thread is not satisfactory for use inasmuch as this thread does not meet specifications satisfactory for acceptable thread to be used in the manufacturing division.

DATA:—

THREAD	TENSILE STRENGTH	SEWABILITY FACTOR	ELONGATION
40/6 Cord X's (#1)	730 gms.	14 oz.	7.2%
40/6 Cord X's (#2)	687 gms.	12 oz.	7.6%
C.P. & Co. Specifications for Acceptable 40/6 Cord Thread	1140 gms.	26 oz.	7.0%

THREAD SIZE
(equivalent cotton count)

40/6 X's #1 — equivalent to 12.7/1's
40/6 X's #2 — equivalent to 13.5/1's
Standard accepted thread — equivalent to 13.1/1's

TWIST – PER INCH

40/6 Cord X's #1 23 S Twist
40/6 Cord X's #2 18 S Twist
Standard accepted thread 23 S Twist

MATERIAL:-

Thread used in this test from the X Thread Company was submitted by Mr. W. H. Flint for testing.

CONCLUSIONS:-

As indicated in the above data, the strength and the sewability factor of the X thread is considerably lower than the acceptable standards. The sewability factor is, of course, of primary importance and would in itself constitute sufficient cause for rejection when not satisfactory. The elongation as noted above compares favorably with our specifications.

JB:McA

PREPARED BY:	REVIEWED BY:	DATE:
	H.J.J.	October 17, 1947

— Specimen No. 9 —

The following report is complete except for final conclusions and recommendations.

Is there anything illogical in the table of contents? Does the table of contents accurately represent the report?

Examine the use of abbreviations, numerals, symbols, and punctuation for simplicity and consistency.

Is the Introduction adequate?

Study the paragraph structure in the section "Discussion of Results."

EXPERIMENTAL BLEACHING FOR 60-BRIGHTNESS PULP

Technical Department Report No. 254

Brunswick Pulp and Paper Company
Brunswick, Georgia
February 6, 1942

E. T. Rogers
W. J. Ervin

TABLE OF CONTENTS

SUMMARY

Faced with a probable reduction of our chlorine supply, we have completed a series of experimental bleaching with the object of obtaining a 60-brightness pulp.

A sample of regular brown stock was obtained and the sample divided into nine batches, which were all bleached in the laboratory with the following variations:

1. Amount of chlorine.
2. Sequence of stages.
3. Chlorine-to-pulp ratio.
4. Number of stages.

The results of the work done shows that we can bleach our normal pulp with a chlorine number of 7.5 to a 60-brightness with less than 100 pounds of chlorine per ton A. D. pulp.

The use of a caustic extraction stage has a decided advantage. It was found that pulp given a caustic extraction had a brightness from 6 to 13 points higher than pulp that had not been given this treatment.

The chlorine number was not lowered by caustic extraction which followed a hypochlorite, but the amount of organic matter extracted was appreciable and results prove the extraction to be beneficial. Caustic extraction is more effective immediately following chlorination, since the chlorine number is lowered, and better removal of organic compounds was experienced.

From the results, it is recommended that a plant run of from two to six hours be made as soon as possible with the following bleaching procedure:

1st stage: Chlorination

> 25% of chlorine No. as chlorine
>   gas.
> 75% lime on wt. of chlorine
> 20 minutes' reaction time.
> pH 7.5-8.0

2nd stage: Caustic extraction

> 1.75% caustic soda on weight of
> fibre.
> 140°–160° F
> 1-hour reaction

3rd stage: No treatment.

4th stage: Sodium hypochlorite.

> 75% of chlorine No. as chlorine in
> hypochlorite.
> Temp. – 110° F–120° F
> Reaction time according to resid-
> ual. To dump with 5–10 pounds of
> residual per bleacher.

The trial run should be made with laboratory checks being made for quality and other data.

Strength losses on laboratory-bleached pulp were very small, the only appreciable loss being in the final hypochlorite stage.

INTRODUCTION

Owing to an expected reduction in our chlorine supply, we will probably be forced to lower our brightness standards to approximately 60 G. E.

The principal problems then will be to use as little chlorine and caustic as possible but at the same time to remove shives to an extent where they will not be objectionable. The removal of shives is best accomplished in a high-density hypochlorite stage. This, however, will probably be more expensive than the use of some chlorine gas.

PROCEDURE

The procedure for the experimental bleaching was all carried out on a laboratory scale. Chlorine water was used instead of chlorine gas, owing to lack of equipment for handling gas. SO_2 water was also used instead of SO_2 gas.

All brown stock used was collected from the brown-stock chests. This stock was stored wringer-dry with a little formaldehyde as a preservative.

The stock as needed was decked and run through a wringer of known dryness. Sufficient wringer-dry pulp was then weighed out to give the desired amount of B. D. pulp for each test. All pulp tests for quality were run at 90 seconds in the Mead Refiner. Brightness was made on a G. E. reflection meter. Shive counts were made on 100 gms. of oven-dry basis.

The pulp sample was divided into nine different batches and each bleached differently.

No. 1. Chlorination – 1st stage

> 30% Chlorine Number as chlorine gas.
> 20 minutes' reaction time.
> Lime, 80% of chlorine used.

Caustic Extraction – 2nd stage

> 13.0% Density.
> Temperature, 140°–160° F.
> 1.5% Caustic soda–basis pulp.
> 1–hour reaction time.

Sodium Hypochlorite – 3rd stage

> 60% Chlorine Number as chlorine in sodium
>   hypochlorite.
> 13.0% Density room temperature (78° F).
> 2 hours' reaction time.

No. 2. Chlorination – 1st stage

> 35% Chlorine Number as chlorine gas.
> 25 minutes' reaction time.
> Lime equivalent to 80% of chlorine used.
> 20 minutes' reaction time and wash.

No. 2. Caustic Extraction – 2nd stage (Cont'd.)

 1.5% Caustic soda–basis pulp.
 Temperature, 140°–160° F.
 13.0% Density.
 1–hour reaction time.

Sodium Hypochlorite – 3rd stage

 55.0% Chlorine Number as chlorine in sodium
  hypochlorite.
 Reaction time, 2 hours at 80° F.
 13.0% Density.

[*Nos. 3–8 similarly.*]

No. 9. Chlorination – 1st stage

 20.0% of Chlorine Number as chlorine gas.
 30 minutes' reaction time.
 Lime, 70% of chlorine used.
 20 minutes' time and wash.

Sodium Hypochlorite – 2nd stage

 1.5% chlorine as hypochlorite.
 13.0% Density.
 Temperature, 105°–130° F.
 30 minutes' reaction time.

Caustic Extraction – 3rd stage

 1.75% caustic soda–basis pulp.
 4.0% density.
 Temperature, 140°–160° F.
 1–hour reaction time.

In each case, the reference to chlorine gas means the available chlorine in chlorine water as determined by thiosulphate titration of liberated iodine. Available sulphur dioxide was determined by iodine titration. Available chlorine in bleach liquor was determined by titration of liberated iodine with sodium thiosulphate.

All lime and caustic was analyzed by titration with 0.773 N (HCl) hydrochloric acid.

Chlorine Numbers were run on all pulps after each stage of bleaching.

The amount of organic matter extracted was determined on samples of several of the pulps following the hypochlorite and caustic stages. This was determined by the Parson and Jackson Method.

All pH valves were run on a Beckman electric pH meter.

DISCUSSION OF RESULTS

The brightness on the bleached pulps numbers 3, 4, 5, and 7 were above 60. These pulps used, respectively, 91.4, 113.0, 107.4, and 105.0 pounds of chlorine per ton A. D. pulp. From the standpoint of chlorine consumption, No. 3 is the logical choice. No. 3 also had lower over-all cost for bleaching than any of the other pulps that met the required brightness.

A study of the pulp-quality graphs shows that in every case the greater loss in strength was in the final hypochlorite stage. In the case of pulp No. 8, where two hypochlorites were used, the bleach exhausted very rapidly in the first stage. There was no strength loss in the first stage of hypochlorite.

Pulps Nos. 1, 2, and 3 were all treated in the same manner, with the following variations: the ratio of chlorine to fibre in the two chlorine stages. Their quality changes are about the same, except in the case of No. 3, which shows a loss of mullen in the final hypochlorite stage. Pulps 1 and 2 show a slight gain. The high temperature on No. 3 would account for the above. Pulp No. 3 appears to the greater promise for our consideration.

Pulp No. 4 shows extremely high Elmendorf in the second hypochlorite stage but very little in the first hypochlorite. A comparison of No. 4 and

No. 8 pulps is of interest, since there was some question as to the value of a caustic extraction stage. A study of data in Table No. I will show that on pulp No. 4 we started with a pulp of higher chlorine number and used the same percent of the chlorine number that was used on No. 8. On No. 8 there was no caustic extraction made. The final brightness on No. 4 was 13 points higher than on No. 8. The cost on No. 4 was higher by $1.56 per ton, but the use of a low-density caustic extraction increases steam costs. The chlorine consumption shown for No. 4 is higher than would be necessary to obtain the desired brightness, since 10 pounds of chlorine per ton BD pulp were used in place of SO_2. It is known that SO_2 can be substituted for chlorine at this stage. These figures show a definite advantage in using caustic extraction between hypochlorite stages, and it will be even more effective if used following a chlorination stage.

Pulp No. 5 gave good brightness without much loss in strength. Chlorine consumption was too high.

Pulp No. 6 could be considered as a possibility, since we have always obtained better brightness in plant operation than in laboratory bleaching. The chlorine consumption was high.

Pulp No. 7 gave good brightness and again shows the advantage of caustic extraction when compared with No. 6. No. 7, with extraction, gave 6.5 points higher brightness than No. 6, which was bleached identically except for omission of the caustic extraction stage. No. 7 shows higher cost, which can be accounted for by the use of steam for low-density extraction and also more caustic. Pulp No. 8 could not be considered, as the brightness was lower than desired. Pulp No. 9 has the advantage of low chlorine consumption, but over-all costs would be high.

Past operation has shown that increased hypochlorite is more effective in bleaching shives out at higher densities. Therefore, it will be to our advantage to use as much chlorine as possible as hypochlorite at a high density.

The method of determining shives did not prove very satisfactory. Since a small sample was used in determining the shives, it is the opinion of the writer that it was not a true representative of the pulp as compared with operation.

— Specimen No. 10 —

Compare the general effectiveness of the following report with the one that precedes. Is there noticeable difference in the accuracy and consistency of the writing?

Notice the long distribution list (actual names are here omitted) in the heading.

Is there good reason for putting the author's name only at the end of the report?

What is the difference between "Conclusions" and "Summary"? Why that order?

Is the problem effectively stated in the Introduction?

THE GOODYEAR TIRE & RUBBER COMPANY

July 8, 1947

Manager
Chemical Engineering Division

cc: R. P. ———   J. D. ———
L. B. ———   J. R. ———
H. J. ———   P. M. ———
J. P. ———   H. P. ———
F. H. ———   D. E. ———

Subject: Preparation of Mercuric Chloride-
Activated Carbon Catalyst by Adsorption from Methanol Solution.

INTRODUCTION:

Mercuric chloride, adsorbed from solutions on
activated carbon, has been the catalyst used in
German production of vinyl chloride. At Pathfinder,
the mercuric chloride has been added to the carbon
by a sublimation process. In order to make a direct
comparison at Pathfinder of life of catalysts prepared by each method, sufficient material for a
charge was prepared by Chemical Engineering according to the German "wet method." Process methods and
product—control data were developed to bring about
the adsorption on activated carbon pellets of desired percentages of mercuric chloride from methanol
solutions. A total of 425 pounds of catalyst containing an average of 20.7% of mercuric chloride,
and 850 pounds of catalyst containing an average of
10.8% of mercuric chloride, were prepared in the
pilot plant and shipped to Pathfinder.

CONCLUSIONS:

1. By varying the concentration of mercuric
chloride in methanol solution, it is possible to
control the quantity of mercuric chloride which will
be adsorbed from such a solution by a known weight
of activated carbon.

[284]

2. While the heat of adsorption of methanol on activated carbon is substantial, the dissipation of that heat is not a serious problem on the pilot-plant scale.

3. A non-agitated fixed-carbon bed can be used.

4. Adsorption makes it impossible to remove all of the methanol from the product by the drying methods investigated.

SUMMARY:

1. It was found feasible to measure the concentrations of mercuric chloride-methanol solutions from specific-gravity determinations.

2. Approximately four hours at 150° F were required to dry the carbon catalyst down to the minimum attainable residual alcohol concentration.

3. A total time cycle of six hours per batch of catalyst was required.

4. Carbon which was reactivated by Pathfinder adsorbed from three to four percent less mercuric chloride than did the carbon as received from Carbide & Carbon.

PROCEDURE:

A. For 20% Catalyst

For every part by weight of activated carbon pellets to be treated two parts by weight of mercuric chloride-methanol solution are prepared. The quantity of mercuric chloride which this solution should contain may be estimated from the appended Chart No. 1. Determination of the mercuric chloride in the prepared solution may be made from specific-gravity measurements by referring them to Chart No. 2. The solution is added slowly to the carbon pellets without agitation and the mixture allowed to stand for half an hour. The pellets are allowed to drain, the drainings are weighed, and the specific gravity determined. Residual solution is rinsed off with one and one-half parts of methanol. This rinse, when drained off, is weighed and the specific gravity determined. One part by weight of pure methanol is added to the pellets as a second rinse, is drained and weighed and its specific gravity measured. The quantity of mercuric chloride in the original solution, less the total mercuric chloride in the drainings and in the two rinses, is then presumed to have been adsorbed on the carbon. The wet product is then placed on perforated metal trays and dried in a forced-convection air dryer for four hours at 150° F.

B. For 10% Catalyst

Because of the lower concentration of mercuric chloride encountered in this preparation, only one rinse, of one part by weight of methanol, is necessary. Otherwise, the two procedures are similar.

DISCUSSION:

The alcohols originally suggested as possible solvents were methanol, ethanol, and isopropanol. Methanol was selected because isopropanol, with its lower volatility, entails rather long drying periods, and it was thought that the hygroscopic nature of ethanol might seriously affect the catalytic properties of the product.

At the outset, the problem involved determining the relationships between solution concentration and percent mercuric chloride adsorbed. Arbitrarily, for every part by weight of carbon pellets employed, two parts by weight of mercuric chloride-methanol solution were used. This ratio assured entire coverage of the pellets with solution even after adsorption was complete. In all laboratory runs, using 40-gram carbon samples, the percent of solution adsorbed ranged from 83 to 95 percent, based on dry carbon, with no apparent correlation between solution concentration and percent of solution adsorbed.

The heat of adsorption was found to be substantial. No calorimetric determinations were made,
but it was found that, in the laboratory, using a
40-gram carbon sample in a glass tube one inch in
diameter, a temperature of 58°C could be obtained
by rapidly adding 80 grams of methanol to the carbon. (Methanol b.p. 64.7°C.)

It was not found possible to determine the
amount of mercuric chloride in the finished product
by analytical methods because the salt could not be
completely removed from the carbon, even by leaching
the pulverized product with boiling methanol or
boiling water. Consequently, the quantity of mercuric chloride adsorbed on a particular quantity of
carbon was estimated by the difference in the concentration of the methanol solutions before and
after treatment. Moreover, in the analyses of these
solutions, advantage was taken of the great difference between the specific gravities of mercuric
chloride and methanol.* The appended plot of specific gravity versus solution concentration at 25°C
was an aid in determining and adjusting the concentrations of any solutions up to 40%.

In all laboratory and production runs, the
solution was added to the carbon pellets instead of
adding the carbon to the solution, on the assumption
that, by adding the solution to the carbon, each
pellet will be treated with solution of the original
concentration. If the pellets were added slowly to
the solution, the last pellets would be treated with
weaker solution than were the first pellets, resulting in a less uniform product. This idea was borne
out in the laboratory using a 9% mercuric chloride-
methanol solution on two 40-gram carbon samples.
Where the solution was added slowly to the carbon
pellets, the concentration of mercuric chloride in
the drainings was 1.7%, while in the case where the
carbon was added slowly to the solution, the con-

---

* Specific gravity of methanol, 0.792 @ 20°C.
Specific gravity of mercuric chloride, 5.44 @ 20°C.
From Handbook of Chemistry, by Lange.

centration of mercuric chloride in the drainings was 2.7%, indicating less adsorption of mercuric chloride in the latter case.

The corrosive action of methanol solutions of mercuric chloride on metals is very serious, even on stainless steel. The metal is oxidized to the chloride, and substantial quantities of reduced mercury result which amalgamate the metals. In all plant batches, glass-lined equipment was used. Moderate protection for iron fittings was obtained by treating the surfaces with an acetone solution of a methyl methacrylate polymer.

In the plant, a 20-gallon reactor accommodated 50-pound carbon charges, and a 50-gallon reactor allowed 125-pound carbon batches. The jacket recirculation system was used to cool the batches during adsorption. An attempt was made to dry the product in the reactor by applying a vacuum and heating the jacket to 150°F. However, even after six hours at 150°F and a vacuum of 25 inches, there still remained over 30% alcohol in the product. Drying in a forced-convection air dryer (Proctor & Schwartz try dryer) at 150°F for four hours gave a product containing 23% methanol, dry basis. At drying temperatures of 200°F and atmospheric pressure, there were definite indications of sublimation of the mercuric chloride.

All of the 10% catalyst was produced in a 30-gallon glass-lined Pfaudler tank using 100 pounds of carbon per batch. The fact that there was no jacket cooling of the material during adsorption did not present a problem. There was a moderate evolution of alcohol vapors from the heated mass, but the relationships between solution concentration and percent mercuric chloride adsorbed still held despite the higher temperatures.

In the preparation of the 10% catalyst, the second rinse was found to be unnecessary, since it contained less than 0.2% mercuric chloride. By using two parts by weight of solution for every part by weight of carbon, and one part by weight of

methanol as a rinse, the accumulated drainings from
a batch when readjusted in concentration with mercuric chloride were sufficient as a starting solution for the succeeding batch, so that there was no
accumulation of alcohol solutions as was the case in
the preparation of the 20% catalyst.

The first lot of activated carbon, from which
the 20% catalyst was made, was first subjected to a
heating operation at the Pathfinder plant to insure
its adsorptivity. The second lot of activated carbon, from which the 10% catalyst was made, had not
been reactivated by Pathfinder. The accompanying
plot of solution concentration versus percent mercuric chloride adsorbed shows that the "reactivated"
carbon adsorbed from three to four percent less mercuric chloride, throughout the range of solution
concentrations up to thirty percent, than the carbon as received.

Sample calculations from a 20% catalyst batch
and from a 10% catalyst batch are appended.

/s/ G. E. Sholtis

G. E. Sholtis
Chemical Engineering Division

GES
mk

Only the preliminary and the final sections of the following report are included. From these alone can you get a reasonably complete understanding of the substance of the report?

How well does the 75-word abstract summarize the 12-page report?

Compare the bibliographical method with the suggestions found in Chapter 7.

U. S. DEPARTMENT OF COMMERCE   NATIONAL BUREAU OF STANDARDS

RESEARCH PAPER RP1698

*Part of Journal of Research of the National Bureau of Standards,
Volume 36, February 1946*

ENGINE TESTS WITH PRODUCER GAS

By Frederic A. Middleton and Clarence S. Bruce

ABSTRACT

Bench tests with a four-cylinder stationary engine were made with gasoline and producer gas from charcoal as the fuels. A comparison of their performance revealed that maximum power from producer gas from charcoal is about 55 percent of gasoline power, and that about 11.4 pounds of charcoal is equivalent to 1 gallon of gasoline. When operating an engine on producer gas the spark should be advanced beyond the setting for maximum power with gasoline.

CONTENTS

I. SCOPE AND OBJECTIVE OF INVESTIGATION

The work reported herein is a portion of an extensive investigation [1] [1] of substitute motor fuels, conducted by the National Bureau of Standards for the Foreign Economic Administration. The objective

---

[1] Figures in brackets indicate the literature references at the end of this paper.

of this phase of the investigation was the evaluation of charcoal as a fuel for automotive purposes and the determination of the performance both of the gas producer and of the engine when operating on producer gas from charcoal.

II. TEST EQUIPMENT

The engine used for this study was a four cylinder International Model U–4 with a displacement of 152.1 cubic inches. It was designed for multifuel uses and was supplied with a . . .

[Sections III, IV, & V omitted]

VI. CONCLUSIONS

Charcoal may be used successfully as an automotive fuel if its limitations and weaknesses are understood.

A 45-percent loss of power can be expected on an unmodified gasoline engine. This may or may not prove permissible, depending on the amount of excess power available over actual needs.

Spark timing must be advanced beyond the setting for gasoline.

Servicing requirements would make the use of gas producers impractical for the average automobile owner in this country, but for commercial uses where a fleet of vehicles was being operated, trained servicemen could handle this problem satisfactorily.

In general, the gas-generating plant performed satisfactorily. The difficulty experienced with the tuyeres melting at their tips is a subject that should be investigated.

This work shows that although different lots of charcoal vary in their suitability as producer fuel, the ash content is not a satisfactory criterion of performance.

VII. REFERENCES

[1] Donald B. Brooks, Single-cylinder engine tests of substitute motor fuels, J. Research NBS 35, 1 (1945) RP1660.
[2] Donald B. Brooks, Correcting engine tests for humidity, BS J. Research 3, 795 (1925) RP118.
[3] D. B. Brooks and E. A. Garlock, The effect of humidity on engine power at altitude, Nat. Adv. Comm. Aeron. Rep. 426 (1932), Eighteenth Annual Report of NACA.
[4] E. A. Allcut, Producer gas for motor transport, Automotive and Aviation Ind. 89, 39 (August 15, 1943).
[5] A. E. Burstall and M. W. Woods, Experiments on a high-speed producer gas engine, Engineer 167, 642 (May 26, 1939).
[6] J. Spiers, The performance of a converted petrol engine on producer gas, Proc. Inst. Automobile Engrs. (London) 36, 117 (1941–42).
[7] Harold C. Weber, Theory of gas producers, Mechanical Engineers' Handbook (McGraw-Hill Book Co., Inc., New York, N. Y., 4th ed., p. 372, 1941).

[8] Harry A. Curtis, Solid fuels, Chemical Engineers' Handbook (McGraw-Hill Book Co., Inc., New York, N. Y., 2d ed., p. 2341, 1941).

[9] E. A. Allcut and R. H. Patten, Gas producers for motor vehicles, National Research Council of Canada, No. 1220, p. 69, Ottawa (1944).

[10] Martin Shepherd, Improved apparatus and methods for analysis of gas mixtures by combustion and absorption, BS J. Research 6, 121 (1931) RP266.

WASHINGTON, November 14, 1945.

Letter of Transmittal, Table of Contents, Introduction, and Summary of the following report are included. Discussion and Appendices are omitted.

Is there good reason for omitting the subtitles under "Summary" from the table of contents?

How well does the letter of transmittal introduce the report?

Are purpose and scope well defined under Section I?

Could these preliminary sections be understood by nontechnical executives?

THE STANDARD OIL COMPANY (OHIO)

TO: Mr. E. E. Kerne   DATE: September 4, 1947

FROM: R. H. Wehrle   SUBJECT: Survey of Mechanical
Condition — API Waste
Water Separators
No. 1 Refinery

In accordance with your instructions of July 30 and in line with our discussions at No. 1 Refinery with Messrs. Cuthbert and Bale on Aug. 7, a detailed survey of the mechanical condition of the API separators at No. 1 Refinery is being prepared.

Mr. R. W. Ballmer, Assistant Process Engineer, No. 1 Refinery, has been assigned to collaborate in this survey.

For purposes of simplicity and efficiency we have divided the survey into the following three phases:

Phase I: Historical report consolidating all available information on the design and failures of the mechanical equipment installed on subject separators.

Phase II:
A. To determine by correspondence and inspection trips the experience of other refiners with API separators.

B. To initiate investigations with equipment manufacturers for more satisfactory mechanical equipment.

Phase III: To prepare a list of recommendations indicated from Phases I and II above, from which the separators at No. 1 Refinery can be put in good mechanical operating condition.

The attached report is intended to constitute Phase I.

TAMullett;Mcg

(s) T. A. Mullett

TABLE OF CONTENTS

SURVEY OF MECHANICAL CONDITION
API WASTE WATER SEPARATORS
NO. 1 REFINERY

I. PURPOSE AND SCOPE OF REPORT

The purpose of this report is to present a general history of the design and failures of the mechanical equipment installed in the API separators at No. 1 Refinery. This report is intended to constitute the first phase of a survey from which it is expected recommendations will be made to put the separators in good mechanical condition.

Although many of the recommendations to be made later may be indicated by this report, it is not intended that this report cover that phase of the survey.

It should be pointed out that the following report represents the result of an examination of a great volume of correspondence covering a period of six years and the consolidation of the opinions of several persons.

Therefore, although it is believed that the information herein presented is accurate and includes the assigned scope, any firsthand additions or corrections will be greatly appreciated.

II. SUMMARY

A. HISTORY & DESIGN

1. Operational difficulties were encountered in early operations and have continued to the present time. Chief problem is one of sludge disposal.

2. Design a compromise. However, capacity appears to be adequate if temperatures, oil gravity, and turbidity are not unfavorable.

[297]

B. MECHANICAL EQUIPMENT — OPERATING PROBLEMS

1. Influent Channel Gates – Recent adjustments of the hand-operated gate have
eliminated minor difficulty here.

2. Influent Channel Screens – Present 1"
mesh screens on inclined bar screen are
not believed to be the most satisfactory
arrangement.

3. Gates from Influent Channel to Distribution Basins – Operation satisfactory.

4. Film Rupture Trays – Raschig rings removed
early in operation because of clogging by
algae. Two remedies suggested at Western
Petroleum Refiners' Association Meeting.

5. Flight Cleaners, Primary & Transverse –
Subject to frequent breakdowns on account
of sludge accumulation. Necessity for
similar installation in secondary basins
indicated.

6. Oil Collecting Pipes – Pitch and size of
drain lines may be insufficient. Packing
joint and positioning mechanism have
proven unsatisfactory.

7. Sludge & Oil Moving Equipment – This is
one of most important problems. No satisfactory method of sludge removal has been
in operation for past five years. Original pumps not satisfactory. Experiments
with eductors continuing.

8. Ultimate Sludge Disposal – This the most
important problem. Many of the other difficulties stem from this difficulty.

From the following report, the main discussion is omitted.

For whom is this report written?

How does the initial Summary differ from the final Conclusions?

Is the Introduction limited to the usual introductory information, or does it do more?

Note how references are handled in the Introduction.

Does the style conform with the principles stated in Chapter 4?

NATIONAL ADVISORY COMMITTEE FOR AERONAUTICS

REPORT NO. 756

THE INDUCTION OF WATER TO THE INLET AIR AS A MEANS OF INTERNAL COOLING IN AIRCRAFT-ENGINE CYLINDERS

By ADDISON M. ROTHROCK, ALOIS KRSEK, Jr., and ANTHONY W. JONES

Aircraft Engine Research Laboratory
Cleveland, Ohio

SUMMARY

Investigations were conducted on a full-scale air-cooled aircraft-engine cylinder of 202-cubic-inch displacement to determine the effects of internal cooling by water induction on the maximum permissible power and output of an internal-combustion engine. For a range of fuel-air and water-fuel ratios, the engine inlet pressure was increased until knock was detected aurally; the power was then decreased 7 percent holding the ratios constant. The data indicated that water was a very effective internal coolant, permitting large increases in engine power as limited by either knock or cylinder temperatures.

INTRODUCTION

The induction of water into the inlet air of an internal-combustion engine has been investigated by various persons as a means of improving engine cooling. Prescott in a paper given in Chicago in 1933 presented data for extremely high permissible power outputs obtained by the use of inducted water to suppress knock. (See reference 1.) Kuhring (reference 2) determined the effect of induction of water and of water-alcohol mixtures on the temperatures of a full-scale aircraft engine. Heron and Beatty (reference 3) have shown that water-alcohol mixtures decrease the temperature of a liquid-cooled single-cylinder test engine. Hives and Smith (reference 4) present brief evidence of the increase of permissible brake mean effective pressure as limited by knock when water is inducted with the incoming air. The effectiveness of water and water-alcohol mixtures as internal coolants in a multicylinder engine has also been investigated at Wright Field. The results of these various investigations show that water is an effective internal coolant.

The use of water as an internal coolant is of particular interest if a suitable aftercooler of the exhaust gases can be designed that will permit the recovery of water formed during the combustion process. Investigations at Langley Memorial Aeronautical Laboratory show that the weight of water formed at a fuel-air ratio of 0.067 is 1.25 (based on exhaust-gas analysis) times the weight of the fuel burned, as compared with an estimated weight of water 1.34 (based on hydrogen-carbon ratio) times the weight of the fuel burned. Consequently, the amount of water in the exhaust is sufficient for appreciable internal cooling of the engine.

If a satisfactory water-recovery apparatus can be designed, several advantages will result:

1. The permissible output from the fuel could be materially increased or the octane number of the fuel required could be materially decreased.

2. The water-recovery apparatus may be mounted in an aircraft wing and used as a wing de-icer.

3. The exhaust flame or glow would be eliminated.

4. Intercoolers or aftercoolers in the supercharging system might be eliminated.

The disadvantages of the system are:

1. Increased weight.
2. Bulkiness of water-recovery apparatus.
3. Increased drag.
4. Difficulties in preventing freezing of water.
5. Difficulties if used in conjunction with turbosupercharger.
6. Difficulties if installed in conjunction with exhaust-jet propulsion.

Information on weights of an aftercooler is given in reference 5, in which Kohr presents data on a water-recovery apparatus built for a small airship. The following information is taken from Kohr's data:

Duration of tests, hours 90
Average airspeed, miles per hour 48
Average air temperature, °F 59
Total weight of fuel used, pounds 15,075
Total weight of water collected, pounds 13,943
Water collected, percent of fuel 92.5
Engine horsepower (estimated) 280
Weight condenser less suspension, pounds.................. 400

The horsepower listed is based on the assumption that the brake specific fuel consumption of the engine was 0.6 pound per horsepower-hour. The weight of the aftercooler is then 1.42 pounds per horsepower.

Improved design should appreciably decrease this weight. Also, the average airspeed of 48 miles per hour is much slower than that of current military aircraft.

Water as an internal coolant is of interest as a means of suppressing knock in short bursts of high power output, that is, during take-off or during combat maneuvers. In these cases it probably would be necessary to use a water-alcohol mixture to prevent freezing. Such a procedure would permit high powers during take-off with a fuel of low octane number.

The use of water injection as an internal coolant may have immediate application in types of aircraft in which, where weight limitations are not severe, the water necessary for continuous operation can be carried in addition to the fuel or can be recovered from the exhaust gases.

In view of the possibilities offered by the use of internal coolants, a series of investigations on a full-scale air-cooled aircraft-engine cylinder were undertaken using water as the coolant. The investigations were made at Langley Memorial Aeronautical Laboratory during the period from December 1941 to March 1942.

APPARATUS AND PROCEDURE

The determination of the effect . . .

RESULTS

Group A

Maximum permissible engine performance.—Figure 1 presents the relation . . .

Constant inlet-air pressure investigations.—For the data in Figure 6, the inlet-air pressure was constant at 35 inches of . . .

Group B

Maximum permissible engine performance.—Figure 8 shows the relation between fuel-air ratio and maximum permissible . . .

Indicator diagrams.—Indicator diagrams for a time-pressure card were taken with a Farnsboro indicator, using a constant fuel-air ratio of approximately 0.07 and water-fuel ratios of 0, 0.5, 1.0, and 1.5 at maximum permissible performance conditions. The pressure and temperature results are . . .

Dilution of crankcase oil.—Considerable dilution of crankcase oil with water occurred during . . .

CONCLUSIONS

Investigation of water induction in a single-cylinder engine over a range of fuel-air ratios from 0.05 to 0.12 indicated the following conclusions:

1. Water injection allowed a fuel to be operated above its normal maximum permissible performance limits.

2. Water injection allowed a fuel to be operated at a higher indicated mean effective pressure, with a lower indicated specific fuel consumption, or with both, than was permitted without an internal coolant.

3. Water injection had a marked cooling effect on the engine head and cylinder. The exhaust-valve guide was the only point cn the head at which the temperature showed a tendency to increase with indicated mean effective pressure. The temperature was less, however, than that obtained with a straight fuel permitting equivalent power.

4. Water injection showed no advantage in fuel economy when the fuel was operated well below its maximum permissible performance limits.

5. Water injection might be a disadvantage if the engine-cooling effects are carried to an extreme and cause crankcase-oil dilution. Operation at normal engine and crankcase-oil temperatures should minimize crankcase-oil dilution.

LANGLEY MEMORIAL AERONAUTICAL LABORATORY
NATIONAL ADVISORY COMMITTEE FOR AERONAUTICS
LANGLEY FIELD, VA., *August 15, 1942.*

REFERENCES

1. Prescott, Ford L.: Military Aircraft Engines of the Future. Mech. Eng., vol. 58, no. 3, March 1936, pp. 157–161.
2. Kuhring, M. S.: Water and Water-Alcohol Injection in a Supercharged Jaguar Aircraft Engine. Canadian Jour. Res., sec. A, vol. 16, Aug. 1938, pp. 149–176.
3. Heron, S. E., and Beatty, Harold A.: Aircraft Fuels. Jour. Aero. Sci., vol. 5, no. 12, Oct. 1938, pp. 463–479.
4. Hives, E. W., and Smith, F. Ll.: High Output Aircraft Engines. SAE Jour., vol. 46, no. 3, March 1940, pp. 106–117.
5. Kohr, Robert F.: Condensation of Water from Engine Exhaust for Airship Ballasting. A. S. I. C., vol. 1, no. 44, May 1, 1924.
6. Rothrock, Addison M., Biermann, Arnold E., and Corrington, Lester C.: Maximum Permissible Engine Performance of Eight Representative Fuels of 100-Octane Number. NACA ARR, Jan. 1942.

Table of contents, foreword, and summary from The National Applied Mathematics Laboratories—A Prospectus, *by the National Bureau of Standards, February 1947*

How formal is the style?

Is it well adapted to the readers Dr. Condon has in mind?

Is there a clear distinction in purpose between the Foreword and the Summary?

From the writing itself, what seems to be the relationship between writer and reader?

FOREWORD

In these days when so much emphasis is properly being placed on economy in Government research operations, it is important to take advantage of the substantial savings which can be effected by substituting sound mathematical analysis for costly experimentation. In science as well as in business, it pays to stop and figure things out in advance.

Applied mathematics is on the threshold of revolutionary developments which will permit numerical answers to be obtained to physical problems at hitherto undreamed-of speeds. It has seemed to me for some time that a strong, easily accessible federal applied mathematics center, operating with low overhead costs, providing economical but competent computational and consulting services, and performing forward-looking research in the newer methods of applied mathematics, is a necessity in the national research program. It is now proposed to establish such a center as a unit of the National Bureau of Standards. The specifications for this center, as set forth in the following Prospectus, have been worked out after much study and many consultations with qualified representatives of industry, educational institutions, and private groups. A modest and conservative scale of operations is proposed for the immediate future, with considerable emphasis on long-range research intended to develop methods of permanent value. However, ample elasticity has been provided in the plans to meet unforeseen demands upon the organization.

It is my expectation that the new center will make an important contribution to the development of our scientific resources and their application to national security and peacetime technology.

/s/

E. U. Condon

SUMMARY

A prospectus is herein set forth for a federal center of applied mathematics, to be operated as a division of the National Bureau of Standards of the Department of Commerce. The center is to be known as the National Applied Mathematics Laboratories. It will specialize in numerical and statistical analysis, and will undertake to offer various services in these fields, and carry on a broad program of research and training. Particular emphasis will be placed on the development of high-speed automatic computing machinery and the mathematical theory needed for its effective use.

The concept of the center originated in the Planning Division of the Office of Research and Inventions of the Navy Department (now the Office of Naval Research), which early in 1946 requested the assistance of the Bureau in establishing a national mathematical computation center. Further cooperative study revealed the desirability of a more fundamental approach, and specifications for a more general type of facility have now been evolved after lengthy consultations with scientific representatives of industrial groups, educational institutions, and other Government agencies. Primary justification for such an organization resides in (i) the economies in time and effort brought about in scientific research by the substitution of mathematical methods for expensive experimentation, (ii) the high first cost of revolutionary automatic computing machinery now under development, (iii) the fact that applied mathematics is a relatively unfashionable subject among the mathematicians of this country in peacetime.

The work of the National Applied Mathematics Laboratories is to be carried on with the guidance of a committee of representatives of interested outside groups, to be called the Applied Mathematics Executive Council. The Laboratories will consist of four major units. The first of these is a section devoted primarily to research and training, to be located in California and to be called the Institute of Numerical Analysis. The second unit is a large computing laboratory, to be located in Washington, D. C., or in New York City. The third unit is a statistical consulting service specializing in the application of modern statistical inference to the physical and engineering sciences, and the fourth unit is a laboratory devoted to the development of automatic digital computing machinery. The last two units are located at the Bureau in Washington, D. C.

A plan of development based on the present mathematical activities of the Bureau has been worked out which is geared to the availability in fiscal 1949 of automatic computing machinery now under construction. The plan envisions a stabilization of operations within two years at a level of about 94 man-years and $532,000 annually. The estimated capital cost of automatic computing equipment is not included in these figures, and is about $700,000.

The following complete typewritten report may be useful in showing both form and function of the various elements in a recommendation report.

How much of the report must a busy executive read to get what he needs?

Are so many subdivisions of the report desirable?

Are titles (main title, sectional heads, titles of tables and figures) all sufficiently clear and concise?

Is "Order of Presentation" a useful division?

Is the material of the report logically arranged?

Examine mechanical details: punctuation, abbreviations, numbers, hyphenation, etc.

Is material in the Appendix best placed there, or would it be more convenient in the body of the report?

Examine footnotes and bibliography.

Report on

OXYGEN–ENRICHMENT OF BLAST IN BLAST
FURNACE OPERATION

Suggested for
THE OAKDALE STEEL CORPORATION

Submitted to

Mr. Guy C. Oakdale

President

By

W. H. Stauffenberg

Consultant

January 14, 1948

103 South Laurel Street
Hazleton, Pennsylvania
January 14, 1948

Mr. Guy C. Oakdale, President
Oakdale Steel Corporation
Steelburg, Pennsylvania

My dear Sir:

In accordance with your letter of December 15, 1947, I have investigated the principle of oxygen-enrichment of the blast in the smelting of iron ore, especially in regard to the possible adaptation to the Corporation's furnaces.

The enclosed report, avoiding the technical details of the principle, considers the possible financial advantages which this adaptation might have for the Corporation.

These advantages seem to be of magnitude sufficient to warrant construction of an oxygen-rectifying plant to be used in conjunction with the proposed blast furnaces.

Respectfully yours,

W. H. Stauffenberg

W. H. Stauffenberg

TABLE OF CONTENTS

TABLE OF CONTENTS, cont'd

INTRODUCTION

SUBJECT

This report deals with the smelting of iron ore by a blast enriched with various percentages of oxygen, especially 25%, and the results obtained by the use of this blast.

PURPOSE

The purpose of the report is to investigate the adaptability of the principle of oxygen–enrichment of the blast to the design and operation of the two blast furnaces, construction of which is deemed necessary by the Corporation to increase the smelting capacity of the steel plant.

SCOPE

It is not intended to introduce details of construction either of the blast furnaces as modified or of the oxygen plant itself. Rather it is desired to consider the apparent financial advantage such adaptation of the process may have to the Corporation.

ORDER OF PRESENTATION

Only the features of operation necessary to the understanding of the principle of blast enrichment are discussed. The advantages to the Corporation are presented with emphasis upon increased production, flexible operation, and financial benefits. Only the pertinent facts of the oxygen–manufacturing equipment, such as the general equipment needed, the cost of the complete rectifier, and costs of operation.

CONCLUSIONS

1. Experiments have proved that 25%–oxygen-enriched blast can boost production of blast furnaces by from 200 to 400 tons per day, to a total production of about 2250 tons of pig iron per day.

2. Enrichment of the blast to 40% oxygen increases the rate to 3300 tons of iron per day, but at a somewhat higher unit cost.

3. Low-grade ores may be smelted with the use of oxygen-enriched blast with greater production possible than with air blast alone.

4. The Corporation would benefit financially from the increased production of iron ore by the use of oxygen.

5. An oxygen plant sufficiently large to meet the demands of two furnaces would deliver 500 tons of oxygen per day at a cost of about $3 per ton.

6. Construction of this plant would require about $2,500,000.

7. Unless furnaces are specially designed, and unless slag formation is carefully controlled, enrichment may be limited to 30%.

RECOMMENDATIONS

1. The Corporation should authorize the construction of an oxygen plant to produce metallurgical oxygen for smelting operations in the two proposed blast furnaces.

2. The Engineering Department should be instructed to draft plans for the necessary modifications to the present plans for the proposed blast furnaces. Briefly, these concern pressure operation, modified stacks, and equipment for introducing the oxygen into the primary air stream.

3. The Engineering Department should also draw up specifications for an oxygen plant capable of manufacturing 500 tons of 95% oxygen per day. The Department should consult with experts in the metallurgical-oxygen field, especially the Linde Air Products Company and the Air Reduction Corporation, both of whom pioneered in the manufacture of commercial oxygen.

PERTINENT OPERATIONAL FEATURES
IN PRESENT AND PROPOSED BLAST FURNACES

No attempt is made to present the details of construction of present or proposed blast furnaces.

Only those details concerned with pertinent operational features are here discussed. The supporting
data used are drawn from Tables I and II, pages 10,
11.

CONVENTIONAL–TYPE BLAST FURNACES

Wind Blown: The amount of wind blown varies
between 45,000 and 75,000 cu ft per min. If greater
volume is blown, excessive velocity disrupts the
movement of the charge.

Top Pressure: Average pressure of 2.5 lb per
sq in. results at the top of the blast–furnace
stack.

Burden Ratio: The burden ratio in lb of iron
ore per lb of dry coke ranges from an average of
2.65 at 45,000 cu ft per min to an average of 2.28
at 75,000 cu ft per min.

Production: Production of pig iron per day by
a 27–ft–hearth furnace ranges from 837 tons when
blown at 45,000 cu ft per min to 1187 tons at 75,000
cu ft per min.

HIGH–PRESSURE BLAST FURNACES

Wind Blown: Wind blown may be varied to a
maximum of 105,000 cu ft per min by the application
of greater top pressure.

Top Pressure: The application of top pressure
of 20 psi restricts the wind velocity so that the
movement of the charge is not disrupted.

Burden Ratio: The burden ratio, substantially
improved by the combination of more wind and greater
top pressure, averages 2.83 at 45,000 cu ft per min
and 2.62 at 105,000 cu ft per min.

Production: Daily production is substantially
boosted by the combination of more wind and high
top pressure, all at an improved iron–coke ratio.
Table I (p. 14) shows daily production of 1467 tons
at 75,000 cu ft per min in the high top pressure
furnace, a marginal increase of 280 tons over the

common type of blast furnace. The pressure furnace can yield 1935 tons per day at 105,000 cu ft per min.

Cost of Modifications in Design: Since prices of turbo-blowers and pressure equipment vary but little between types of furnaces, design of furnaces for pressure operation entails no increase in construction costs.

HIGH-PRESSURE FURNACES WITH OXYGEN-ENRICHED BLAST

Wind Blown: For most efficient operation, wind rate should range between 60,000 and 105,000 cu ft per min.

Top Pressure: Top pressure of 20 lb per sq in. is necessary for this rate of blast.

Burden Ratio: The burden ratio with oxygen-enriched blast remains essentially the same as in the high-pressure furnace with air blast.

Production: High-pressure furnaces operated with 25%-oxygen blast show a marginal increase of 200 to 315 tons of pig iron per day over the production of high-pressure furnaces operated with air. A daily production rate of 2250 tons per furnace seems assured.

When the blast is enriched further, pig iron production rate is much increased, reaching a maximum of 3300 tons when 40%-oxygen blast is used.[1] Best economy of operation is not assured at this rate, but the ability of the furnace to produce this ample amount may be very significant in time of imperative need.

[1] Old, B. S., Almeida, A. R., Hyde, R. W., and Pepper, E. L., "Economics of the Blast Furnace," Iron Age, Vol. 160, No. 12, p. 62, September 18, 1947.

ADVANTAGES OF OXYGEN-ENRICHED BLAST

PRODUCTION INCREASED

Increased production is the greatest near-term advantage obtained by using oxygen-enriched blast. The marginal increase of 315 tons per day over the output of the high-pressure air-blast furnace is significant during the present period of scarcity of steel. This marginal increase, boosting output per furnace to 2250 tons, occurs under good operational conditions, economy of operation being considered. Furthermore, a production-rate increase to 3300 tons is significant, inasmuch as demand for steel is expected to be great for several years. Consequently, enrichment of the blast seems to be a worth-while measure.

FLEXIBILITY OF OPERATION

Altering the volume of wind, the top pressure, and the degree of enrichment permits a flexibility of blast furnace operation so that either increased production or decreased unit cost may be emphasized. Although best economy of blast furnace operation is not assured at the production rate of 3300 tons, for example, consideration must be given to the advantage of having an adequate supply of pig iron available for the plant's refining furnaces. The ability to adjust this supply to meet the demands of refining schedules their economy to balance a less economical smelting operation. Smoother coordination of blast-furnace-rolling-mill sequence is thus possible.

OPERATION USING LOW-GRADE ORES

An experimental furnace using low-grade ores averaged 115 tons per day with 25%-oxygen blast and 96 tons with air blast. Pounds of coke consumed per ton of iron produced dropped to 1746 from 1870.[1]

[1] Neustaetter, Kurt, "Blowing Oxygen-Enriched Air into Blast Furnace," Blast Furnace and Steel Plant, Vol. 35 No. 3, p. 329, March 1947.

The ability of oxygen blast to raise the rate of production from both high-grade and low-grade ores is of interest. Since the reserves of high-grade ores in the United States are rapidly being depleted,[1] the price is subject to upward pressure. Reserves of low-grade ores are adequate and should be considered for longer-term operation. The ability of the furnaces to smelt low-grade ores provides some assurance against closing down the furnaces if either the available supply of high-grade ore is diminished or the cost becomes excessive.

Beneficiation of low-grade ore to 55% iron content is expected to provide a satisfactory substitute for the high-grade ore, but the process has not been perfected. Using beneficiated ore, oxygen, and pressure, the furnaces should be capable of producing at the rate of 2500 tons per day, as shown in Table III (p. 15).

INTANGIBLE ADVANTAGES

Improvement of Delivery Schedules: Greater flexibility of production and increased rate of production will aid in shortening delivery time, enabling the plant to accept and fill orders which might otherwise be diverted to other manufacturers.

Improved Competitive Position: The Corporation's competitive position is much improved if it is able to deliver steel on shorter order because of a higher rate of production. Diversion of orders to producers of competitive materials, such as aluminum, will be diminished. Furthermore, customers urgently in need of steel look to the mill which can deliver sooner. Ability to deliver results in consumer good-will.

If necessary, low-grade ores may be utilized, better rate of production being maintained than that possible by using air blast alone. Beneficiation of low-grade ores undoubtedly would be more

[1] Reserves of rich ore have been estimated at 15 years' supply.

economical than continued use of the lean ores, but oxygen-enriched blast used on unbeneficiated lean ores can furnish the necessary buffer between stoppage of supply of rich ore and adequate supply by beneficiation.

SATISFACTORY UNIT PRODUCTION COST

Unit cost of production when oxygen is used compares favorably with unit cost when high-pressure air blast alone is used. Both are lower than unit cost of pig iron produced by the conventional blast furnace. Figure No. 1 (p. 16) shows probable savings of $1 to $2.50 per ton when high-pressure air blast is used. Chart No. 2 (p. 16) shows similar savings when 25%-oxygen blast is used.

The most economical rate of operation is about 85,000 cu ft per min. While unit cost is from 50 to 75 cents greater when the furnace is operated at 105,000 cu ft per min, production rate is boosted by about 400 tons. The criterion deciding operating rate is whether stress is upon production or upon unit cost.

These calculated unit costs are predicated upon the cost of oxygen at $3 per ton, which is the best estimate at the present time. However, a lower figure ($2 per ton)[1] predicted by some engineers would reduce unit costs 10 to 15 cents.

EFFECT UPON REFRACTORIES

The use of oxygen has been found to have no deleterious effect upon hearth or stack refractories.[2]

[1] Farley, Ralph W., "Iron and Steel Manufacture," Metal Progress, Vol. 51, No. 6, p. 973, June 1947.

[2] Thring, M. W., "Use of Oxygen in British Steel Industry," Journal of the Iron and Steel Institute, Vol. 156, Part 2, p. 288, June 1947.

FACTORS LIMITING THE USE OF OXYGEN

HEAT REQUIREMENTS

The heat leaving the hearth must meet the stack requirements. That is, the preheating of the charge is dependent upon the sensible heat carried to the stack by the gases leaving the hearth. As the percentage of oxygen—enrichment increases, the sensible heat in the exhaust gas decreases, owing to smaller volume of gas and to the somewhat lower hearth temperature. In order to avoid condensation at the top of the stack, exit gases should be above 230 degrees F. Oxygen-enrichment may be limited to about 30% unless the stack is shortened.[1]

RETARDED SLAG FORMATION

Slag formation may be retarded owing to low-ered hearth temperature, which results from too much oxygen. Enrichment is limited unless special emphasis is placed upon producing a lower-melting slag.

LIMITED DISCUSSION ON THE OXYGEN PLANT

REQUIRED OUTPUT

An oxygen plant capable of furnishing 500 tons per day would be required to supply the two proposed furnaces of the standard 27-ft-hearth size.[2] The oxygen, 95% pure, is supplied directly to the turbo-blowers and mixers at low pressure, 3 lb per sq in.

CONSTRUCTION COST

A plant of the required capacity is estimated to cost about $2,500,000.[3] This cost includes all necessary blowers, compressors, coolers, rectifier,

[1] Bennett, William, "Oxygen in the Blast Furnace," Abstract, Chemical Engineering, Vol. 54, No. 10, p. 114, October 1947.

[2] Old, B. S., op. cit., p. 67.

[3] Ibid.

etc. Electric power lines will be erected from the steel plant's central power station, which is deemed capable of supplying the necessary power.

OPERATING COSTS

Estimates of the cost of supplying oxygen range from $3 per ton[1] down to $2 per ton. Maintenance costs are expected to be low.[2] These costs, of course, are predicated upon nonintermittent operation such as is usually encountered in the blast furnace smelting.

CONCLUSION

The data, herein reproduced in tables or available in the references cited, seem to indicate that oxygen–enrichment of blast applied at high pressure to blast furnaces causes a substantial improvement in the rate of production. Up to 2250 tons of pig iron per day may be smelted when wind is blown to a maximum of 105,000 cu ft per min with very good economy of operation, while a maximum output of 3300 tons per day is possible at higher unit cost. In addition, greater flexibility in operation is possible, so that stress may be placed upon either economy in operation or maximum production.

In addition to showing better performance with high–grade ore, oxygen–enrichment of the blast should aid in smelting low–grade ores with greater production at lower unit cost than is possible with air blast alone. The ore–to–coke ratio, unchanged with rich ore, seems improved when lean ore is smelted.

An oxygen plant capable of producing 500 tons of oxygen per day (sufficient for two blast furnaces) would cost about $2,500,000. Cost of producing this metallurgical oxygen would be about $3 per ton.

The limit of oxygen–enrichment of the blast is apparently decided by hearth and stack temperatures and by the unit cost of the oxygen.

2 Farley, Ralph W., op. cit., p. 973.

TABLE I[1]

Normal and Pressure Operation of Blast Furnace with Air Blast

Wind Blown cfm	Top Pressure psi	Burden Ratio lb ore/ lb coke	Pig Iron tons/ day	Coke Rate lb/ton iron
45,000	2.5	2.65	837	1468
	10	2.79	883	1394
	20	2.83	895	1380
60,000	2.5	2.39	998	1632
	10	2.72	1150	1429
	20	2.80	1196	1380
75,000	2.5	2.28	1187	1710
	10	2.59	1359	1502
	20	2.77	1467	1402
90,000	2.5 (Cannot Operate)			
	10	2.42	1520	1608
	20	2.72	1724	1430
105,000	2.5 (Cannot Operate)			
	10	2.31	1690	1680
	20	2.62	1935	1480

1 Old, B. S., Almeida, A. R., Hyde, R. W., and Pepper, E. L., "Economics of the Blast Furnace,"
Iron Age, Vol. 160, No. 12, p. 62, September 18,
1947.

TABLE II[1]

Normal and Pressure Operation with 25%-Oxygen-Enriched Blast

Wind Blown cfm	Top Pressure psi	Burden Ratio lb ore/ lb coke	Pig Iron tons/ day	Coke Rate lb/ton iron
45,000	2.5	2.60	977	1497
	10	2.78	1049	1399
	20	2.82	1063	1380
60,000	2.5	2.34	1168	1660
	10	2.69	1351	1447
	20	2.79	1412	1391
75,000	2.5	2.26	1400	1720
	10	2.52	1576	1544
	20	2.75	1736	1412
90,000	2.5 (Cannot Operate)			
	10	2.37	1765	1643
	20	2.70	2039	1440
105,000	2.5 (Cannot Operate)			
	10	2.29	1987	1702
	20	2.57	2250	1515

1 Old, B. S., op. cit.

TABLE III[1]

Blast–Furnace Operation with Air and with 25%-
Oxygen–Enriched Blast, Beneficiated Ore
(55% Iron), Normal and High Pressure

Wind Blown cfm	Top Pressure psi	Oxygen Percentage	Pig Iron tons/ day	Coke Rate lb/ton iron
75,000	2.5	21	1306	1539
	10	21	1496	1471
	20	21	1613	1380
75,000	2.5	25	1540	1548
	10	25	1733	1513
	20	25	1908	1383
90,000	2.5	21	(Cannot Operate)	
	10	21	1672	1575
	20	21	1896	1401
90,000	2.5	25	(Cannot Operate)	
	10	25	1940	1610
	20	25	2243	1411
105,000	2.5	21	(Cannot Operate)	
	10	21	1859	1647
	20	21	2129	1450
105,000	2.5	25	(Cannot Operate)	
	10	25	2186	1667
	20	25	2475	1484

1 Old, B. S., op. cit., p. 66.

TABLE IV[1]

Manufacturing Costs for Various Conditions of Wind,
Top Pressures, and Oxygen in Blast, Compared to
Normal Cost per Ton of Pig Iron

Top Pressure psi	Oxygen Percentage	Wind Blown cfm	Pig Iron tons/day	Mfg. Cost per Ton (oxygen $3/ton)
2.5	25	67,000	1300	X
2.5	25	82,000	1500	X+0.30
10	21	71,000	1300	X-1.60
10	21	89,000	1500	X-1.20
10	25	58,000	1300	X-1.55
10	25	69,000	1500	X-1.25
20	21	66,000	1300	X-2.30
20	21	77,000	1500.	X-2.45
20	21	89,000	1700	X-2.35
20	25	55,000	1300	X-2.15
20	25	64,000	1500	X-2.35
20	25	74,000	1700	X-2.40

1 Ibid., p. 67.

Figure 1. UNIT COST OF PIG IRON AT VARIOUS PRESSURES - AIR BLAST [1]

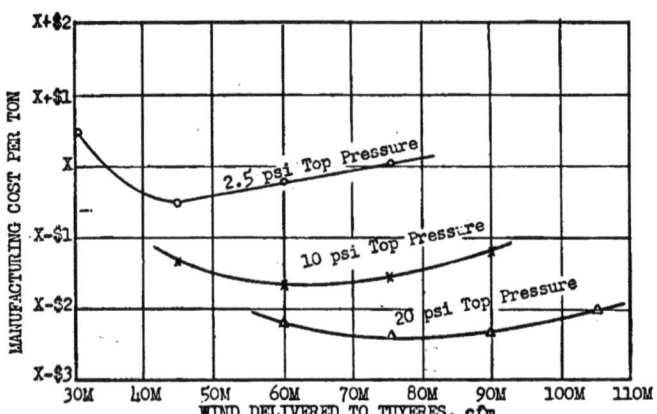

("X" is manufacturing cost at normal pressure and 75,000 cfm.)

Figure 2. UNIT COST OF PIG IRON, VARIOUS PRESSURES, OXYGEN USED [2]

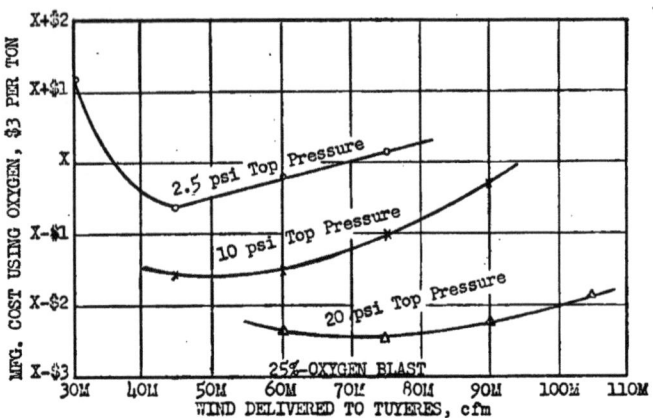

("X" is unit cost using air blast at 2.5 psi and 75,000 cfm.)

[1] Old, B. S. op. cit. p. 63
[2] Ibid. p. 65

BIBLIOGRAPHY

Bennett, William, "Oxygen in the Blast Furnace," Abstract, Chemical Engineering, Vol. 54, No. 10, p. 114, October 1947.

Bennett, William, "Use of Oxygen-Enriched Blast," Abstract, Mechanical Engineering, Vol. 69, No. 9, p. 769, September 1947.

Durrer, Robert, "The Production of Iron and Steel with Oxygen-Enriched Blast," Journal of the Iron and Steel Institute, Vol. 156, Part 2, pp. 253–256, June 1947.

Farley, Ralph W., "Iron and Steel Manufacture," Metal Progress, Vol. 51, No. 6, p. 973, June 1947.

Lobo, Walter E., "Low-Cost Metallurgical Oxygen," Iron Age, Vol. 160, No. 3, pp. 49–53, July 17, 1947.

Neustaetter, Kurt, "Blowing Oxygen-Enriched Air into the Blast Furnace," Blast Furnace and Steel Plant, Vol. 35, No. 3, pp. 329–331, March 1947.

Old, B. S., Almeida, A. R., Hyde, R. W., Pepper, E. L., "Economics of the Blast Furnace," Iron Age, Vol. 160, No. 12, pp. 60–68, September 18, 1947.

Thring, M. W., "Possibilities for Extended Use of Oxygen in the British Iron and Steel Industry," Journal of the Iron and Steel Institute, Vol. 156, Part 2, pp. 285–288, June 1947.

Anonymous, "Gaseous-Oxygen Pilot Plant Now Producing 200 Tons Daily," Chemical Engineering Progress, Vol. 43, No. 7, p. 16, July 1947.

Anonymous, "Steel-Making Oxygen Presents Problems," Iron Age, Vol. 160, No. 6, pp. 113–115, August 7, 1947.

THE LETTER OF APPLICATION

ALTHOUGH the letter of application is only indirectly a concern of the report writer, the authors feel that a brief discussion of its form and content is of sufficient importance to him to warrant its inclusion in the appendix. The treatment given here is intended merely as a guide to the average applicant; for elaboration the student is referred to the bibliography on letter-writing in Appendix B, Part II.

In writing any letter of application, consider the problem from four points of view: appearance, conventional practice, content, and presentation. These are the things by which your letter will be judged.

Appearance

1. Use plain white paper of good quality and standard size (8¾ x 11) with envelope to match. Avoid stationery bearing the letterhead of any social or business organization.

2. Typewrite your letter or have it typewritten. Unless you have specific instructions to the contrary, nothing in the letter except your signature should be handwritten. Use a black typewriter ribbon, and either black, blue-black, or blue ink for your signature.

3. Frame your letter on the page. The center of the letter, as a whole, including the heading, should be just above the center of the page, making the lower margin somewhat wider than the others. Leave ample margins on all four sides and try to arrange your wording in such a way that the right-hand margin will be reasonably uniform.

4. Be neat. Avoid blots, erasures, crossed-out words. Be sure that the ribbon is well inked and that the type is clean enough to print distinctly. Type evenly.

Conventional Practice

The conventional requirements of a letter of application differ little from those of the ordinary business letter as explained in Chapter 2, except in placing increased emphasis on courtesy and respectfulness, and in demanding absolute mechanical accuracy. In addition to these generalities:

1. Be consistent in your letter form. Use the block or the modified block, but do not use some of each.

2. Be consistent in punctuation. Use either open or close punctuation, but not some of each. The open is simpler, just as neat, and generally preferable.

3. Check and recheck your spelling. Use standard spelling forms.

4. Avoid abbreviations unless their use improves the appearance of the letter or unless the official name of a firm you are mentioning includes an abbreviation.

5. Use complete sentences (except on a data sheet).

6. Avoid stilted and hackneyed phrases quite as much as slang and colloquialisms.

7. Do not employ roundabout, awkward phrasing simply to avoid using "I" and "my." However, use these pronouns as seldom as possible, and keep them out of eye-catching places in your letter, especially the beginning (first word) of a paragraph.

8. Address an individual whenever possible; when not, address the personnel director.

9. Use "Respectfully yours" or "Yours respectfully" for your complimentary close.

Content

It is obvious that the letter of application should result from a careful consideration of two variables: the qualifications of the applicant and the requirements of the potential employer. It is equally obvious that no one but the individual applicant is in a position to determine the nature of both of these variables as they exist in his particular case. Too much emphasis cannot be placed on the need for his study of this problem before he outlines his letter. A textbook can do no more than make general suggestions, list the conventional inclusions, and give a few examples.

The following elements should appear in a letter of application —not all of them as separate paragraphs, and not necessarily in this order:

1. A direct statement of the purpose of the letter; that is, the direct and immediate application for a *specific* job or type of job.

2. Your reason for applying to this particular firm. If you are not answering an advertisement or if you do not have a "lead,"

the analysis you have made of the employer's requirements should supply your reason.

3. Your reason for applying for this particular job. If you have no additional reason, the details of your education, training, or experience probably explain this point.

4. Your education. If you do not use the data sheet method of presenting your information (as explained in the next section), you should select from the following items only the most significant. Even the data sheet need not include all of them.

High school record
College curriculum
   Major subject
   Minor subjects
   Courses related to job sought
College average or rank in class
Ability to read, understand, or speak foreign language
Extracurricular activities and interests

5. Your experience. If you are a student with little or no professional experience, mention *any* work you have done; an employer is often interested in knowing that you have been willing to deliver papers, mow lawns, work on road construction. If you earned part of your college expenses, say so.

A man with an experience record has a different problem. He must stress only what best meets the employer's requirements, even if it means the use of a separate data sheet to include the details.

In listing previous employment use the reverse chronological order. Give the name and business address of your employer, the exact title of the position you held, the dates you entered and left the job, a description of the work you did, and your reason for leaving. Also include the name and title of your immediate superior.

6. Personal information. From the following, select the items which meet the demands of the situation. If a data sheet is used, more details may be included.

Age	Married or single
Place of birth	Number of dependents
Lineage	Church affiliation
Nationality	Club affiliations

State of health
Height and weight
Eyesight and hearing

In addition, many applicants include a photograph. Unless, however, your physical appearance has some direct bearing on your ability to hold the job you are seeking, an offer to send a photograph on request is just as good.

7. References. Give at least three references, but none without permission. Choose them carefully from teachers who know your work, tradesmen with whom you have dealt, responsible citizens of your community, or persons for whom you have worked. Give their complete business addresses and identify each so that your relationship is apparent. These references and addresses should be blocked (unless you have used the indented style) and indented from your regular margins.

8. Request for the interview. For most letters of application the obtaining of an interview is the fulfillment of the letter's purpose. Such a request supplies a good positive close for your letter. Remember to state when and where you can be reached and when you will be available.

Presentation

The *order* of presentation has been indicated in the foregoing section. This order, of course, is variable: it would and it should be changed to meet the requirements of specific situations. Also, the employment of a separate data sheet would change the content of the letter proper and might also change the arrangement.

The *method* of presentation is more important than the order, and perhaps no less important than the content. However, it is subject to only the most general of rules.

1. The first paragraph—usually containing only the direct application itself—should be brief, emphatic.

2. The last paragraph should also be brief, emphatic, and positive. Usually it is a straightforward request for an interview.

3. The other paragraph, or paragraphs, should be centered about the points the writer wishes to emphasize most. If he uses a data sheet, perhaps one paragraph will be sufficient. If not, he may use several, depending largely on the amount and variety of his experience.

4. In general:
    a. Be direct and concise.
    b. Do not exaggerate; it is much better to understate.
    c. Stress what you have done, not what you will do.

d. Make no statements about your ability which you do not substantiate with concrete facts.

e. If possible, show that you have an understanding of what the requirements of the job are. This may be accomplished by the selection of things you include in your letter or by the emphasis you place on certain of them, but it can be done by actually linking your qualifications to the requirements of the job you are after.

f. Do not use flattery.

5. Use of a Data Sheet:

The letter of application is sometimes supplemented by a "data sheet," a separate page which resembles the questionnaire sent out by many companies in response to letters of application. (The student, incidentally, should not interpret this practice as indicating that no attention is paid his letter: filed observations about it are often the means of determining whether the applicant is worth the time of an interview.) The data sheet gives a complete and detailed record of the applicant and his history, complete enough so that *when it is filed separately it constitutes an adequate record.*

This tabular method is especially useful to the man who possesses considerable experience and wishes to stress in the letter itself only the most significant points. It is less useful to the student, whose experience is likely to be so slight that the inclusion of a data sheet makes either his first sheet "thin" or his second repetitious. He can use it to advantage, however, when the situation calls for the listing of many details—individual courses, complete information on his personal appearance, habits, lineage, and the like.

When used, the data sheet should:

a. Meet the same requirements of appearance demanded of the letter proper.

b. Contain sections giving the details of (1) education, (2) experience, (3) personal information, (4) references. Very often a small photograph is also included.

c. Have the items in each of these sections arranged in tabular form. Standard abbreviations are permissible, and single words or simple phrases should be used for identification— not complete sentences.

Study the form and content of the following examples of the letter of application:

228 West Prospect Avenue
Vernal Falls, New York
——— March 22, 1949

Personnel Director
Panamerico Chemical Company
710 Pine Street
New York, New York

Dear Sir:

Please consider this an application for a job as shift chemist in one of your plants, either in this country or in South America.

In June I shall graduate from the School of Chemistry at State University, where I have majored in physical chemistry. Other subjects I have taken include mathematics, organic and inorganic chemistry, and enough Spanish to speak the language fairly well. My scholastic average is in the upper third of a class of 1200. Although I have had to earn my board and room by waiting on table and firing furnace, my extra-curricular activities include membership on the editorial staff of a campus periodical and in the university camera club.

During vacations I have been needed on my father's farm, but the last two summers I have worked evenings as an oiler and pump packer for the Vernal Ice Company.

I am 22, American, and in good health. Permission has been given me to use the following persons as references:

Mr. R. C. Kent, Manager Mr. Paul Camp, President
Vernal Ice Company   Vernal National Bank
Vernal Falls, N.Y.   Vernal, New York

     Prof. W. R. Cushman
     School of Chemistry
     State University
     Albany, New York

If you desire any further references or information I shall be glad to send it. I should very much appreciate the opportunity of coming to New York for an interview on any Saturday.

      Respectfully yours,

      Anson H. Field

      Anson H. Field

FIG. 17. Letter of Application Without Data Sheet

4210 Atherton Street
Danbury, Connecticut
May 1, 1950

Mr. Harvey Eastman
Power Engineer
Western Salt Company
Trona, California

Dear Mr. Eastman

I should like to apply for a job in the instrument section
of your Testing Division, or as a junior engineer in your
Engineering Department.

Mr. E.J. Thacker, Sales Engineer for the Arvin Meter Company
of Hartford, tells me that you have ordered a considerable
number of flowmeters and pressure gages for your new soda-
products plant. Since I have spent the last two summers as
a parts inspector in the Arvin plant, and since I shall be
graduated from Stratton University next month in Mechanical
Engineering with a major study in power-plant operation, I
feel that I possess the qualifications you require of a novice
engineer.

The enclosed data sheet will supply details of my education
and experience, and the names and addresses of the persons
who can best evaluate my work.

I shall be glad to come to your New York office for an interview and can make the trip on a few days' notice at any time.

Yours respectfully,

John K. Bratzler

John K. Bratzler

FIG. 18a. Letter of Application

<u>DATA SHEET</u>

John K. Bratzler
4210 Atherton Street
Danbury, Connecticut

<u>PERSONAL DATA, June 1950</u>
Age 22   No dependents   Health good
Height 5 ft, 11 in.   American citizen   Hearing good
Weight 185 lb   Eyesight fair

<u>EDUCATION</u>
Stratton University (1950)
Degree: B.S. in Mechanical Engineering
Rank in class: Second fifth
Major study: Power-Plant Operation

Important courses (and credit hours):

<u>Basic</u>	<u>Technical</u>	<u>General</u>
Mathematics (18)	Thermodynamics (9)	English (9)
Physics (10)	Machine Design (9)	Psychology (3)
Drawing (5)	Electric Applications (6)	Report Writing (3)
Chemistry (6)	Fluid Mechanics (4)	Economics (6)
Metallurgy (3)	Engineering Materials (6)	History (3)

Danbury High School (Connecticut), 1946

<u>ACTIVITIES AND ORGANIZATIONS</u>
Gamma Xi Fraternity, Chapter Secretary
Junior member ASME
Cabinet representative, College of Engineering

<u>EXPERIENCE</u>
Summers of 1948, 1949:
Parts inspector, Arvin Meter Company
Superior: Mr. C.L.Jameson
Summer of 1947:
Truck driver, Carmel Lumber Company
Employer: Mr. Stephen Cornell, Carmel, N.Y.
Summer of 1946:
Laborer on highway construction, Town of Danbury, Conn.
Employer: Mr. J.C. Lonert, Road Commissioner

<u>REFERENCES (by permission)</u>:

Mr. C.L. Jameson, Head   Mr. J.C. Lonert
Inspection Department   Road Commissioner
Arvin Meter Company   Town of Danbury
Hartford 7, Connecticut   Danbury, Connecticut

Prof. S.M. Semp, Head
Department of Mechanics
College of Engineering
Stratton University
Albany 5, New York

FIG. 18b. Data Sheet

BIBLIOGRAPHY OF BOOKS AND PERIODICALS USEFUL TO THE REPORT WRITER

I

REFERENCE ABSTRACTS AND INDEXES

Today the volume of technical literature is so great that a systematic search for information on a special subject would be impossible without the following indexes.

The Agricultural Index. Monthly and cumulative. A subject index to a selected list of more than 200 agricultural publications.

The Art Index. Irregularly and cumulative. A subject and author index to fine arts periodicals, books, and museum bulletins, covering archeology, architecture, ceramics, decoration and ornament, graphic arts, landscape architecture, painting, and sculpture.

Battelle Library Review. Monthly. An annotated bibliography of industrial and scientific research. Especially valuable in ceramics, fuel technology, and metallurgy.

Bibliography of Scientific and Industrial Reports. Monthly. By the U. S. Department of Commerce. Classified by subject and indexed by author. Many foreign reports listed.

Chemical Abstracts. Semimonthly. Abstracts material (in English) from some 3600 publications from all over the world. Indexed by author, subject, and chemical formula. Cumulative index decennially (last in December 1946).

Cumulative Book Index. Monthly and cumulative. Indexes American (and some other) books by author, subject, and title.

The Engineering Index. Annually. Contains references to important articles, papers, and reports in some 1500 current engineering, scientific, and industrial publications from all parts of the world. These publications include periodicals; society transactions, bulletins, and proceedings; reports and bulletins of government agencies, engineering colleges, experiment stations, research laboratories, and other technical agencies.

The Industrial Arts Index. Monthly and cumulative. A subject index to a selected list of some 250 engineering, trade, and business periodicals and pamphlets.

International Index to Periodicals. Monthly and cumulative. An author and subject index to a selected list of periodicals of the world. "Devoted chiefly to the humanities and science."

The New York Times Index. Monthly and cumulative annually. Lists and digests contents of the *Times* and supplies publication dates of general and international news.

U. S. Government Monthly Publications Catalog. Monthly. Bound and indexed annually. Lists and describes the publications of all government agencies. An invaluable source of reference material in every field.

The U. S. Quarterly Book List. Quarterly. A highly selective bibliography, including short reviews, of currently published books in the United States only. Relevant headings: Social Sciences; Biological Sciences; Physical Sciences; Technology.

II

BOOKS

Handbooks, Texts, and Booklets Relating to the Composition of Reports

American Standards Association, *Abbreviations for Scientific and Engineering Terms.* Bulletin Z10.1–1941. New York: American Standards Association, 1941.

American Standards Association, *Abbreviations for Use on Drawings.* Bulletin Z32.13–1946. New York: American Standards Association, 1946.

American Society of Mechanical Engineers, *Style Manual for Engineering Authors and Editors.* New York: A.S.M.E., 1939.

Baker, Ray Palmer, and Howell, Almonte C., *Preparation of Reports,* Revised Edition. New York: Ronald Press, 1938.

Crouch, W. George, and Zetler, Robert L., *A Guide to Technical Writing.* New York: Ronald Press Co., 1948.

Gatner, E. S. M., and Cordasco, F. G. M., *University Handbook for Research and Report Writing,* Revised Edition. Brooklyn: Lambs Book Exchange, 1947.

Government Printing Office, *Manual of Style,* Revised Edition. 1945.

Harbarger, Sada A., *et al., English for Engineers.* Fourth Edition. New York: McGraw-Hill Book Co., 1943.

Howell, A. C., *Handbook of English in Engineering Usage.* New York: John Wiley & Sons, 1940.

Hubbell, G. S., *Writing Documented Papers.* New York: Barnes & Noble, 1946.

Jones, W. Paul, *Writing Scientific Papers and Reports.* Dubuque, Iowa: W. C. Brown, 1946.

Nelson, J. Raleigh, *Writing the Technical Report.* Second Edition. New York: McGraw-Hill Book Co., 1947.

Oliver, Leslie M., *Technical Exposition.* New York: McGraw-Hill Book Co., 1940.

Rhodes, Fred H., *Technical Report Writing.* New York: McGraw-Hill Book Co., 1941.

Schmitz, R. M., *Preparing the Research Paper,* Third Edition. New York: Rinehart and Co., 1947.

Smellie, D. G., "Research Reports," Chapter IX of *Research in Industry*. New York: D. Van Nostrand Co., Inc., 1948.

Sypherd, Wilbur O., *et al.*, *Engineer's Manual of English*, Revised Edition. Chicago: Scott, Foresman & Co., 1943.

Trelease, Samuel F., *The Scientific Paper*. Baltimore: Williams & Wilkins, 1947.

Walker, Harry C., *Analysis and Presentation of Engineering Problems*, Second Edition. Nashville: Cullon & Gherter Co., 1946.

Handbooks and Texts on English and Letter Writing

Aurner, Robert Ray, *Effective English in Business*, Second Edition. Cincinnati: South-Western Publishing Co., 1940.

Babenroth, A. Charles, and Parkhurst, C. C., *Modern Business English*, Fourth Edition. New York: Prentice-Hall, Inc., 1949.

Butterfield, William Henry, *The Business Letter in Modern Form*, Enlarged Edition. New York: Prentice-Hall, Inc., 1941.

Conat, W. H., *Letter Writing in Business*. New York: Gregg Publishing Co., 1945.

Frailey, Lester F., *Handbook of Business Letters*. New York: Prentice-Hall, Inc., 1948.

Hotchkiss, George B., and Kilduff, E. J., *Advanced Business Correspondence*, Fourth Edition. New York: Harper & Brothers, 1947.

Perrin, Porter G., *Writer's Guide and Index to English*. Chicago: Scott, Foresman & Co., 1942.

Smart, Walter Kay, and McKelvey, Louis W., *Business Letters*. New York: Harper & Brothers, 1941.

University of Chicago, *Manual of Style*, Tenth Edition. Chicago: University of Chicago Press, 1937.

Williams, Cecil B., *Effective Business Writing*. New York: The Ronald Press, 1947.

Handbooks and Texts on Graphs, Charts, and Statistics

American Standards Association, *Engineering and Scientific Graphs for Publication*. Bulletin Z15.3–1943. New York: American Standards Association, 1943.

Arkin, Herbert, and Colton, Raymond R., *An Outline of Statistical Methods*. New York: Barnes & Noble, Inc., 1939.

Brinton, Willard Cope, *Graphic Presentation*. New York: Brinton Associates, 1939.

Columbia University, *Selected Techniques of Statistical Analysis for Scientific and Industrial Research and Production and Management Engineering*. New York: McGraw-Hill Book Co., 1948.

Croxton, F. E., and Cowden, D. J., *Practical Business Statistics*. New York: Prentice-Hall, Inc., 1937.

Davies, Owen L., *Statistical Methods in Research and Production*. London: Oliver & Boyd, 1947.

Fisher, Ronald A., *Statistical Methods for Research Workers*. London: Oliver & Boyd, 1946.

Hays, Samuel, *Outline of Statistics*. New York: Longmans, Green & Co., 1947.

Jordan, Richard C., and Edwards, Marion J., *Aids to Technical Writing*. Minneapolis: University of Minnesota Engineering Experiment Station, 1944.

Mode, Elmer B., *Elements of Statistics*. New York: Prentice-Hall, Inc., 1941.

Modley, Rudolf, *How to Use Pictorial Statistics*. New York: Harper & Brothers, 1937.

Simon, Leslie Earl, *An Engineer's Manual of Statistical Methods*. New York: John Wiley & Sons, 1941.

Smart, L. E., and Arnold, S., *Practical Rules for Graphic Presentation of Business Statistics*. Columbus: Ohio State Bureau of Business Research, 1947.

Weld, Walter E., *How to Chart*. Norwood, Mass.: Codex Book Co., 1947.

Publications of Source and Reference Material

The American Year Book. Thomas Nelson & Sons.

The Census Volumes (Department of Commerce; Bureau of the Census):

Agriculture	Manufacturers
Construction Industry	Retail Distribution
Drainage of Agricultural Lands	Unemployment
Irrigation of Agricultural Lands	Wholesale Distribution

Foreign Commerce Yearbook. Department of Commerce.

Minerals Year Book. Department of the Interior; Bureau of Mines.

Moody's Manual of Investments, American and Foreign:

> Industrial Securities
> Municipal Securities
> Public Utility Securities
> Railroad Securities

The Municipal Year Book. International City Managers' Assn.

N.A.P.A. Handbook of Commodity Data Sheets. National Assn. of Purchasing Agents.

Bulletin of the Public Affairs Information Service. The P.A.I.S., New York.

The Statesman's Year Book. Macmillan & Company.

Statistical Abstract of the United States. Department of Commerce.

Tax Diary and Manual. Prentice-Hall, Inc.

The World Almanac. The New York *World-Telegram*.

III

TECHNICAL PERIODICALS

To facilitate reference, the following selected British and American periodicals have been somewhat loosely classified according to their content. Most of them are indexed in one or more of the indexes listed in Part I of this appendix. British publications are marked with an asterisk. Frequency of publication is indicated by the following symbols:

W—weekly	BW—biweekly	SW—semiweekly
M—monthly	BM—bimonthly	SM—semimonthly
Q—quarterly	6x, 9x etc.—number	SQ—semiquarterly
A—annually	of times annually	SA—semiannually

For complete information on periodicals, consult *The Dictionary of Newspapers and Periodicals,* published by N. W. Ayer & Son, Inc. in Philadelphia.

Aeronautics

Aero Digest	New York	M
Aeronautical Engineering Review	New York	M
Aeronautics•	London	M
Air Transport	New York	M
Aircraft Engineering•	London	M
Aircraft Production•	London	M
American Aviation	New York	SM
Automotive and Aviation Industries	Philadelphia	SM
Aviation Maintenance and Operation	New York	M
Aviation Week	New York	W
Canadian Aviation	Toronto	M
CAA Journal	Washington	M
Flight and Aircraft Engineer•	London	W
Journal of Aeronautical Sciences	New York	M

Agriculture, Agronomy, and Forestry

(*See also* Biology)

Agricultural Engineering	St. Joseph, Mich.	M
Agricultural Engineering Record•	London	Q
American Agriculturist	Ithaca, N. Y.	BW
American Fertilizer	Philadelphia	BW
American Forests	Washington	M
American Fruit Grower	Cleveland	M
American Lumberman	Chicago	BW
Biodynamics	Chester, N. Y.	irreg.
Chemurgic Digest	New York	SM
Cosgrove's Magazine	Grand Rapids, Mich.	M
Empire Journal of Agricultural Research•	London	Q
Experiment Station Record	Washington	M
Extension Service Review	Washington	M
Farm Journal	Philadelphia	M
Farm Research	Geneva, N. Y.	Q
Farm Science Reporter	Ames, Iowa	Q
Farmer's Bulletin	Washington	irreg.
Fire Control Notes	Washington	Q

Food Research	Champaign, Ill.	BM
Horticultural Abstracts•	Kent	Q
Journal of Agricultural Research	Washington	SM
Journal of Agricultural Science•	London	Q
Journal of the American Society of Agronomy	Geneva, N. Y.	M
Journal of Forestry	Washington	M
Journal of Official Agricultural Chemists	Menasha, Wis.	Q
Journal of Wildlife Management	Menasha, Wis.	Q
Lumber Industry Report	Washington	M
Nature Magazine	Washington	10x
Paper Trade Journal	New York	W
Scientific Agriculture	Ottawa	M
Soil Conservation	Washington	M
Soil Service	Baltimore	M
Southern Pulp and Paper Manufacture	Atlanta	M
Timber of Canada	Ottawa	M
Timberman	Portland, Ore.	M
Tropical Woods	New Haven	4x
West Coast Lumberman	Seattle	M
Wood•	London	M
Wood-Worker	Indianapolis	M

Architecture

(*See also* Civil Engineering)

American Builder and Building Age	Chicago	M
Architect and Building News•	London	W
Architect and Engineer	San Francisco	M
Architectural Forum	New York	M
Architectural Record	New York	M
Builder•	London	W
Journal of American Institute of Architects	Washington	M
Journal of Royal Institute of British Architects•	London	M
Progressive Architecture	New York	M

Biology and Physiology

(*See also* Agriculture)

American Anthropologist	Menasha, Wis.	Q
American Botanist	Indianapolis	Q
American Journal of Botany	Burlington, Vt.	M
American Journal of Medical Sciences	Philadelphia	M
American Journal of Physical Anthropology	Philadelphia	Q
American Journal of Physiology	Baltimore	M
American Naturalist	Lancaster, Pa.	BM
Anatomical Record	Philadelphia	M

*Annals of Applied Biology**	London	Q
*Annals of Botany**	London	Q
*Annals of Eugenics**	London	Q
Applied Anthropology	Boston	Q
Bacteriological Review	Baltimore	Q
Biological Abstracts	Philadelphia	irreg.
Biological Bulletin	Woods Hole, Mass.	BM
*British Chemical and Physiological Abstracts**	London	M
Chemical Abstracts	Washington	SM
Chemical Reviews	Washington	BM
Ecological Monographs	Durham, N. C.	Q
Ecology	Durham, N. C.	Q
Entomological News	Philadelphia	M
*Eugenics Review**	London	Q
Genetics	Brooklyn	BM
Growth	Philadelphia	Q
Human Biology	Baltimore	Q
Hygeia	Chicago	M
Industrial Hygiene	Washington	M
Journal of Biological Chemistry	Baltimore	M
Journal of Cellular and Comparative Physiology	Philadelphia	BM
Journal of Entomology and Zoology	Claremont, Cal.	Q
Journal of Experimental Zoology	Philadelphia	9x
Journal of General Physiology	New York	M
*Journal of Genetics**	London	3x
Journal of Health and Toxicology	Baltimore	BM
Journal of Heredity	Baltimore	M
Journal of Morphology	Philadelphia	BM
Journal of Parisitology	Colorado Springs	BM
*Journal of Physiology**	London	irreg.
*Man**	London	M
*Nutrition Abstracts and Reviews**	Aberdeen	Q
Pests and Their Control	Kansas City, Mo.	M
Physiological Reviews	Baltimore	Q
Physiological Zoology	Chicago	Q
Plant Physiology	Lancaster, Pa.	Q
*Quarterly Journal of Microscopical Science**	London	Q
Quarterly Review of Biology	Baltimore	Q
Stain Technology	Geneva, N. Y.	Q
Yale Journal of Biology and Medicine	New Haven	6x

Ceramics

Brick and Clay Record	Chicago	M
Bulletin of the American Ceramic Society	Columbus, O.	M
Ceramic Age	Newark, N. J.	M
*Ceramic Digest**	London	SA
Ceramic Forum	Pittsburgh	M

Ceramic Industry	Chicago	M
China and Glass	New York	M
Crockery and Glass	East Stroudsburg, Pa.	M
Glass Industry	New York	M
Journal of American Ceramic Society (Including *Ceramic Abstracts*)	Columbus, O.	M
Journal of the Society of Glass Technology°	Sheffield	M
Transactions of the British Ceramic Society°	Stoke-on-Trent	M

Chemistry

(*See also related headings*)

American Dyestuff Reporter	New York	BW
Analyst °	Cambridge	M
Analytical Chemistry	Washington	M
Archives of Biochemistry	New York	M
Canadian Chemistry and Process Industries	Toronto	M
Chemical Abstracts	Washington	SM
Chemical Age°	London	W
Chemical and Engineering News	Washington	W
Chemical and Metallurgical Engineering	New York	M
Chemical Engineering	New York	M
Chemical Engineering Progress	Philadelphia	M
Chemical Industries	New York	M
Chemical Processing Review	Chicago	M
Chemical Reviews	Baltimore	BM
Chemist	New York	9x
Chemistry and Industry°	London	W
Enamelist	Cleveland	M
India Rubber World	New York	M
Industrial and Engineering Chemistry	Washington	SM
Isotopics	Cleveland	M
Journal of American Chemical Society	Washington	M
Journal of American Oil Chemists	Chicago	M
Journal of American Pharmaceutical Association	Washington	M
Journal of Chemical Education	Washington	M
Journal of Colloid Science	New York	M
Journal of Electrochemical Society	Baltimore	M
Journal of Organic Chemistry	Baltimore	BM
Journal of Physical Chemistry	Baltimore	9x
Journal of Polymer Science	New York	M
Modern Plastics	New York	M
Oil, Paint, and Drug Reporter	New York	W
Oil and Soap	Chicago	M
Paint, Oil, and Chemical Review	Chicago	BW
Paper Industry and Paper World	Chicago	M
Paper Makers' Journal	Albany, N. Y.	M

Rayon Textile Monthly	New York	M
Rubber Age	New York	M
Soap and Sanitary Chemicals	New York	M
Textile Colorist and Converter	New York	M
Textile Research Journal	New York	M
Textile.World	New York	M
Transactions of American Institute of Chemical Engineers	New York	BM
Transactions of the Faraday Society*	London	M
Transactions of Institution of Chemical Engineers*	London	irreg.
Wood Preserving News	Chicago	M

Civil Engineering

American Builder and Building Age	Chicago	M
American City	New York	M
American Highway	Washington	Q
Better Roads	Chicago	M
Civil Engineering	New York	M
Concrete	Chicago	M
Concrete Products	Chicago	M
Construction	Baltimore	M
Construction Digest	Indianapolis	BW
Construction Methods	New York	M
Construction News	Little Rock	M
Contractors' and Engineers' Monthly	New York	M
Excavating Engineer	S. Milwaukee	M
Journal of American Concrete Institute	Detroit	6x
Journal of American Water Works Association	New York	M
Journal of Institution of Civil Engineers*	London	M
Mass Transportation	Chicago	M
Modern Railroads	Chicago	M
Municipal Engineers Journal	New York	Q
Pacific Road Builder and Review	San Francisco	M
Photogrammetric Engineering	Washington	Q
Practical Builder	Chicago	M
Proceedings of the A.S.C.E.	New York	10x
Public Roads	Washington	M
Public Works	Washington	M
Railway Age	New York	W
Railway Electric Engineering	New York	M
Railway Engineering and Maintenance	Chicago	M
Roads and Bridges	Toronto	M
Roads and Streets	Chicago	M
Sewage Works Engineering	New York	M
Sewage Works Journal	Chicago	BM
Surveying and Mapping	Washington	Q
Surveyor and Municipal and County Engineer*	London	W

Traffic Engineering	New York	M
Water and Sewage	Toronto	M
Water and Sewage Works	Chicago	M
Water and Water Engineering°	London	M
Water Works and Sewage	New York	M
Water Works Engineering	New York	SM
Western Construction News	San Francisco	M

Coal, Coke, Combustion, and Fuel

(See also related headings)

Coal Age	New York	M
Coal-Heat	Chicago	M
Coal Herald	Boston	M
Coal Mining	Pittsburgh	M
Coal Technology	New York	Q
Coke and Gas°	London	M
Colliery°	London	M
Colliery Guardian°	London	W
Combustion	New York	M
Fuel°	London	M
Journal of the Institute of Fuel°	London	6x
Mechanization	Washington	M
Utilization	Washington	M

Electricity and Power

(See also Physics)

Allis-Chalmers Electrical Review	Milwaukee	Q
Electrical Construction and Mainte- nance	New York	M
Electrical Engineering	New York	M
Electrical Manufacturing	New York	M
Electrical Review°	London	W
Electrical South	Atlanta	M
Electrical West	San Francisco	M
Electrical World	New York	W
Electrician°	London	W
Electric Light and Power	Chicago	M
Electrified Industry	Chicago	M
Electronic Industries and Electronic Instrumentation	New York	M
Electronic News	Chicago	M
Electronics	New York	M
General Electric Review	Schenectady	M
Illuminating Engineer	New York	10x
Industry and Power	St. Joseph, Mich.	M
Journal of the Institution of Electrical Engineers°	London	M
Light and Lighting°	London	M
Modern Power and Engineering	Toronto	M

National Engineer	Chicago	M
Power	New York	M
Power Generation	Chicago	M
Power Plant Engineering	Chicago	M
Public Power	Washington	M
Rural Electrification News	Washington	M
Science Abstracts, Section B°	London	M
Southern Power and Industry	Atlanta	M
Steam Engineer°	London	M

Gas, Oil, and Petroleum

American Gas Association Monthly	New York	M
American Gas Journal	New York	M
American Petroleum Institute Quarterly	New York	Q
Drilling	Dallas	M
Gas	Los Angeles	M
Gas Age	New York	BW
Gas Journal °	London	W
Gas World °	London	W
Industrial Gas	New York	M
Journal of the Institute of Petroleum°	Suffolk	M
Lubrication	Cleveland	W
National Petroleum News	New York	M
Oil and Gas Journal	Tulsa	W
Oil Digest °	London	M
Petroleum°	London	M
Petroleum Engineer	Dallas	M
Petroleum Processing	Cleveland	M
Petroleum Refiner	Houston	M
Petroleum Technology	New York	BM
Petroleum Times°	London	BW
Producers Monthly	Bradford, Pa.	M
World Oil	Houston	W
World Petroleum	New York	M

General and Miscellaneous

American Engineer	New York	M
A.S.T.M. Bulletin	Philadelphia	6x
Bulletin of the General Contractors Association	New York	M
Bulletin of Research, National Board Fire Underwriters	New York	M
Bulletin of the Western Society of Engineers	Chicago	Q
Canadian Journal of Research	Ottawa	M
Compressed Air Magazine	Phillipsburg, N. J.	M
Design News	Detroit	M
Draftsman	New York	M
Engineer°	London	W
Engineering°	London	W

Engineering News-Record	New York	W
Engineer's Digest	New York	M
Experiment Station Record	Washington	M
Explosives Engineer	Wilmington, Del.	BM
Fasteners	Cleveland	irreg.
Fire Engineering	New York	M
Firemen	Boston	M
Fortune	New York	M
Industrial Marketing	Chicago	M
Industrial Research	New York	M
Industrial Standardization	New York	M
International Engineer	Washington	M
International Fire Fighter	Washington	M
Journal of American Statistics Association	Washington	Q
Journal of Engineering Education	Pittsburgh	10x
Journal of the Franklin Institute	Philadelphia	M
Journal of Research of the National Bureau of Standards	Washington	M
Modern Packaging	New York	M
National Research Council Bulletins	Washington	irreg.
National Safety News	Chicago	M
Official Gazette of the U. S. Patent Office	Washington	W
Proceedings of American Society for Testing Materials	Philadelphia	A
Professional Engineer	Chicago	4x
Public Service Management	St. Paul	M
Public Utilities Fortnightly	Washington	BW
Quarterly Journal of Applied Mathematics	Providence	Q
Safety	New York	M
Safety Engineering	New York	M
Technology Review	Cambridge	10x

Geology

Bulletin American Association of Petroleum Geologists	Tulsa	M
Bulletin of the Geological Society of America	New York	M
Economic Geology	Lancaster, Pa.	SQ
Geological Magazine°	Hertford	BM
Geophysics	Houston	Q
Journal of Geology	Chicago	SQ
Journal of Paleontology	Tulsa	BM
Journal of Sedimentary Petrology	Madison, Wis.	SA
Pan-American Geologist	Des Moines	M
Quarterly Journal of Geological Society°	London	Q
Rocks and Minerals	Peekskill, N. Y.	M

Geography and Meteorology

Annals of the Association of American Geographers	Lancaster, Pa.	Q
Bulletin of the American Society of Meteorology	Boston	10x
Canadian Geographical Journal	Ottawa	M
Climatological Data	Washington	M
Economic Geography	Worcester, Mass.	Q
Geographical Journal •	London	M
Geographical Review	New York	Q
Geography•	London	Q
Journal of Geography	Chicago	9x
Monthly Weather Review	Washington	M
New Zealand Geographer•	Christchurch, N. Z.	SA
Professional Geographer	varies	SA
Quarterly Journal of Royal Meteorological Society•	London	Q
Scottish Geographical Magazine•	Edinburgh	Q

Heating, Air-Conditioning, and Refrigeration

Air Conditioning and Refrigeration News	Detroit	M
Coal Herald—Stoker and Air-Conditioner	Boston	M
Domestic Engineering	Chicago	M
Heating, Piping, and Air-Conditioning	Chicago	M
Heating and Ventilating	New York	M
Ice and Refrigeration	Chicago	M
Industrial Heat Engineer•	London	BM
Industrial Heating	Pittsburgh	M
Insulation	New York	M
Refrigerating Engineering	New York	M
Refrigerating Industry	Cleveland	M
Refrigeration	Atlanta	M
Refrigeration Service Engineer	Chicago	M

Industrial Engineering

Advanced Management	New York	M
Arbitration Magazine	New York	BM
Equipment and Materials Reporter	Los Angeles	W
Factory Expediter's Production Information	Chicago	M
Factory Management and Maintenance	New York	M
Industrial Equipment News	New York	M
Industrial Maintenance	Philadelphia	M
Industrial Medicine	Chicago	M
Industrial Relations	Chicago	M

Industrial Standardization	New York	M
Industrial Trends	New York	SM
International Labor Review	Washington	M
Journal of Accountancy	New York	M
Labor Information	Washington	M
Management Review	New York	M
Manufacturers Record	Baltimore	M
*Mass Production**	London	M
Materials and Methods	New York	M
*Mechanical Handling**	London	M
Mill and Factory	New York	M
Modern Industry	New York	M
Modern Machine Shop	Cincinnati	M
Modern Management	New York	8x
Modern Materials Handling	Boston	M
New Equipment Digest	Cleveland	M
Personnel	New York	BM
Personnel Journal	New York	10x
Product Design and Development News	New York	M
Product Engineering	New York	M
Product Engineering and Management	Detroit	M
Production Equipment	Chicago	M
Supervision	New York	M

Marine and Military Engineering

American Marine Engineer	Washington	M
Infantry Journal	Washington	M
Journal of American Society of Naval Engineering	Washington	M
Marine Engineering and Shipping Review	New York	M
Military Engineer	Washington	M
*Motor Ship**	London	M
Motorship	New York	M
Nautical Gazette	New York	M
Ordnance	Washington	BM
U. S. Naval Institute Proceedings	Annapolis	M

Mechanical Engineering

(See also Electricity and Power *and other related topics*)

American Machinist	New York	BW
*Automobile Engineer**	London	M
Automotive Industries	Philadelphia	SM
Diesel Power and Diesel Transportation	New York	M
Diesel Progress	New York	M
*Gas and Oil Power**	London	M

Journal of Applied Mechanics	New York	Q
Journal and Proceedings Institution of		
Mechanical Engineers°	London	4x
Locomotive	Hartford	Q
Machine Design	Cleveland	M
Machinery	New York	M
Mechanical Engineering	New York	M
Motor	New York	M
Oil Engine and Gas Turbine°	London	M
Railway Mechanical Engineering	New York	M
S.A.E. Journal	New York	M
Tool Engineer	New York	M
Transactions of the A.S.M.E.	Detroit	M

Metals, Mining, and Minerals

(See also related headings)

Aluminum and Magnesium	New York	M
American Foundryman	Chicago	M
American Mineralogist	Ann Arbor, Mich.	BM
Blast Furnace and Steel Plant	Pittsburgh	M
Canadian Metals and Metallurgical		
Industries	Toronto	M
Canadian Mining and Metallurgical		
Bulletin	Montreal	M
Canadian Mining Journal	Ottawa	M
Chemical and Metallurgical Engineer-		
ing	New York	M
Corrosion	Houston	M
Corrosion and Material Protection	Pittsburgh	BM
Die Castings	Cleveland	M
Electroplating°	Teddington	M
Engineering and Mining Journal	New York ·	M
Foundry	Cleveland	M
Foundry Trade Journal°	London	W
Industry and Welding	Cleveland	M
Iron Age	Philadelphia	W
Iron and Steel Engineer	Pittsburgh	M
Journal of Institute of Metals and		
Metallurgical Abstracts°	London	M
Journal of the Iron and Steel Institute°	London	M
Light Metal Age	Chicago	M
Metal Finishing	New York	M
Metal Industry°	London	W
Metallurgia°	Manchester	M
Metal Progress	Cleveland	M
Metals Review	Cleveland	M
Metals Technology	New York	SQ
Mineralogical Magazine°	London	Q
Mineralogist	Portland, Ore.	M
Mines Magazine	Denver	M
Mining and Metallurgy	New York	M

Mining Congress Journal	Washington	M
*Mining Magazine**	London	M
Mining Technology	New York	BM
Mining World	San Francisco	M
Modern Metals	Chicago	M
Pit and Quarry	Chicago	M
Progressive Miner	Springfield, Ill.	SM
Rock Products	Chicago	M
Rocks and Minerals	Peekskill, N. Y.	M
*Sheet Metal Industries**	London	M
Sheet Metal Worker	New York	M
Steel	Cleveland	W
Steel Facts	New York	BM
Steel Processing	Pittsburgh	M
Transactions American Society for Metals	Cleveland	A
*Transactions of Institution of Mining Engineers**	London	M
Welding Journal	New York	M

Physics and Science
(including Radio, Television, and Photography)

American Journal of Physics	New York	BM
American Journal of Roentgenology	Springfield, Ill.	M
American Journal of Science	New Haven	M
American Photography	Boston	M
American Scientist	Burlington, Vt.	Q
Audio Engineering	Pittsfield, Mass.	M
Bell Laboratories Record	New York	M
Bell System Technical Journal	New York	Q
Bulletin of the Atomic Scientists	Chicago	M
Camera	Baltimore	M
Communications	New York	M
FM and Television	New York	M
General Electric Review	Schenectady	M
Instruments	Pittsburgh	M
Journal of Acoustical Society of America	New York	Q
Journal of Applied Physics	New York	M
Journal of Chemical Physics	New York	M
Journal of the Franklin Institute	Philadelphia	M
Journal of Mathematics and Physics	Cambridge	Q
Journal of the Optical Society of America	New York	M
*Journal of Scientific Instruments**	London	M
Journal of the Society of Motion Picture Engineers	New York	M
Nature	New York	M
Nucleonics	New York	M
Philips Technical Review	New York	M
*Photographic Journal**	London	M

Physical Review	New York	SM
Proceedings of the I.R.E.	New York	M
Proceedings of the National Academy		
of Sciences	Washington	M
Radio Engineer's Digest	New York	M
Radio News	Chicago	M
Science	Lancaster, Pa.	W
*Science Abstracts, Section A**	London	M
Science Illustrated	New York	M
Science News Letter	Washington	W
*Science Progress**	London	Q
Scientific Monthly	New York	M
Telegraph and Telephone Age	New York	M
Telephone Engineer and Management	Chicago	M
Telephony	Chicago	W
Tele-Tech	Orange, Conn.	M

IV

SOURCES OF GOVERNMENT REPORTS

The student of report writing can with advantage spend considerable time in examining the form, make-up, and style of public reports. These reports constitute an unequaled source of technical information often available nowhere else. The student should examine their make-up carefully, however: there is as much to learn from the bad as from the good. The following lists suggest some of the more productive of the common sources.

Publications of the States

The states, with their many departments, bureaus, and institutions, publish a tremendous number of reports in a wide variety of fields. Aside from the literature published irregularly by colleges and universities, the publications emanating from the following sources are perhaps of greatest general interest:

Agricultural Experiment Stations

Alabama (Auburn)
Alaska (Sitka)
Arizona (Tucson)
Arkansas (Fayetteville)
California (Berkeley)
Colorado (Fort Collins)
Connecticut (New Haven)
Connecticut (Storrs)
Delaware (Newark)
Florida (Gainesville)
Georgia (Experiment)
Georgia (Tifton)

Hawaii (Honolulu)
Idaho (Moscow)
Illinois (Urbana)
Indiana (Lafayette)
Iowa (Ames)
Kansas (Manhattan)
Kentucky (Lexington)
Louisiana (Baton Rouge)
Maine (Orono)
Maryland (College Park)
Massachusetts (Amherst)
Michigan (East Lansing)

Minnesota (University Farm, St. Paul)

Mississippi (State College)
Missouri (Columbia)
Missouri (Mountain Grove)
Montana (Bozeman)
Nebraska (Lincoln)
Nevada (Reno)
New Hampshire (Durham)
New Jersey (New Brunswick)
New Mexico (State College)
New York (Cornell, Ithaca)
New York (Geneva)
North Carolina (Raleigh)
North Dakota (State College Station, and Fargo)
Ohio (Wooster)
Oklahoma (Stillwater)
Oregon (Corvallis)
Panhandle Experiment Station (Goodwell, Oklahoma)
Pennsylvania (State College)
Puerto Rico (Rio Piedras)
Rhode Island (Kingston)
South Carolina (Clemson)
South Dakota (Brookings)
Tennessee (Knoxville)
Texas (College Station)
Utah (Logan)
Vermont (Burlington)
Virginia (Blacksburg)
Virginia Truck Exp. Station (Norfolk)
Washington (Pullman)
Washington (Puyallup)
West Virginia (Morgantown)
Wisconsin (Madison)
Wyoming (Laramie)

State Bureaus of Mines or Resources

Alabama . . . . Department of Industrial Relations
Arizona . . . . Department of Mineral Resources
Arkansas . . . . Department of Mining
California . . . . Department of Natural Resources
Colorado . . . . Executive Department
Florida . . . . Geological Survey
Georgia . . . . Division of Mines, Mining, and Geology
Hawaii . . . . Department of Public Lands
Idaho . . . . Bureau of Mines
Illinois . . . . Department of Mines and Minerals
Indiana . . . . Department of Commerce and Industry
Iowa . . . . Department of State Mine Inspectors
Kansas . . . . Mine Examining Board
Kentucky . . . . Department of Mines and Minerals
Louisiana . . . . Department of Minerals
Maine . . . . Secretary of State
Maryland . . . . Bureau of Mines
Michigan . . . . Department of Conservation
Minnesota . . . . Division of Land and Minerals
Mississippi . . . . State Mineral Lease Commission
Missouri . . . . Bureau of Mines
Montana . . . . Industrial Accident Board
Nevada . . . . Bureau of Mines
New Hampshire . . . . State Planning and Development Commission
New Jersey . . . . Department of Conservation and Development
New Mexico . . . . Bureau of Mines and Mineral Resources
New York . . . . Department of Labor
.North Carolina . . . . Department of Labor
North Dakota . . . . Division of Mines and Mining Experiments
Ohio . . . . Department of Industrial Relations
Oregon . . . . Department of Geology & Mineral Resources

Pennsylvania .... Department of Mines
Tennessee .... Department of Labor
Utah .... Industrial Commission
Virginia .... Department of Labor and Industry
Washington .... Department of Conservation & Development
West Virginia .... Department of Mines
Wisconsin .... Industrial Commission
Wyoming .... Land Department

Engineering Experiment Stations

Alabama Polytechnical Institute	Auburn
University of Arizona	Tucson
University of Arkansas	Fayetteville
University of California	Berkeley
Carnegie Institute of Technology	Pittsburgh
Clemson College	Clemson, S. C.
Colorado A & M College	Fort Collins
University of Connecticut	Storrs
Cornell University	Ithaca, N. Y.
University of Delaware	Newark
University of Florida	Gainesville
Georgia School of Technology	Atlanta
Harvard University	Cambridge, Mass.
University of Idaho	Moscow
University of Iowa	Iowa City
Iowa State College	Ames
Johns Hopkins University	Baltimore
Kansas State College	Manhattan
University of Kentucky	Lexington
Louisiana State University	Baton Rouge
University of Maine	Orono
University of Maryland	College Park
Michigan State College	East Lansing
University of Minnesota	Minneapolis
Mississippi State College	State College
University of Missouri	Columbia
Montana State College	Bozeman
University of Nebraska	Lincoln
University of New Hampshire	Durham
New Mexico College	State College
New York University	New York
North Carolina State College	Raleigh
Ohio State University	Columbus
Oklahoma A & M College	Stillwater
Pennsylvania State College	State College
Purdue University	Lafayette, Ind.
Rensselaer Polytechnic Institute	Troy, N. Y.
Rhode Island State College	Kingston
Rutgers University	New Brunswick, N. J.
South Dakota State College	Brookings
University of Tennessee	Knoxville
Texas A & M College	College Station

Virginia Polytechnic Institute	Blacksburg, Va.
Washington State College	Pullman
West Virginia University	Morgantown
University of Wisconsin	Madison
University of Wyoming	Laramie

Publications of the Federal Government

Recent decades have seen a tremendous increase in the number of governmental divisions—"authorities," "administrations," commissions, bureaus, services—governmental agencies which among them publish bulletins or reports on almost every aspect of national life. The importance of these publications to the technical man cannot be easily exaggerated. To the report writer they supply a practically unlimited source of reference material and offer a great variety of report forms and types, many of which can be profitably studied. It is obviously impossible to do more than indicate here how these publications may be most easily consulted. The following outline used in conjunction with the *United States Government Publications Monthly Catalog* will serve a double purpose: it will point out just what governmental publishers of technical papers exist, and it will suggest where particular reference material is to be sought:

Department of Agriculture:
    Agricultural Economics Bureau
    Agricultural Research Administration
    Commodity Exchange Authority
    Extension Service
    Rural Electrification Administration
    Soil Conservation Service
Atomic Energy Commission
Civil Service Commission
Department of Commerce
    Census Bureau
    Civil Aeronautics Authority
    Coast and Geodetic Survey
    National Bureau of Standards
    Patent Office
    Weather Bureau
The Congress
    (Reports of various special committees)
Federal Communications Commission
Federal Power Commission
Federal Security Agency
    Education Office
    Food and Drug Administration
    Public Health Service

Federal Works Agency
Department of Interior
    Fish and Wildlife Service
    Geological Survey
    Mines Bureau
    Reclamation Bureau
Interstate Commerce Commission
Department of Justice
Department of Labor
    Employment Service
    Bureau of Labor Statistics
Library of Congress
National Advisory Committee for Aeronautics
National Labor Relations Board
National Mediation Board
National Military Establishment
    Air Force Department
    Army Department
    Navy Department
Securities and Exchange Commission

PERMISSIBLE ABBREVIATIONS

(See rules, Chapter 4)

American Standard Abbreviations for Scientific and Engineering Terms

Prepared by the Sectional Committee on Letter Symbols and Abbreviations for Science and Engineering, and designated as an American Standard by the American Standards Association* in March, 1941, this list should eliminate much of the confusion arising from the lack of standardization in technical abbreviations. The list is published by the American Society of Mechanical Engineers (29 West 39th Street, New York, N. Y.) and is sponsored by the following organizations:

> American Association for the Advancement of Science
> American Institute of Electrical Engineers
> American Society of Civil Engineers
> American Society for Engineering Education
> The American Society of Mechanical Engineers

"These [the following] forms are recommended for readers whose familiarity with the terms used makes possible a maximum of abbreviations. For other classes of readers editors may wish to use less contracted combinations made up from this list. For example, the list gives the abbreviation of the term 'feet per second' as 'fps.' To some readers 'ft per sec' will be more easily understood."

absolute	abs
acre	spell out
acre-foot	acre-ft
air horsepower	air hp
alternating current (as adjective)	a-c
ampere	amp
ampere-hour	amp-hr
amplitude, an elliptic function	am.

---

* The American Standards Association has also published Bulletin Z32.13-1946, *Abbreviations for Use on Drawings*. The only significant difference in the two sets of abbreviations is that those for use on drawings are consistently capitalized throughout.

Angstrom unit	A
antilogarithm	antilog
atmosphere	atm
atomic weight	at.wt
average	avg
avoirdupois	avdp
azimuth	az or α
barometer	bar.
barrel	bbl
Baumé	Bé
board feet (feet board measure)	fbm
boiler pressure	spell out
boiling point	bp
brake horsepower	bhp
brake horsepower-hour	bhp-hr
Brinell hardness number	Bhn
British thermal unit	Btu or B
bushel	bu
calorie	cal
candle	c
candle-hour	c-hr
candlepower	cp
cent	c or ¢
center to center	c to c
centigram	cg
centiliter	cl
centimeter	cm
centimeter-gram-second (system)	cgs
chemical	chem
chemically pure	cp
circular	cir
circular mils	cir mils
coefficient	coef
cologarithm	colog
concentrate	conc
conductivity	cond
constant	const
continental horsepower	cont hp
cord	cd
cosecant	csc
cosine	cos
cosine of the amplitude, an elliptic function	cn
cost, insurance, and freight	cif
cotangent	cot
coulomb	spell out
counter electromotive force	cemf
cubic	cu
cubic centimeter	cu cm, cm^3 (liquid, meaning milliliter, ml)

cubic foot .... cu ft
cubic feet per minute .... cfm
cubic feet per second .... cfs
cubic inch .... cu in.
cubic meter .... cu m or m³
cubic micron .... cu μ or cu mu or μ³
cubic millimeter .... cu mm or mm³
cubic yard .... cu yd
current density .... spell out
cycles per second .... spell out or c
cylinder .... cyl

day .... spell out
decibel .... db
degree .... deg or °
degree centigrade C
degree Fahrenheit .... F
degree Kelvin .... K
degree Réaumur .... R
delta amplitude, an elliptic function .... dn
diameter .... diam
direct-current (as adjective) .... d-c
dollar .... $
dozen .... doz
dram .... dr

efficiency .... eff
electric .... elec
electromotive force .... emf
elevation .... el
equation .... eq
external .... ext

farad .... spell out or f
feet board measure (board feet) .... fbm
feet per minute .... fpm
feet per second .... fps
fluid .... fl
foot .... ft
foot-candle .... ft-c
foot-Lambert .... ft-L
foot-pound .... ft-lb
foot-pound-second (system) .... fps
foot-second (*see* cubic feet per second)
franc .... fr
free aboard ship .... spell out
free alongside ship .... spell out
freezing point .... fp
frequency .... spell out
fusion point .... fnp

gallon .... gal
gallons per minute .... gpm

gallons per second .... gps
grain .... spell out
gram .... g
gram-calorie .... g-cal
greatest common divisor .... gcd

haversine .... hav
hectare .... ha
henry .... h
high-pressure (adjective) .... h-p
hogshead .... hhd
horsepower .... hp
horsepower-hour .... hp-hr
hour .... hr
hour (in astronomical tables) .... h
hundred C
hundredweight (112 lb) .... cwt
hyperbolic cosine .... cosh
hyperbolic sine .... sinh
hyperbolic tangent .... tanh

inch .... in.
inch-pound .... in-lb
inches per second .... ips
indicated horsepower .... ihp
indicated horsepower-hour .... ihp-hr
inside diameter. .... ID
intermediate-pressure (adjective) .... i-p
internal .... int

joule .... j

kilocalorie .... kcal
kilocycles per second .... kc
kilogram .... kg
kilogram-calorie .... kg-cal
kilogram-meter .... kg-m
kilograms per cubic meter .... kg per cu m or kg/m^3
kilograms per second .... kgps
kiloliter .... kl
kilometer .... km
kilometers per second .... kmps
kilovolt .... kv
kilovolt-ampere .... kva
kilowatt .... kw
kilowatthour .... kwhr

Lambert L
latitude .... lat or ϕ
least common multiple .... lcm
linear foot .... lin ft

liquid .... liq
lira .... spell out
liter l
logarithm (common) .... log
logarithm (natural) .... log$_e$ or ln
longitude .... long. or λ
low-pressure (as adjective) .... l-p
lumen l
lumen-hour .... l-hr
lumens per watt .... lpw

mass .... spell out
mathematics (ical) .... math
maximum .... max
mean effective pressure .... mep
mean horizontal candlepower .... mhcp
megacycle .... spell out
megohm .... spell out
melting point .... mp
meter .... m
meter-kilogram .... m-kg
mho .... spell out
microampere .... μa or mu a
microfarad .... μf
microinch .... μin.
micromicrofarad .... μμf
micromicron .... μμ or mu mu
micron .... μ or mu
microvolt .... μv
microwatt .... μw or mu w
mile .... spell out
miles per hour .... mph
miles per hour per second .... mphps
milliampere .... ma
milligram .... mg
millihenry .... mh
millilambert .... mL
milliliter .... ml
millimeter .... mm
millimicron .... mμ or m mu
million .... spell out
million gallons per day .... mgd
millivolt .... mv
minimum .... min
minute .... min
minute (angular measure) .... ′
minute (time) (in astronomical tables) .... m
mole .... spell out
molecular weight .... mol. wt
month .... spell out

National Electrical Code .... NEC

ohm	spell out or Ω
ohm-centimeter	ohm-cm
ounce	oz
ounce-foot	oz-ft
ounce-inch	oz-in
outside diameter	OD
parts per million	ppm
peck	pk
penny (pence)	d
pennyweight	dwt
per	See Chapter 4
peso	spell out
pint	pt
potential	spell out
potential difference	spell out
pound	lb
pound-foot	lb-ft
pound-inch	lb-in
pound sterling	£
pounds per brake horsepower-hour	lb per bhp-hr
pounds per cubic foot	lb per cu ft
pounds per square foot	psf.
pounds per square inch	psi
pounds per square inch absolute	psia
power factor	spell out or pf
quart	qt
radian	spell out
reactive kilovolt-ampere	kvar
reactive volt-ampere	var
revolutions per minute	rpm
revolutions per second	rps
rod	spell out
root mean square	rms
secant	sec
second	sec
second (angular)	″
second-foot (*see* cubic feet per second)	
second (time) (in astronomical tables)	s
shaft horsepower	shp
shilling	s
sine	sin
sine of the amplitude, an elliptic function	sn
specific gravity	sp gr
specific heat	sp ht
spherical candle power	scp
square	sq
square centimeter	sq cm or cm^2
square foot	sq ft

square inch .... sq. in.
square kilometer .... sq km or km²
square meter .... sq m or m²
square micron .... sq μ or sq mu or μ²
square millimeter .... sq mm or mm²
square root of mean square .... rms
standard .... std
stere .... s

tangent .... tan
temperature .... temp
tensile strength .... ts
thousand .... M
thousand foot-pounds .... kip-ft
thousand pound . ... kip
ton .... spell out
ton-mile .... spell out

versed sine .... vers
volt v
volt-ampere .... va
volt-coulomb .... spell out

watt .... w
watthour .... whr
watts per candle .... wpc
week .... spell out
weight .... wt

yard .... yd
year .... yr

Other Abbreviations

afternoon .... p.m.
Agent .... Agt.
Agricultural Adjustment Administration .... AAA
American Federation of Labor .... AF of L
American Society of Civil Engineers .... ASCE
American Society of Mechanical Engineers .... ASME
American Society for Testing Materials .... ASTM
American Standards Association .... ASA
and so forth .... etc.
and what follows .... et seq.
anno Domini (in the year of our Lord) .... A.D.
anonymous .... anon.
ante meridian (forenoon) .... a.m.
April .... Apr.
Architect . (title) .... Archt.
Assistant (title) .... Asst.
Associated Press .... AP
Association .... Assn.
Attorney (title) .... Atty.

August .... Aug.
Avenue .... Ave.

Bachelor of Arts (title) .... B.A.
Bachelor of Science (title) .... B.S.
before Christ .... B.C.
brake mean effective horsepower .... bmep
Brotherhood of Locomotive Engineers .... BLE
Brothers (in title) .... Bros.
Browne & Sharpe gage .... B&S gage
Building (part of address) .... Bldg.

Captain (title) .... Capt.
cash on delivery .... c.o.d.
Ceramic Engineer (title) .... Cer.Engr.
Certified Public Accountant .... CPA
Chapter (preceding a specific number) .... Chap.
Chemical Engineer (title) .... Ch. E.
Citizen's Military Training Camp .... CMTC
Civil Aeronautics Authority .... CAA
Civil Engineer (title) .... C.E.
Civilian Conservation Corps CCC
Colonel (title) .... Col.
Commandant (title) .... Comdt.
Company (in firm name) .... Co.
compare .... cf.
Congress of Industrial Organizations .... CIO
Construction Engineer (title) .... Constr. Engr.
Consulting Engineer (title) .... Cons. Engr.
Contracting Engineer (title) .... Contr. Engr.
Corporation (in firm name) .... Corp.

December .... Dec.
decimeter, decimeters .... dm
Department (as part of title) .... Dept.
Doctor (title) .... Dr.
Doctor of Philosophy (title, degree) .... Ph.D.
Doctor of Science (title, degree) .... Sc.D.

Electrical Engineer (title) .... E.E.
Engineer of Mines (title) .... E.M.
et cetera (and so forth) .... etc.
extreme-pressure .... EP

February .... Feb.
Federal Communications Commission .... FCC
Federal Housing Administration .... FHA
Federal Radio Commission .... FRC
Federal Trade Commission .... FTC
Figure, Figures (preceding specific number or numbers) Fig., Figs.
following (pages) .... ff.
for example .... e.g.

General (title) .... Gen.
General Headquarters .... GHQ

hectoliters .... hl.
Honorable (title) .... ·Hon.

in the same place .... ibid.
inclusive .... incl.
Incorporated (in firm name) .... Inc.
Industrial Engineer (title) .... I.E.
Institute (in title) .... Inst.
intelligence quotient .... IQ
International News Service .... INS
Interstate Commerce Commission ICC

January .... Jan.
Junior (in title or name) .... Jr.

Lieutenant (title) .... Lt., Lieut.
Limited (in firm name) .... Ltd.

Major (title) .... spell out
Manager (title) .... Mgr.
Manufacturing (in firm name) .... Mfg.
March .... Mar.
Master of Arts (degree, title) .... M.A.
Master of Science (degree, title) .... M.S.
Mechanical Engineer (title) .... M.E.
Medicinae Doctor .... M.D.
mercury .... hg
Metallurgical Engineer (title) .... Met.Engr.
miles per gallon .... mpg
morning (ante meridiem) .... a.m.

nota bene (note well) .... n.b.
November .... Nov.
Number, Numbers (preceding specific number or num-
    bers; Table No. 7., Nos. 5 and 6) .... No., Nos.

October .... Oct.
opere citato (in the work cited) .... op. cit.

page, pages .... p., pp.
per cent .... %
percentage .... spell out
post meridiem (afternoon) .... p.m.
Post Office .... P.O.
preferred (referring to stock) .... pfd.
President (title) .... Pres.
Private (title) .... Pvt.
Professor (title) .... Prof.

Quartermaster Corps .... QMC

Railroad .... R.R.
Railway .... Ry.
Reserve Officers' Training Corps .... R.O.T.C.
Reverend (title) .... Rev.

Secretary (title) .... Sec., Secy.
Securities Exchange Commission .... SEC
Senior (title) .... Sr.
September .... Sept.
Sergeant (title) .... Sgt.
Society of Automotive Engineers .... SAE
Street, Streets .... St., Sts.
Superintendent (title) .... Supt.

Tennessee Valley Authority .... TVA
that is .... i.e.
Treasurer (title) .... Treas.

United Press .... UP
United States Army .... USA
United States Marine Corps .... USMC
United States National Guard .... USNG
United States Navy .... USN

videlicet (namely) .... viz.
Volume, Volumes .... Vol., Vols.

which see .... q.v.

Abbreviations for States and Territories

Alabama	Ala.	Mississippi	Miss.
Arizona	Ariz.	Missouri	Mo.
Arkansas	Ark.	Montana	Mont.
California	Calif.	Nebraska	Neb.
Canal Zone	C. Z.	Nevada	Nev.
Colorado	Col.	New Hampshire	N. H.
Connecticut	Conn.	New Jersey	N. J.
Delaware	Del.	New Mexico	N. M.
Florida	Fla.	New York	N. Y.
Georgia	Ga.	North Carolina	N. C.
Illinois	Ill.	North Dakota	N. D.
Indiana	Ind.	Oklahoma	Okla.
Kansas	Kan.	Oregon	Ore.
Kentucky	Ky.	Pennsylvania	Pa.
Louisiana	La.	Philippine Islands	P. I.
Maine	Me.	Puerto Rico	P. R.
Maryland	Md.	South Carolina	S. C.
Massachusetts	Mass.	South Dakota	S. D.
Michigan	Mich.	Tennessee	Tenn.

Texas	Tex.	Washington	Wash.
Vermont	Vt.	West Virginia	W. Va.
Virginia	Va.	Wisconsin	Wis.
Virgin Islands	V. I.	Wyoming	Wy.

Alaska, Guam, Hawaii, Idaho, Iowa, Midway Island, Ohio, Samoa, Utah, and Wake should not be abbreviated.

SPELLING FORMS

THE FOLLOWING LIST, in addition to providing easy reference to the approved forms of some of the more troublesome words used by the technical writer, also illustrates present practice in combining words regularly found together (see Chapter 4 and the examples at the end of this appendix). In compiling the list, the authors have included most of the spellings recommended by the Society of Automotive Engineers under "Authorized Spelling Forms" in their *Style Sheet* of November, 1939.

A

aboveboard
abscissas
accelerator
accessible
accidentally
accommodate
accumulate
achievement
acidproof
acquire
aeration
aftercooler
aileron
air brake
air chamber
air compressor
aircraft
air duct
airflow
air gap
air heater
air liner
airplane
air pump
air-speed meter
airtight
align (not "aline")
all-metal (adj.)
all right

alternating-current (adj.)
alternating current (noun)
altogether
ammeter
among (not "amongst")
angle iron
antiknock
anyone
apparent
armor plate
ashpit
auxiliary

B

babbitt
backfire
backlash
back pressure
backward (not "backwards")
balance wheel
ball-and-socket joint
ball-bearing (adj.)
ballonet
baseplate
battleship
Baumé (not "Beaume")
bearing surface
bedplate
bedrock
bell-crank

belt wheel
benefited
benzene
beside ("next to")
besides ("in addition to")
biplane
blast furnace
blowby
blowhole
blow-off (noun or adj.)
blowpipe
blueprint
board feet
boilermaker
boiler room
boiling point
bolt-circle
bolted-on (adj. only)
boring mill
brake band
brake drum
brake lining
breakdown (noun, adj., not verb)
built-up (adj. only)
bulkhead
bulls-eye
buoyant
busbar
bylaw
bypass
byproduct

C

caliber
camshaft
candlepower
capscrew
carburetion
carburetor
carload
case-harden
cast-in-block
cast-iron (adj.)
catalog
center
centerline
changeable
cipher
circuit breaker
closed-in (adj.)
clutch housing
coal-dust (adj.)

coal dust (noun)
coefficient
cold-drawn (adj.)
combustion-chamber (adj.)
committee
comparative
comparison
competition
connecting-rod (adj.)
controlled
convenience
cooperation
coordinate
counterbore
counterclockwise
counterflow
countershaft
countersunk
crankcase
crankpin
crankshaft
cribwork
cross-arm
crosshead
cross-link
cross-section
cutoff (adj. or noun)
cylinder-head (adj.)

D

damper
dashpot
data (plural)
dead-center
deadweight
decalage
decision
deficient
de-icing
desiccated
desirable
develop
development
device
dewpoint
diaphragm
Diesel
differential
direct-connected
direct-current (adj.)
direct current (noun)
disc

distill
downstream
downtake
draft (not "draught")
drafting room
draftsman
dragline
drawbar
drawing board
drill-press (adj.)
driveshaft
drop forge
drop-forging
dry batteries
dry cell
drydock
dry point
dustproof

E

efficiency
elastic limit
electrochemical
embed
emphasize
en bloc
encase
enclose
end-point
end thrust
engineman
engine room
environment
equipped
everyday (adj.)
everything
exceed
exhaust
existence
experience
explanation
eyebolt

F

faceplate
falsework
fan belt
feedwater
fiber
financial
firebox
firebrick

fireclay
firedoor
fireproof
fire-resistant
flash point
flat car
floor board
flowmeter
flue gas
flywheel
foot-candle
footnote
foot-pound
force pump
foreign
foreman
formulas
forward (not "forwards")
4-cylinder (adj.)
4-cycle (adj.)
4-wheel drive
framework
friction clutch (noun)
friction surface (noun)
fuel tank
full-floating axle
fundamental fuse box
fuselage

G

gage
gas-engine (adj.)
gas engine
gasoline (not "gas")
gas-tight
gate valve (noun)
gearbox
geared-up (adj.)
gearshaft
gearwheel
generator room
government
gray (iron)
grease cup
guidance

H

half-size
half-speed (adj.)
halftone
handbook
handhole

handwheel
hangar
hardpan
headlamp
headlight
head resistance
headstock
heat-treatment
heavier-than-air (adj.)
height
high-frequency (adj.)
high-gear (adj.)
high-pressure (adj.)
high-speed (adj.)
high-tension (adj.)
horsepower
hundredths
hydrocarbon

I

I-beam
ignition
inasmuch as
incidentally
inclinometer (not "clinomter")
indexes (not "indices")
indispensable
infra-red
input
in so far as
inspection lamp
instrument board
insulator
intake
intercooler
internal-combustion (adj.)
interrelate
irresistible
iso-octane

J

jackscrew
jackshaft

K

keyseat
keyway
kilovolt-ampere
kilowatt-hour

L

laboratory
lagscrew

lampblack
landing gear
layout
layshift
lead screw
left-hand (adj.)
L-head cylinder
lighter-than-air (adj.)
lightweight
limewater
lineshaft
liquefy
locknut
longeron
louvers
low-pressure (adj.)

M

machinability
machine-shop (adj.)
machine shop (noun)
machine tool (noun)
maintenance
manageable
manhole
mathematics
media
meter
miniature
misfire
mold
monoplane
motorboat
motor car
motorcoach
motorcycle
motorship
motor truck
motor vehicle
muckbar
mud drum
multicylinder
multiple-disc (adj.)

N

necessary
network
nickel
ninety
non-condensing
non-inflammable
non-rigid

no one
noticeable
nozzle

O

occasion
occurred
occurrence
offset
oil bath
oil-filler cup
oil groove
oil pump
oil tank
oil-tight
oil-well (adj.)
olefin
omitted
open-hearth (adj.)
optimistic
ore bed
orebody
out-of-balance (adj.)
output
overall (dimension)
overflow
overload
overrunning

P

paraffin
parallel
passenger car (not "pleasure car")
patternmaker
payload
payroll
peak load
peephole
permissible
pickup
piecework
pig iron
pile-driver
pinhole
pipe line
pipe wrench
piston-ring (adj.)
planing mill
plow
poppet valve
power factor
powerplant

practically
practice
precede
preeminent
preheat
preignition
pressure gage
principal (meaning "chief")
principle (meaning "rule")
proceed
propeller
proved (not "proven")
pushbutton
push-rods

Q

quantitative
quantity
questionnaire
quicklime

R

radius-rod
railcar
railroad
railway
rainfall
reach rod
rear-axle housing
reduction of area (not "in")
reference
referred
remote-control (adj.)
repetition
replaceable
rhythm
right-hand (adj.)
right-of-way
roadbed
roadway
rocker arm
rockshaft
rod mill
roller-bearing (adj.)
roundhouse
running board
runway

S

safety valve
sandblast
sand bricks

sawteeth
schedule
science
scleroscope
screwdriver
screw eye
searchlight
semi-floating
separate (adj. or verb)
setscrew
set-up
sheet-iron (adj.)
sheet iron (noun)
shining
shop order
short-circuit
shutdown
side-by-side
side-slip
sightseeing
sinkheadsiphon
skilful
sleeve valve
slide rule
slipstream
slow-speed (adj.)
smokebox
smoke flue
so-called
some day
somehow
someone
something
somewhere
spark gap
spark-plug (adj.)
specimen
standpipe
staybolt
steam chest
steam engine
steam heat
steam jacket
steam plant
steamtight
steam turbine
steering gear
step-up
stockholder
stopcock
streamline
stud bolt

subcommittee
subdivision
sub-frame side-member
succeed
sulfur
superheater
superimpose
superinduce
supersede
surface elevation
sweepback
switchback
symmetry

T

tailrace
tailshaft
tailstock
take-off
tanbark
taxiing
tee fitting
temperature
templet
tensile strength
textbook
T-head cylinder
thermocouple
thumbscrew
tidewater
tie-rod
time. table
today
toeboard
tomorrow
ton-mileage
toolmaker
toolroom
torque-arm
toward (not "towards")
tractor
trademark
T-rail
train shed
transatlantic
transcontinental
transmission case
transoceanic
transpacific
triplane
try-out
T-square

tune-up
turntable
turret lathe
twin-engined
twist drill
two-wire

U

U-bolt
U-gage
ultraviolet
underframe
underpinning
uniflow
universal joint
up-stroke
up-to-date

V

vacua
vacuum
valuable
valve gear
valve-in-head
valve spring
valve-stem guide
vapor
variety
V-bolt
voltmeter
V-thread
V-type

W

washout
water column
water flow

water gage
water jacket
waterpower
water pump
watershed
water supply
watertight
waterwheel
water works
watt-hour
wattmeter
well-balanced
well-known
wheelbase
wide-open
widespread
wilful
windshield
windstorm
wire-drawing
woodworking
workman
worldwide
worm gear
wormwheel
worth-while (adj.)
wristpin
wristplate
wrought-iron (adj.)
wrought iron (noun)

X

x-ray

Y

yield point

* * * *

Remember that all compound attributive adjectives (adjectives standing before the noun they qualify) are hyphenated in reports:

This plant uses the well-known Solvay Process.
But: The process is well known.

Wrought-iron pipe has proved superior here.
But: The casing is wrought iron.

Power is supplied by four high-speed motors.
But: The motors must be run at high speed.

The building is not wired for alternating-current appliances.
But: This is alternating current.

INDEX

Lightning Source UK Ltd.
Milton Keynes UK
UKHW012359291218
334537UK00011B/1044/P